Space, Text, and Gender

Women talking.

SPACE, TEXT, AND GENDER

An Anthropological Study of the Marakwet of Kenya

HENRIETTA L. MOORE

THE GUILFORD PRESS
New York London

For Themselves
and for Ian Hodder

©1996 The Guilford Press
A Division of Guilford Publications, Inc.
72 Spring Street, New York, NY 10012
Marketed and distributed outside North America by
Longman Group Limited.

Printed in the United States of America

This book is printed on acid-free paper.

Last digit is print number: 9 8 7 6 5 4 3 2 1

Library of Congress Cataloging-in-Publication Data
Moore, Henrietta L.
   Space, text, and gender : an anthropological study of the Marakwet
of Kenya / Henrietta L. Moore.
      p. cm. – (Mappings)
   Originally published: Cambridge ; New York : Cambridge University
Press, 1986. With new pref.
   Includes bibliographical references and index.
   ISBN 0-89862-825-3
   1. Marakwet (African people)–Social life and customs. 2. Women,
Marakwet–Social conditions. 3. Space and time. 4. Spatial behavior–
Kenya–Sibou. 5. Sex role–Kenya–Sibou. 6. Gender identity–Kenya–
Sibou. 7. Sibou (Kenya)–Social conditions. 8. Sibou (Kenya)–Economic
conditions. I. Title. II. Series.
DT433.545.M32M65 1996
306'089'96–dc20   95-46816
                                                                              CIP

Preface

The studies of space and gender have been linked together in anthropology for some time. The origins of this partnership can be traced back to Durkheim's idea of socially differentiated space, and before that to Lewis Henry Morgan's work on kinship and territory. It is now axiomatic that spatial relations represent and reproduce social relations, and it is the view that relations of likeness exist between social distinctions and spatial boundaries that links the study of gender to the study of space. Daughters-in-law who reside in the corners of tents, high-status women who never leave the house, rites of passage, foot-binding, inauspicious axes and directions, the waxing and waning of the moon, are all facets of the social and conceptual topography of human society. In this study I focus on relations of space, and on aspects of Marakwet society and culture as presented in the lived space of everyday life. It would be impossible to describe and analyze all the "spatial" features of Marakwet life, and I am aware that I have concerned myself almost exclusively with a limited range of spatial relations. My focus is on the organization of household space in an attempt to understand one particular form of cultural representation, how it is produced and how it changes. My broader aim is to discuss the relationship between symbolic forms and the social and economic conditions within which those forms are produced, maintained, and ultimately transformed. With this end in view, I have used the idea of "cultural text" to construct an analytical framework and to try and pursue some of the theoretical issues raised by such an inquiry. In choosing this focus, I have given less attention to other important aspects of Marakwet life: for example, affinal relationships, economics, the conflict of old and young, the rites and associated rituals of birth, marriage and death, all of which could have been considered in some detail and are not. Nonetheless, I hope that the book sheds some light on the more general problems of understanding cultural representation, and thus belies what may seem initially to be an unduly narrow focus.

Fieldwork among the Marakwet was carried out from March to July 1980
and from November 1980 to August 1981. During the course of my research
a number of institutions have allowed me the use of their facilities, and a
great number of people have given me advice and assistance. I should like
here to acknowledge my gratitude to them all. My research in Cambridge
and in Kenya was funded by the Department of Education and Science. I
am also pleased to acknowledge assistance from the British Institute in Eastern
Africa; the Smuts Memorial Fund, Cambridge; the Crowther–Beynon Fund,
Cambridge; the Anthony Wilkin Fund, Cambridge; and the Tweedie Exploration Fund, Edinburgh. Permission to carry out the work was obtained from
the Government of Kenya and the Office of the President, under Permit Number OP.13/001/10 C83/3. During my research in Kenya I worked under the
auspices of the National Museums of Kenya, and I should like to thank the
many people within that organization who were of help to me, especially
the Director, Richard Leakey.

My visits to Nairobi were made both pleasant and profitable by the kindness and help of the staff of the British Institute in Eastern Africa. I owe particular thanks to the former Director, Dr. Neville Chittick, whose unexpected
death during the preparation of this book saddened the many researchers who
remember his generosity and support. While in the field I was supported by
the agency and assistance of many individuals. I cannot mention all those
who gave so generously of their time and support, but I should like to record
my thanks to Dr. and Mrs. Peter Robertshaw, Dr. and Mrs. Brian Carson
and the staff of the AIC Mission at Kapsowar, Father Leo Staples, and the
Sisters and Fathers of the Catholic Mission at Chesongoch. Dr. Ian Hodder
supervised the PhD thesis on which this book is based, and I owe much to
his encouragement and constructive criticism. During my research I have
benefited greatly from discussions with members of the Institute of African
Studies, Nairobi; the British Institute in Eastern Africa; and the Faculty of
Archaeology and Anthropology, Cambridge. The preparation of this book
was made possible through the support of the African Studies Center, Cambridge.

Research and writing are always corporate efforts, and although I cannot
mention all those who have helped me I should particularly like to thank
Edwin Ardener, David Brooks, Sheena Crawford, Ian Hodder, Joan Scanlon,
Marilyn Strathern, and Deborah Swallow for reading earlier drafts of this
work, and for making the time to comment and provide encouragement. It
would not be possible to thank the people of Sibou and Tot adequately for
their patience and support during my long and inquisitive stay. I can only say
that working with them has added a great deal to my life and to my understanding of others' lives. I cannot mention all those who helped me, but I
would particularly like to thank Jacob Kipkore and his family, Mzee Ezekia,
Chief Kisang, and the staff of Tot Health Center. My work was made pos-

sible by my assistants: Samuel Chebet, Josphat Kilimo, Samuel Kilimo, Sally Chebiwot Kipkore, and Joseph Kisang. I should like to offer special thanks to Sally, who was my constant companion and guide throughout my stay in Kenya. I am deeply grateful to all my Marakwet friends for their kindness and support, they know more than I that what is written here is just a beginning.

—Henrietta L. Moore
Cambridge
November 1984

Preface to
the Paperback Edition

*There is no theory that is not a fragment, carefully preserved,
of some autobiography.*

— PAUL VALERY

Space has proliferated in the social sciences, exploding into contemporary theory in expanding fragmentary positions. In the ten years since this book was first published, there has been a strange confluence of theoretical terms. Theorists, notably geographers, writing about space–time relations have become preoccupied with terms (locales, regions) which seek to ground the contexts of social action, while others, notably feminists, Chicana and Black scholars, and postcolonial theorists, have developed different terms (local, position, borderlands) to characterize the multiple and overdetermined nature of discourses of difference and identity.[1] These arenas of writing overlap to a considerable extent, partly because of the influence of discourses of deconstruction and difference in the social sciences and humanities, and partly because all the theorists involved are responding to the local/global forms of fragmented capitalisms. In this preface, I want to say something about how I locate myself and this book in relation to these different scholars of "space" and "place."

---

[1] Compare, for example, Giddens's (1984; 1985) terms (locale, regionalization, distanciation) with Probyn's (1990) concepts (locale, location, local). Probyn is concerned with the "sites from which we speak," the space–time constitution of subjectivity, and experience. Giddens's concerns are different, but certainly include questions of context, contextualization, and identity.

GENDERED THEORIES: NEUTRAL SPACES

Several theorists have demanded that we recognize how representations of space are important constitutive elements of major theoretical perspectives (Pred, 1990a; Soja, 1989; Giddens, 1984; 1985). These writers all emphasize that social systems consist of social practices situated in space–time and produced and reproduced through the actions of knowledgeable social actors. Their positions differ from earlier writers in that they reject views which characterize space as static, neutral, or passive, as well as those that depict it as a backdrop for, or simple container of, social action. They reject the abstract, metaphorical space of earlier social theory, which emphasized geographical comparison as a subset of historical trajectories; they look instead into the concrete lived spaces of daily lives, and into how quotidian repetitive social practices expand outwards into social structures, social systems, and social institutions.

This shift in the analysis of space and the space–time constitution of social relations has been most noticeable within geography, where it has drawn primary inspiration from the social theory of Anthony Giddens. But also, it parallels developments in many other fields which emphasize the importance of a praxis-based approach to the understanding of human agency.[2] In anthropology, praxis-based theories elaborating on the work of Bourdieu and Foucault have become canonical in the last decade, and new ethnographies regularly draw on a corpus of ideas about the routines of social life and their relationship to bodily dispositions, linguistic discourses, power relations, and social structures.[3] What distinguishes anthropological writing from the more geographical approaches is its continuing concern with symbolism, with the microspecificities of day-to-day routines and practices, and an increasing emphasis on the relationship between language, embodiment, and space. There are, of course, theorists who bridge these differences, but for the most part geographers and anthropologists continue to work on different scales.[4] The

---

[2] The main impetus for this theoretical perspective in geography initially came from Anthony Giddens's "structuration theory" (Giddens, 1984; 1985), although scholars subsequently criticized Giddens for privileging historical over spatial analysis, and for failing to demonstrate in detail how space–time relations constitute social relations in concrete situations, thus leading him to ignore, among other things, the importance of gender to the ordering of spatial relations (Soja, 1983; Thrift, 1983; 1985; Gregory, 1989; Murgatroyd, 1989). Recent work in geography has drawn extensively on the theoretical work of Lefebvre and Foucault, and a growing interest in colonial and postcolonial geographies has resulted in an increasing dialogue between geographers and cultural theorists of all kinds, including anthropologists (Soja, 1989; Gregory, 1994; Keith and Pile, 1993).

[3] For recent examples, see Ong, 1987, and Hardin, 1993. For an overview of the development of anthropological theory and the relationship of praxis-based approaches to earlier theories, see Ortner, 1984.

[4] Examples would include, among others, Pred, 1990a; 1990b; Carney and Watts, 1990; Pred and Watts, 1992; Agnew and Duncan, 1989; Duncan and Ley, 1993; as well as a body of feminist work including Katz and Monk, 1993; Rose, 1993; Dyck, 1990; Deutsche, 1991; Valentine, 1989; and Mackenzie, 1989.

question of scale is an important one because of its connection to the larger problem of the conceptualization and representation of space in social theory. John Agnew has argued that theorists in the social sciences in general exhibit very little self-consciousness about their representations of space and scale. So little effort is expended in analyzing assumptions about space that Agnew feels moved to call these unreflexive and unreflected-upon notions "hidden geographies" (Agnew, 1993). These "hidden geographies" work their effects in the texts of those who employ them, where abstract spatial metaphors are often used as mechanisms for categorizing and selecting data. This is a means of imposing unexamined spatial perceptions onto nonspatial social processes as part of the mechanism of interpretation. The issue here concerns both the imposition of the theorist's own unexamined views of space and the concomitant assumption that space is neutral. Recent feminist writing in geography has criticized the very male nature of the space(s) discussed in time–geography and the lack of attention devoted to the gendered nature of space in lived contexts.[5]

In the following chapters, I draw on the work of Pierre Bourdieu and Paul Ricoeur to develop a theory of interpretive action. The repetitive quotidian activities of Marakwet life produce and are produced by sets of structuring principles only made manifest in practice. The organization of space is not simply a backdrop to social activity, but is the active and interactive context within which social relations and social structures are produced and transformed. Space in this context is never neutral, but neither is it ever fixed or static. This means that while it is never ungendered, it is also never unambiguously or statically gendered. It cannot be attributed fixed meanings. The organization of space is the product of enacted practices and, given the nature of resources and power relations in Marakwet life, its meanings are always open to negotiation and renegotiation. This is a view of space that takes account of the way in which it is constitutive through practice of social relations and social meanings.

The Marakwet make no clear-cut distinction between public and private, although they do have a strong sense of spatial topography and of the nature of lived space: which means that compound space, village space, and the space of the fields are not the same kinds of places. The association between compounds and individuals and between people and the land has much to do with their strong sense of spatial topography, but the differing nature of compound, village, and field cannot be glossed by a distinction between the public and the private. However, as I show in Chapter 8, the experience of space is one which is bound up with the experience of modernity and with alternative discourses brought to bear from the world outside the valley, and thus ideas about privacy and a particular view of the family unit were gaining ground

---

[5] See Rose (1993, chap. 2) for a summary.

during my fieldwork in 1980–1. It might seem strange that I do not discuss the public/private distinction in the following chapters given its saliency in anthropological theorizing in general, and in feminist theorizing in particular.[6] However, it was not a salient distinction for the Marakwet and I tried to stay close to the ideas about position that were much more important for people both in a day-to-day sense and a discursive sense (see Chapter 4). The Marakwet see men and women as having different relations to space and time, and this is reflected in the organization of domestic space, in language, in attitudes to household and clan responsibilities, and in ritual. However, on the day-to-day level, one's position in space is signaled by one's relative location on the Cherangani escarpment. The world of the Marakwet is a sloping world; constant movement up and down the escarpment, from the village to the fields on the valley floor, is the basis for economic life.

I learned about the importance of the sloping world and of the difference between men's and women's location on it by moving about with women and men and literally noticing the differences. This was a difference concretized and naturalized for all the Marakwet villagers I met, but I would never have had any real access to it without using my body as both subject and object of knowledge. It was the way I was positioned in space that gave me access to the spatial understandings of the Marakwet. The theoretical argument that space and time are involved in the constitution of social meanings and social relations was not something I arrived at intellectually. I rediscovered it when I came back to the United Kingdom to write, but only because it was by then inscribed on my own body.[7] I also firmly believe that I was assisted in developing a particular explanatory framework based on these assumptions because they were simultaneously part of both a Marakwet discourse and of my own theoretical understanding.

It seems puzzling to me now that I did not write about this at the time. I cannot even remember whether I really thought it. Looking back, I realize that in spite of my theoretical preoccupations, I still had a residual idea that space was neutral in theoretical terms, even though I knew it was very far from neutral for the Marakwet or for me in real life, whether in Kenya or the United Kingdom. The notion of neutrality came from the fact that I did not or could not acknowledge the assumptions about space underlying my own or others' theoretical views. It is easy, with hindsight, to make arguments about the masculinist nature of social theories, and by extension, of the spatial categories and processes implied in those theories, but in 1981 I had yet to learn about the deconstruction of grand social theory; I still thought it an unproblematically objective way of knowing the world. Or, at least,

---

[6] See Moore (1988, chap. 2) for a summary of the debate.
[7] Jackson (1983) describes the importance of acquiring knowledge in the field through active physical participation as opposed to observation or questioning.

part of me did. I simultaneously understood that Marakwet men and women did not perceive space in the same way, and that the organization of domestic space was experienced very differently by old and young, new wives and widows, and boys and girls, as well as by men and women. It was this insight that led me to develop an interpretative theory of the social meanings of domestic space which would allow room for these different interpretations, while taking account of the fixed nature of spatial forms. This drew me inexorably into a discussion of the politics of interpretation, ideology, and power differences as I struggled to explain why some interpretations should be preferred over others (see Chapters 9 and 10).

I recognize even now that I am reluctant to write about how I came to a particular theoretical understanding through my own physical involvement in a social and spatial world constructed by the Marakwet. I have often discussed this process of theory formation in seminars, but my reluctance to put these ideas down on paper has something to do with an anxiety about how to express myself. I am committed to the idea that theories and the espousal of particular theoretical positions are often the result of personal experiences and predilections that can remain opaque, if not invisible to us (Moore, 1994a). I am equally committed to the idea that anthropologists are frequently influenced by the philosophical and discursive views of the people they work with, and that anthropological theories are often the result of an unacknowledged process of dialogue and mutual recognition.

This is not a popular view in spite of the recent discussions in anthropology about the necessity of incorporating dialogue and polyphony into our texts, and about recognizing the hierarchical politics of representation. Anthropologists may be happy to talk of the ethnocentric and imperialist nature of their representations of others and to recognize the power claims inherent in the anthropologist's textual strategies, but what this leads to is a liberal desire to recognize the partial and constructed nature of anthropological accounts and to share textual authority with others. Anthropologists, including feminist anthropologists, talk much less about the influence of "others" theories on their own processes of theorization; "others" theories are after all cultural beliefs and are supposed to be the object of anthropological theorization.[8]

FEMINIST POSITIONS

The relationship between the anthropologist and the people she works with has been a subject of heated debate in the last ten years. Current feminist

---

[8] See Moore (1996) for a fuller discussion of anthropology's reluctance to see "others" as producers of social theory.

theory emphasizes the importance of placing the analyst in the same frame of reference as the subject(s) of study and acknowledging the constitutive nature of position and perspective in the construction of knowledge. The situation of feminist anthropologists has been much complicated by the differing ways in which feminist and anthropological discourses have handled questions of experience, difference, and identity.[9] Some feminist theorists have emphasized that personal experience can act as a legitimate source of authority, and there has been a noticeable shift in recent theoretical work toward valorizing the autobiographical.[10] What is at stake here is the recognition of the local and concrete situations from which women act and speak, both those who are analysts and those who are the subjects of analysis. Acknowledging specificities is part of a larger project of recognizing differences between women, and of ensuring that diverse experiences and alternative analytical formulations are not subsumed within an homogenized Western feminist framework.

Recent work in anthropology, the so-called "new ethnography," has taken a somewhat different turn and sought to undermine the authoritative experience of the anthropologist. Anthropologists have traditionally based their claims to represent "others" on their having done fieldwork and in the process acquiring personal knowledge of the society being studied.[11] The questioning of anthropological authority has been part of a larger interrogation of Western theorizing and knowledge construction. The process of radical "othering" on which subject–object relations are premised has been criticized as phallocentric and ethnocentric. Anthropological knowledge is not alone in this, but it does provide commentators of all kinds with a particularly marked exemplar of the issues at hand because of the discipline's history and its self-definition as "the study of other cultures."[12]

Both feminism and anthropology have wanted, for slightly different reasons, to question privileged subject positions and to examine dominant narratives and knowledge constructions by undermining the priority of the place from which they begin (Bhabha, 1990: 207). Dominant forms of scholarship emphasize clarity, coherence, and structured forms of argumentation, all of which serve to validate the subject position of the scholar and *his* interpretation. The narratives of others may be conflictual, using forms of address and argument that are not valorized or recognized within dominant scholarship, and thus may not be heard. Both feminism and anthropology want to reveal

---

[9] See the debate in *Signs* about the relationship between feminism, postmodernism, and anthropology (Strathern, 1987; Kirby, 1989; 1991; Mascia-Lees et al., 1989; 1991).

[10] Recent examples would include Miller, 1991, and Krieger, 1991.

[11] See Moore (1994b) for a summary and discussion of this debate.

[12] See Kirby (1993) for a critique of the failure of feminist anthropologists to take on board postmodernist discourse and its insights concerning the ethnocentric and phallocentric nature of knowledge construction.

and contest these processes of exclusion, and undermine the radical processes of othering on which they are based.

The question of how this is to be done is not resolved. Critics of the new ethnography have pointed out that experimental ethnography – changing modes of writing to include multiple voices, dialogue, and polyphony – does little to tackle the very real issues of power differences between anthropologist and informants. Feminist scholars have argued that altering modes of representation is not enough, that we must also change our practices and reconsider the ways in which we conceptualize difference. What anthropologists rarely do, including feminist anthropologists, is consider the relationship between the experience of difference(s) and the manner in which we subsequently theorize and represent them. When I wrote this book in 1984, deconstructionist and postmodernist theories were not commonplace in anthropology. However, debates about anthropological writing and the construction of anthropological knowledge did exist, and they focused on questions of ethnocentrism and the nature of anthropological models. There was also a lively discussion about why the experience of fieldwork was rarely depicted in ethnographic texts, amidst a general call for more so-called "confessional," that is autobiographical, accounts of fieldwork. The "new ethnographers" are not in any way the direct heirs to this line of thinking. Their work is more concerned with the politics of representation and the construction of difference, while the debates in the 1970s and early 1980s were principally about the adequacy of anthropological models and descriptions, but without any intention of questioning the purpose and politics of anthropology in general. There is no doubt that anthropology has benefited enormously from the critique put forward by the "new ethnographers" and from its ongoing dialogue with postmodernism. However, what has been lost in the process is any discussion of how anthropologists and the people they work with manage and think about the differences they encounter in the fieldwork situation.

I recognize, again with hindsight, that one of the reasons I chose to write a theoretical study was because I felt exceedingly insecure about how to write about my experiences of fieldwork using what I then saw as the anthropological genres available to me. I knew at the time that this was, in part, an act of cowardice, rather than simply a failure of the imagination. "The main purpose of the work is theoretical and I have not attempted to write a conventional monograph on the Endo. If, in the end, some sense of their life endures, this is their achievement, not mine" (Chapter 1, p. 12). These are the final words of the original introduction. When asked to account for them at several points over the last ten years, I have consistently explained that I could not bring myself to write in certain ways. I have always had a horror of the "As, I was standing under the palm tree" mode of anthropological writing. The romanticization and exoticization of fieldwork as text has always disturbed me. The reasons for this are intimately connected to the image of the anthropologist as public arbiter of cultural difference; where the differences will be first exaggerated only to be later incorporated and subsumed. I had a very strong sense when I came back from the field that I could not possibly portray myself in relation to the Marakwet in that way, as an all-knowing observer. Part of the experience of fieldwork both for myself and for the Marakwet I worked with was that some differences were irreducible and ultimately unknowable. We could know each other and discuss a whole range of topics and issues, but we were not and could not be the same. However, there was more to it than this because I had to recognize and accept that I was happy about this, that I did not wish to be the same, and that some differences were unknowable insofar as they were not available for or amenable to anthropological or any other kind of inquiry. By this I mean that I did not always understand the nature, significance, and meaning of differences; they simply existed as difference – at least in my perception. I do not believe that this is something confined to the anthropological field-work situation, or to ostensive "cultural" differences. It is probably a feature of all intersubjective engagement, even with people of the same gender, race, class, and culture, that establishing commonalities is a matter of trust and of relating one's own position to the position of others.

It is precisely for this reason that a knowledge of shared circumstances and familiarity with shared discourses does help. However, experiencing differences and representing them are not the same thing. One persistent problem was a question about the commonalities of women's experiences. What, if anything, did I share with Marakwet women? On one level, the answer to this question was obvious, absolutely nothing. But, on another, the answer was far from clear and remained resolutely undecidable.

The question, "Can we know difference, can we know what it consists of?" is at the center of contemporary feminist and postmodernist theorizing. But, the current emphasis on difference and on its theorization once again obscures the experience of difference(s) in the fieldwork situation. The difference of self/other is not the only form of difference in play in the context of anthropological fieldwork, and it can never be assumed to map straightforwardly onto the distinction anthropologist/informant. Recent postmodernist and feminist theorizing has shifted theoretical attention from subjects defined by difference between themselves to subjects defined by difference within themselves. The differences in play for all of us are the relations between our multiple selves: the differences which constitute us as subjects and are internal to us.

One consequence of taking this perspective on subjectivity and identity is that we have to question the ontological status of experience and its homogenized, finished nature as the property of a self-knowing individual. Recognizing the differences of which we are constituted involves acknowledging that gender, race, class, sexuality, and other forms of difference are experienced simultaneously but can be and often are in contradiction with each other.[13] Each subject is the site of competing subjectivites, and experience has to be understood and theorized on several different levels. It is not enough to say, "You are different from me and therefore you have completely different experiences from me."

The confusing thing about recognizing differences in the field is that I did not always experience myself as different from the women I worked with. There were a number of similarities or perceived similarities between us that provided recognition, pleasure, identification, and communication. Not all these similarities were long-lived, some were momentary and depended on inter-subjectivity and, on occasion, the ability to feel and apprehend something through another person. Since I was not always, or perhaps ever, apprehended simply as a categorical white, British woman, I did not communicate with others as if they were categorical black, Kenyan women. Such categorical distinctions were, of course, always present and constituted a forcible reminder of colonialism and of black–white politics in the postcolonial state. I was also very aware at the time that the experience of colonialism had consistently placed an emphasis on Kenya's black population understanding and coming to terms with the values, lifeways, and demands of white colonialists. The anthropologist reactivates this compulsive oppression, albeit unwittingly and in a slightly different register. I might have thought I was the one negotiating and making sense of cultural difference, but as the embodiment of a set of categorical identities, I was already partially known and understood. It was in many ways the Marakwet understanding of "white" culture that made the anthropological endeavor possible. But, our selves were never simply or only engaged as black/white subjects. Differences are always experienced relationally and it is through intersubjective engagement that we come to have some sense of ourselves and of others. Differences are never erased, but they can be lived simultaneously with a sense of constructed similarities, of things shared.[14] These similarities, like the differences I mentioned earlier, are also undecidable, in part, because subject positions within discourses are not fixed, but are continuously negotiated and renegotiated. Writing about these issues is formidably difficult. Looking back, I do wish that I had positioned myself more clearly in relation to the discipline of anthropology and its politics. I also wish that I had discussed the relationship between myself, the women I lived with, and the work I was engaged in.

---

[13] Scholars of color have discussed the simultaneity and often conflicting nature of multiple subject positions based on race, class, and gender; and their work has done most to theorize the understanding of the relationship between agency, subjectivity, narrative, and experience (see, e.g., Anzaldua, 1987; 1990; Moraga and Anzaldua, 1981; Sommer, 1988).

[14] Walkerdine has discussed the problem of recognition in the research context: "Often when interviewing the participants I felt that 'I knew what they meant,' that I recognized how the practices were regulated or that I understood what it was like to be a participant" (1986: 192).

In writing the text, I did deal with issues of positionality and perspective, but not my own. I wanted to advance a theoretical position that would describe women, even in circumstances of patriarchal control, as active social agents. The crux of my argument is one about physical space and the material world. The interpretive actions of Marakwet women and men are not always contained in language (see Chapter 5). Language may be a very important part of culture and social life, but not all social phenomena can be reduced to language. The interpretations and instances of social action I concern myself with in this book are about positions, about doing things differently within constructed space, about using the nonlinguistic to social effect. Issues of power, sedimentation, and hierarchy are crucial here. How can alternative interpretations be made when the organization of the material world appears fixed, socially inscribed within a particular configuration of power relations? These are some of the questions I address and try to answer in this book. It is clear that I could have placed Marakwet interpretations and perspectives alongside my own within the text. I thought I was dealing with issues of agency, and within a very neglected dimension, but there is a very big difference between theorizing definitions of agency and creating the dialogical space for that agency to be recognized as such. However, when reading this book it is important not to search for and privilege voices too much. It is true that my own and the voices of the women and men I lived with are absent for different, if connected, reasons, but I do want to draw attention to forms of gendered agency that are about position and embodiment within constructed space–time, and which are still neglected in the social sciences in favor of the spoken word.

–HENRIETTA L. MOORE
London
December 1996

Contents

 ᴄ

PART I. The Background and Setting of the Study

1	*Introduction*	3
2	*The Marakwet*	13
3	*Sibou Village*	26
4	*Space, Time, and Gender*	55

PART II. Cultural Texts and Social Change

5	*Of Texts and Other Matters*	79
6	*Ash and Animal Dung: The Organization of Domestic Space among the Endo*	98
7	*Interpreting Space*	115
8	*Wages and Westernization: The Changing Spaces of the Endo*	129

PART III. Interpretation and Representation

9	*Invisible Women*	165
10	*Text, Ideology, and Power*	200

Appendix 1	207
Appendix 2	209
Afterword	211
References	219
Index	231

Woman of Africa
Sweeper
Smearing floors and walls
with cow dung and black soil
Cook, ayah, the baby on your back
Washer of dishes,
Planting, weeding, harvesting
Store-keeper, builder
Runner of errands,
Cart, lorry, donkey . . .
Woman of Africa
What are you not?

—OKOT P'BITEK
Song of Ocol

There is more ado to interpret the interpretations than to interpret the things, and there are more books upon books than upon any other subject. We do nothing but write glosses upon one another.

—MICHEL DE MONTAIGNE

The frontiers of a book are never clear-cut: beyond the title, the first lines, and the last full stop, beyond its internal configuration and its autonomous form, it is caught up in a system of references to other books, other texts, other sentences: it is a node within a network . . . [The book's] unity is variable and relative. As soon as one questions that unity, it loses its self-evidence; it indicates itself, constructs itself, only on the basis of a complex field of discourse.

—MICHEL FOUCAULT (1972: 23)

PART I

THE BACKGROUND
AND SETTING
OF THE STUDY

CHAPTER 1

Introduction

It is now commonplace to say that the organization of space may be analyzed as a communication system or symbolic code analogous to language.
This insight, which is the product of the application of Saussurian linguistics
to anthropology, informs the contemporary analysis of a wide variety of cultural forms.

> All the various non-verbal dimensions of culture, such as styles in clothing, vil-
> lage lay-out, architecture, furniture, food, clothing, music, physical gestures, postural
> attitudes and so on are organised in patterned sets so as to incorporate coded in-
> formation in a manner analogous to the sounds and words and sentences of a
> natural language. (Leach, 1976: 10)

Structuralist and semiotic approaches to the study of cultual representation
have proved rich and very profitable in anthropology. There have, of course,
been both hostile and sympathetic critics, but few have ever been inattentive
or dismissive. The purpose of resurrecting some well-worn criticisms is not
to enter into these debates, but simply to establish a context for the theoretical and ethnographic material which follows – a way of setting the parameters
to the debate, while acknowledging the very real debt which is owed.

THE STRUCTURAL/SEMIOTIC APPROACH

Within the structural/semiotic approach cultural forms are produced, like language, from an underlying set of relationships according to rules of combination and articulation.[1] Such an approach is particularly valuable for the study

---

[1] I use the term "structural/semiotic" to refer to analyses which are concerned with signs and
sign systems, and their combination into codes and messages. I do not intend the distinction

of space, because it establishes a series of homologies between the spatial, symbolic, and social orders.[2] These homologies are partially the product of structural/semiotic analysis, where the material and the mental are joined together in the notion of boundary, constituted through the ways in which humans perceive, build and classify their social and natural worlds.[3]

Through classifying the world, people separate themselves from nature and in so doing create a cultural order which is not that of nature. Classificatory systems may be understood as systems of meaning, where meaning is given through a series of structural contrasts or oppositions. Such systems are models of intelligibility which are projected onto the world and which, in their myriad forms – dress, cuisine, house space – are all transformations of the same underlying logic. The natural world is thus divided into cultural categories, and the same conceptions and categories are to be apprehended in the social structure of society, the organization of the cosmos, the layout of ritual, and a wide variety of cultural activities and representations from the symbolic to the quotidian. The use of conceptual and material boundaries to mark and maintain differences means that the same spatial "grid" may underlie the social and symbolic distinctions between people, between those people and their world, and between their world and the world of their gods. Space is thus often analyzed as a reflection of social categories and systems of classification. The meanings assigned to elements of the spatial order in this kind of analysis are given and fixed by virtue of their relationship with the total cultural order. There is, of course, a wide variety of approaches, and it would be impossible to specify the different ways in which individual scholars have handled the study of space. However, it is important to emphasize that contemporary studies are dominated by a theoretical concern with the classification of social meanings, which is inherited from the early work of Durkheim and Mauss (Durkheim, 1976 [1915]; Durkheim and Mauss, 1963).

The analysis of space as a symbolic code and/or as a reflection of social categories and classifications presents a number of difficulties which are discussed below.

Contextuality

As we have noted, if space can embody social meanings then it can be treated as a kind of language. This portrayal of space opens it to a structuralist

---

structural/semiotic versus structuralist to be understood in a rigorous sense. My aim is to distinguish work which is concerned with the production and perception of meaning from that which is more rigidly concerned with the unconscious structures of the mind and binary oppositions. There is not always a clear-cut distinction in writings on the subject.

[2] See, for example: Ardener, 1981; Bulmer, 1973; Callaway, 1981; Hobart, 1978; Hugh-Jones, 1979; Rapoport, 1977.

[3] See, for example: Douglas, 1966, 1973; Leach, 1964; Lévi-Strauss, 1963; Tambiah, 1973.

or semiotic concern with internal relations of meaning. However, it has been pointed out that an emphasis on the internal logic of symbol systems brackets off the possibility of understanding how such systems are used and situated in defined historical contexts.[4] Finding structuralism ahistorical, critics have tried to shift attention from the analysis of abstract systems of symbols – *langue* – to the concrete utterances and practices of individuals in particular social contexts.[5] As a result, a number of writers have observed that the meaning of symbols is given by their operationalization in different contexts, rather than merely by their position in an abstract system of differences.[6] The possibility of linking signs and symbols to the specific social conditions in which they are used opens the analysis of cultural forms, including language, to a concern with the social and strategic production of meaning. For example, Barthes is able to analyze food, clothes, washing powder and wrestling as systems of signs which, through the higher-order system of signification he calls "myth," become forms of representation which naturalize certain meanings and interests (Barthes, 1973). Sign systems are thus firmly situated both in social practices and in wider social strategies. This "advanced" semiotic position dominates contemporary anthropological analyses of cultural forms.

But even when the location of signs and symbols within concrete social situations emphasizes the importance of context, there is still a "false contextuality" of sorts. For, although it is acknowledged that systems of signification may be ideological – serving or naturalizing particular interests, mystifying the reality of social relations – there is no sustained attempt to link such systems to actual relations of production and/or to the necessary emergence of specific historical conditions of meaning; except, of course, in a general way, by characterizing the relationship between cultural systems and social reality as one of misrepresentation. Misrepresentation is a function of ideology and forms a frequent part of anthropological and Marxist analyses of systems of signification, including the ordering of space. The production and maintenance of authoritative practices and discourses, in conjunction with concrete sets of historical relations and processes, are not given sufficient attention in contemporary anthropology. (Though it must be said that the work of Pierre Bourdieu is a notable exception.)[7] This deficiency is partially due to the problem of reflectionism.

---

[4] Writers from a wide range of disciplines have criticized this position, but examples from anthropology include: Bourdieu, 1977; Leach, 1970; 1976: 55–64; Scholte, 1978.

[5] The importance of context and contextuality has found expression in a wide variety of disciplines. The early work on speech acts has been influential in anthropology (Austin, 1960; Searle, 1969). For the purpose of this text, I have found Eagleton (1976; 1983) and Macherey (1978) particularly useful.

[6] Barth, 1975: 158; Fernandez, 1977; Tambiah, 1973; 1981; Turner, 1974: 22–5.

[7] Bourdieu, 1977; 1981. Other exceptions include: Moore, 1981; Turton, 1978. The relationship between ideology, cultural representations and determinate historical conditions is a major focus of concern outside anthropology; for example: Barrett, 1979; Coward and Ellis, 1977; Hall, 1978; Wolff, 1981.

"Reflection Theory"

A theoretical preoccupation with essential meanings, characteristic of the structural/semiotic approach is linked in anthropology with a particular view of culture. Culture is a difficult term which may be defined in myriad ways. But, in one very frequently used sense, culture is understood as the basic organizing principle of social life, and is defined as the integrated set of shared categories, meanings and predispositions which marks each society as unique. In such formulations, social structures are at the same time systems of social meaning and classification, as well as being categorizations of the social and natural worlds.[8] The result is that, when it comes to the problem of how cultural forms are related to the real world, it is assumed that these forms reflect society in a fairly direct way. This does not deny the possibility of misrepresentation: as I have said, it is acknowledged that cultural forms may be ideological and thus provide a distorted reflection of "social reality" in order to mask and maintain existing social relations.[9] In this sense, misrepresentation is little more than distorted reflection. However, what is clear is that neither the concept of reflection, nor that of distortion, accounts adequately for the relationship between cultural forms and social relations. More importantly, neither concept helps us to understand either the working of ideological formations or why some representations appear as closer or more accurate "reflections" of the historical conditions which generate them than others. This point is taken up again in Part II, where, following Bourdieu and others, I discuss the relationship between systems of signification and socioeconomic conditions in terms of a theory of production.

Social Change

The concept of culture as a pregiven set of meanings from which cultural practices and representations are derived makes it very difficult to conceptualize social change except as a process of creation and contradiction which would arise outside the given social structure. Asad makes this point well when he discusses Douglas's theory of grid-group:[10]

---

[8] See Asad's (1979; 1983) and Bloch's (1977) critiques of Douglas, Leach, Gellner, and Geertz.

[9] A debate which, in its crudest form, is a reworking of the structural–Marxist problematic concerning the determining infrastructure versus the determined superstructure: see Althusser and Balibar, 1970; Friedman, 1974; Godelier, 1977.

[10] Douglas's theory of grid-group is derived from Bernstein's work and is concerned with how individuals are controlled by society: "Group is obvious—the experience of a bounded social unit. Grid refers to rules which relate one person to others on an egocentric basis" (Douglas, 1973: viii). Douglas links types of social organization derived from grid-group interrelation to types of cosmology: "If we have social units whose external boundaries are clearly marked, whose internal relations are confused, and who persist on a small scale at a low level of organization, then we should look for the active witchcraft type of cosmology" (1973: 113).

Thus for Douglas the transformation of social structure is impossible, or impossible to understand, because there is no social object that is specified independently of a system of human meanings, and because such a system, like a given language, has the function of rendering the structure of cultural experience and of political action isomorphic. As in *Natural Symbols,* the meaningful statements and actions produced in those conditions are neatly fused together. Nothing can be said or done with meaning if it does not fit into an *a priori* system, the "authentic" culture which defines the essential social being of the people concerned. The process of radical transformation is described quite literally as "an emptying of meaning" – and quite rightly so if the representation of essential meanings is the mark of an authentic culture. (Asad, 1979: 618)

Asad's argument is that social life is comprised of more than just systems of meaning, and that although communication is an essential domain of human activity it is not identical with social life itself. He portrays Douglas's contextuality – her concern with the social reality of cosmologies – as a "false contextuality," because there is no real account of the material conditions of existence, the historical aspects of the material and social bases of collective life. Asad maintains that the relationship of systems of signification to social and economic conditions should be approached through the question "How do particular social and economic conditions maintain or undermine given forms of authoritative discourse as systems?" (Asad, 1979: 607). This is the question I ask in Part II, where I use the organization of domestic space to link the production and reproduction of symbol systems to the determinate historical and cultural conditions which govern their genesis and transformation.

Social Actors

The structural/semiotic approach – combined, as it so often seems to be, with the definition of culture as a set of pregiven meanings – raises the problem of practical action and of the knowledge and intentions of social actors. Structuralist analysis aims to reveal the real meanings underlying surface manifestations, and it is understood that these meanings are never directly perceivable by the social actors themselves. Such an approach takes no account of the activities of individual actors or the meanings they ascribe to those activities. While there are, of course, structural anthropologists who do try to take account of actors' "meanings," the essential problem remains: how much sense does it make to provide a "meaningful" analysis of cultural phenomena which has no "meaning" for the people themselves?[11] Lévi-Strauss acknowledges

[11] The problem of the relationship between actors' and observers' models is a matter of irresoluble debate. Several scholars have pointed out the gap between anthropological interpretation and the cultural reality of the actors concerned: Beattie, 1968: 415; Goody, 1977: 73; Griaule, 1965; Holy, 1976; 1983; Hugh-Jones, 1979; Sperber, 1975; Turner, 1967.

that he eliminates the conscious self-understandings of social actors, but he justifies it as a "methodological bracketing" (Lévi-Strauss, 1971: 560, 572). This "bracketing" of the reflexive understanding of social actors produces a situation where individuals are subordinate to society or, at least, to a pregiven set of social meanings. Individuals play the game, but they cannot change the rules. This situation is akin to that produced by the functionalist idea that individuals are subordinate to the workings of the system and that social action is governed by the internalization of rules or norms. However, social action and the meanings of social actions cannot be adequately explained by reducing them to the rules or structures of logic which underlie them. Bourdieu illustrates this with reference to Lévi-Strauss's analysis of gift exchange. He demonstrates that to reduce the exchange of gifts to the laws of reciprocity which supposedly govern such exchanges does not help us to understand the nature of gift giving. In fact, it eliminates the essential nature of what a gift is (Bourdieu, 1977: 3–9). On this basis he asserts that some attempt has to be made to link structures with the strategies and intentions of social actors and thus argues for a reintegration of action and structure.[12]

Anthony Giddens criticizes structural theories which see social action as completely determined, but he is equally critical of theories of action which ignore the existence of the historical and institutional determinants of social praxis. His argument is similar to aspects of Bourdieu's work, in that he presents a theory which would connect the strategies and intentions of social actors to the production and reproduction of institutional structures (Giddens, 1976: 156). Like Bourdieu, he conceptualizes structures as enabling, rather than constraining (Giddens, Ibid.: 161), and he stresses that structures are involved in the generation and negotiation of meanings and action (Giddens, 1976; 1979: chap. 2). The reintegration of the intentions, strategies and meanings of social actors with the production and reproduction of symbolic forms is a central concern of Part II, where I try to show that the meaning of any spatial order is not intrinsic, but must be invoked through practice.

The difficulties raised in the above section are well known and form the basis of a number of critical projects. However, for the immediate purposes of this study, the salient criticisms may be paraphrased in the following way:

1. In stressing the importance of ideas and meanings not enough attention is paid to the social and economic contexts of symbol systems or to the determinate historical and cultural conditions which govern their production and transformation.
2. The concept of culture as a pregiven set of meanings – to which all action and discourse must be related – makes it very difficult to pro-

[12] This is the basis for Gidden's theory of structuration, introduced in 1976 and set out in 1979.

vide a theory of change or to understand how human actions both produce structures and are in turn structured by them.

3. The analysis of symbolic forms must acknowledge the interpretation of social actors as other than simply contingent explanations.

The problem of analyzing social change, of linking ideological transformations to shifts in economic and social circumstances, is what first drew me to the Marakwet and to the study of cultural representations. This book discusses the relationship between ideas and beliefs, their representation in the organization of domestic space, and their interconnection with the socioeconomic circumstances which make that representation both possible and powerful. The aim of the argument is to show how socioeconomic conditions and cultural values and ideas work together to produce and transform cultural representations.

THE PLAN OF THE STUDY

The Marakwet are not well represented in writings on East African ethnography; they have never featured in a major monograph. The first part of this study presents the essential outlines of Marakwet history and ethnography, thus providing the necessary background to the more detailed study of space and gender relations presented below.

Part I begins with an overview of the published work on Marakwet history and social geography. During the colonial period, the Marakwet territory was administered as a Native Reserve, and different parts of the territory experienced colonial rule in very different ways.[13] The "highland" Marakwet, who live in the Cherangani region (see Figure 2), had direct and sustained contact with administrators and missionaries from the 1930s onward; while the "valley" Marakwet–including the Endo, who form the basis of this study–had very infrequent contact with both "the white man" and the nation-state of Kenya until the 1970s. The choice of study location was partially determined by the fact that within the last decade the people of Endo have moved from a situation of relative isolation to one of rapid social change. Chapter 3 introduces the village of Sibou, which is the central point of the study. The specific features of social organization, village layout and compound plans are placed in the context of the more general aspects of social geography discussed in Chapter 2. The topography of the valley villages is impressive, and an understanding of "life on the escarpment" is impossible without some sense of the "sloping" world of the Marakwet (Plate I). Chapter 4 aims to provide some sense of that world and of Marakwet concepts

[13] Moore, 1983; 1985.

PLATE I. A view eastward over the Kerio valley, showing the impressive topography of the Cherangani range and its influence on settlement.

of time and space. The intimate relationship between space and time is further complicated by the cross-cutting nature of gender categories. Both physical and social space have "gendered" qualities which make the conceptual and natural worlds mutually realizable. These abstract qualities of gender are related in complex ways to the spacial and temporal positions which men and women have in Marakwet social structure at different times.

Part II begins the analysis of space proper. The first chapter in the section is theoretical. It sets out an "interpretative" approach to the study of space based on an analogy with textual exegesis. The idea that cultural representations may be open to alternative "readings" forces the analysis away from a structural/semiotic concern with given meanings toward the problem of meaning–creation. The main thesis of the chapter is that meanings are not inherent in the organization of domestic space, but must be invoked through the activities of social actors. The discussion goes on to examine how the spatial order comes to have meaning; why alternative meanings exist; and how it is that some interpretations may be thought more appropriate than others. The ability to define a particular interpretation as appropriate or not is seen to be both a function and a dimension of political power. The aim of the argument is to develop a theoretical perspective which integrates aspects of semiotic analysis with the examination of ideology, power and strategy in social relations. The result is a theoretical approach which is less dependent on the anthropologists' models and more intimately related to the practical folk models of the social actors concerned.

In Chapter 6, the analysis of a sample of household compounds from Sibou village shows the degree of variability in compound organization. This variability reflects both the demands of different stages in the life-cycle and the importance of strategic choice on the part of individuals. The analysis also demonstrates a pattern of association and segregation of key features, including house structures, refuse, and human burial. This pattern is then shown to relate to a value system which arises, in part, from conflicts and tensions between the sexes. Within marriage, conflicts between men and women are part of a wider conflict between household and patriclan.

Chapter 7 provides an analysis of the organization of domestic space in the light of the theoretical concerns expressed in Chapter 5. It leads directly into Chapter 8, where an account is given of the contemporary, observable changes in domestic architecture and in the organization and use of domestic space among the Endo. In these changed circumstances, spatial order takes on a different value. The modern, square houses and their compounds represent a break with the traditional order: a break which the Endo express verbally and spatially. Both the contents of the houses and the houses themselves seem to become an expression of the economic success of the family unit. The danger of suggesting that the organization of space simply reflects social order or socioeconomic conditions is avoided by showing that what is reflected is a "representation" of the unity of the individual family rather than its real unity. The issue pursued – why is this "representation" presented and how is it maintained? – concentrates on how and why "representation" works, rather than on "representation" as a distortion or misrepresentation of reality. The final part of the chapter prefigures the argument in Part III and discusses the relationship between ideology and changing socioeconomic circumstances.

Part III examines the relationship between men and women in Endo society through their differing positions with respect to knowledge and power. The issue of male dominance is raised and discussed in relation to the possible existence of specific "male" and "female" models of experience. What is clear is that the view of gender relations expressed in the organization of space has a "male bias," in so far as it represents social and economic relations in a way which is advantageous to men. This "representation" is dominant in the cultural discourse of the Endo. The argument goes on to examine how certain representations become dominant and how they are maintained. A relationship is established between "dominant representations" and "dominant interpretations," linking the reproduction of ideological formations to the repeated renegotiation of power relations.

The layout of the book is intended to provide an easy progression from the ethnography of the Marakwet, through the theoretical concerns of the study, and back to the ethnography again. However, the ethnographic material which is presented is necessarily selective. The main purpose of the work is theoretical and I have not attempted to write a conventional monograph on the Endo. If, in the end, some sense of their life endures, this is their achievement, not mine.

CHAPTER 2

The Marakwet

$\mathcal{C}$

The Marakwet are part of the Kalenjin tribal group and live in the Cherangani hills and along the Kerio valley in western Kenya (see Figure 1).[1] Prior to the colonial period the Marakwet did not exist as a single, coherent unit ("tribe"), and the word "Marakwet" is the corruption of a term (Markweta) which originally applied to one section of the present-day group (Kipkorir, 1973: 1; Sutton, 1973: 6). The present Marakwet "tribe" consists of five sections (Almo, Cherangani, Endo, Kiptani, and Markweta)[2] which, prior to British intervention, were without tribal cohesion and probably possessed only as many similarities with each other as they did with other groups outside this artificial unit (see Figure 2).[3] The fact that the Marakwet did not exist as a recognizable unit before the advent of the colonial administration may be one of the reasons why the early travel accounts make no mention of them (von Hohnel, 1894; Peters, 1891; Gregory, 1896). In fact, as far as I know, the only reference to the Marakwet prior to 1910 is contained in a short passage by Thomson, where he mentions not the people so much as their irrigation furrows (Thomson, 1885: 310). In 1910, Dundas published an article which mentioned two groups called the Ndo and the Maragwetta, and he listed a number of sections which are recognizable as units which still exist today (Dundas, 1910: 61–5). The only other substantial reference to the Marakwet is in Beech's work on the Suk (now called the Pokot), where he mentions the Endo and the Maragweta (Beech, 1911: 2–3) and subsequently relates some of the customs of the Suk to those of their neighbors, including

---

[1] The boundaries of the Marakwet area fall within the grid references 1 17°N to 0 45°N latitude and 35 0°E and 35 42°E longitude.
[2] Sometimes mention is made of another group called the Borokot (see Kipkorir, 1973: 4).
[3] The arbitrary combination and division of indigenous ethnic groups, in order to create convenient units for administration and security purposes, was a feature of colonial policy throughout Africa.

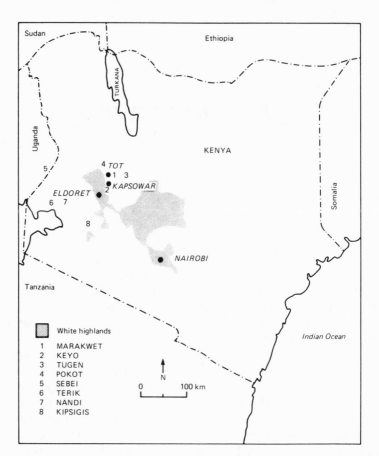

FIGURE 1. The location of the Marakwet and other Kalenjin peoples.

the Endo (Beech, 1911: 27–37). Apart from these references, the Marakwet are almost entirely absent from the literature until the 1950s; on the rare occasions when they are mentioned (e.g., by Evans-Pritchard, 1940: 250) it is clearly assumed that they are not worth discussing because they are so similar to the Suk and/or the Keyo.[4] The result is that the precolonial and early twentieth-century history of the Marakwet is obscure; there is no information on how the different sections were related prior to British intervention and no way of telling whether the similarities and differences between the Marakwet and other Kalenjin groups were great or small.[5] This

[4] Beech published an article in 1913 in which he compared the dialect of the Endo with the language of the Suk; he clearly regarded the Endo as a separate and distinct tribe (Beech, 1913: 70–2).
[5] Recent linguistic work suggests that the Endo dialect is more similar to Pokot (Suk) than it is to some of the more southerly Marakwet groups and that the individual Marakwet sections do indeed have stronger links with some of their non-Marakwet neighbors than they do with each

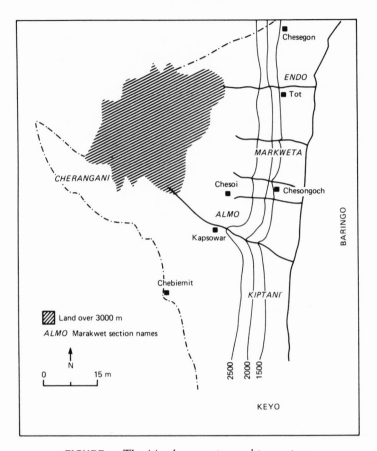

FIGURE 2. The Marakwet region and its sections.

situation has not been improved by recent work on the Kalenjin, which deals
almost exclusively with the group's early history (2000 B.C.–1500 A.D.).
Nevertheless, a brief account of some of the recent ethno-historical and linguistic work is necessary, in order to give some idea of the current state of
research on the Kalenjin and to provide a context for the contemporary study
of the Marakwet which is to follow.

THE KALENJIN AND THEIR HISTORY

The history of the Marakwet may be little known and obscure, but the history of the Kalenjin is much discussed and rather complex. Kalenjin means

other (Rottland, 1981; Sutton, 1976: 23). Writing in 1910, Dundas claims that the Ndo were
a mixture of Pokot (Suk) and Maragwetta and that all Ndo spoke Pokot fluently (Dundas, 1910: 62).

"I tell you"; as a name it is of recent coinage, and covers a group or cluster of tribes who are thought to constitute a distinct linguistic and cultural group.[6] At the present time the Kalenjin number over a million people and are divided into eight main groups: the Pokot (or Suk), the Marakwet, the Sebei, the Terik, the Keyo, the Tugen, the Nandi and the Kipsigis (see Figure 1).[7] The Kalenjin are linguistically classified as "Nilotes," and according to Greenberg they constitute the southern section of the Nilotic branch of the Eastern-Sudanic family, which is part of the Chari–Nile group (Greenberg, 1963).[8] Recent attempts to reconstruct the history of the Kalenjin have been based on examining linguistic similarities and developments, with some occasional use of ethnographic and archaeological evidence. These studies have tried to establish the antiquity of the Kalenjin dialect, to stress that the language and culture of the Kalenjin people evolved in the western highlands of Kenya, to refute the claim that the Kalenjin migrated into the area only four or five hundred years ago. To this end Ehret has identified a pre-Southern Nilote culture, which includes such traits as age sets, individual households, the extraction of upper incisors and the absence of hereditary chieftainship, and which he dates to around 2000 B.C. (Ehret, 1971: 36). These pre-Southern Nilotes occupied an area on the Kenya–Ethiopia–Sudan border, but both Ehret and Sutton agree that by the time of Christ there were Southern Nilotes in the western highlands of Kenya (Ehret, 1971: 44). Sutton sums up the main thesis of the argument extremely clearly:

> It was probably in their present territory of the western highlands of Kenya, especially the more northerly parts of this region, that the Kalenjin evolved as a cultural and linguistic group. Very probably too, it was in this same region that the "Highland" (or Southern) division of Nilotic speech from which Tatoga as well as Kalenjin descends, first developed, after splitting from what were to become the two other Nilotic divisions – Western and Eastern – somewhere around the borders of the southern Sudan and the Ethiopian massif 2,000 yrs ago or more. This conspectus, albeit rather crude, emerges from observations of the basic divisions and relationships within the present Nilotic languages and of their geographical distribution. (Sutton, 1973: 14)[9]

---

[6] For more information on this point and the political background to the term, see Kipkorir, 1973: 70–6.

[7] An additional group, the Okiek, are sometimes mentioned as part of the Kalenjin; it is usually claimed that, unlike all the other groups, they are hunters/gatherers (Sutton, 1973: 8–9; Kipkorir, 1973: 1).

[8] "Nilotic" should be taken to include all languages previously designated "Nilo-Hamitic" and sometimes called "para-Nilotic." For a classification scheme, see Ogot and Kiernan, 1968: chap. 4. This classification is not unproblematic, and there is some controversy as to how the Kalenjin developed as a separate grouping within the Chari–Nile group. For expansion of this point, see Moore, 1977.

[9] For further information on linguistic classification and nomenclature, see Tucker and Bryan, 1962: 149.

Ehret and Sutton further develop their point concerning the antiquity and the indigenous development of the Kalenjin, by stressing the amount of time needed for the development of distinct subdivisions (e.g., a distinct Pokot dialect) within the Kalenjin branch of Highland Nilotic (Sutton, 1973: 15; Ehret, 1971: 166).

The work of Sutton and Ehret has to be set against previous reconstructions of Kalenjin history, which suggested a late migration into the western highlands. The chief proponent of this view was Huntingford, who argued that about five hundred years ago, the Kalenjin migrated from the region around Lake Rudolf (now Turkana), toward Mount Elgon and then dispersed from this point to form the present Kalenjin tribes (Huntingford, 1950: 104–6; 1953: 2; 1963: 72–8). Huntingford's argument is predominantly based on oral testimonies, and he does not appear to account for the way in which oral traditions often telescope chronological time and thus tend to speak of migrations and the founding of clans as if they took place no more than two hundred years ago (see Dundas, 1910: 56–8; and Massam, 1927: 14, for examples). Sutton is of the opinion that oral histories should not be regarded as references to the original Kalenjin migrations and settlements; rather, he sees these stories as related to secondary movements and the redefinition of already existing groups. He further rejects the short chronology based on oral testimonies, because he argues that it does not allow sufficient time for Kalenjin expansion (and subsequent contraction) beyond their present territory.[10] On the basis of word borrowings from Kalenjin into other tongues, Sutton and Ehret postulate considerable Kalenjin movements, south, west, and east of their present position during the last five centuries (Sutton, 1976: 39–43; Ehret, 1968: 170ff; 1971: chap. 9). While this thesis is not in conflict with what we know from oral histories, there has been no systematic attempt to link the movements described in the oral accounts with the linguistic evidence or with an etymological study of "tribal" place-names.[11]

Although recent work on the Kalenjin has illuminated and given coherence to much of the group's early history, it is obvious and unavoidable that this narrative should remain conjectural and uncertain in some of its details. The lack of detail may be unsurprising with regard to the early period (2000 B.C.–1500 A.D.), but it is frustrating and unfortunate when we come to consider the events of the last two hundred years or so. The precolonial history

---

[10] About 500 years ago Kalenjin speech and culture reached their greatest dominance, not only in the western highlands, but also over a wide region to the west, south and east. In subsequent centuries there were limited expansions to the south and north, but the general process was one of contraction, and the Kalenjin were increasingly restricted to the western highlands. This was due partly to Bantu expansion and partly to the great Maasai movements which reached their climax in the eighteenth century (Sutton, 1976: 39–48; Distefano, 1976: 22–31).

[11] Kohler and Distefano both discuss the nature of some of these movements for the various Kalenjin groups and try to place them in the context of the few recorded oral accounts (Kohler, 1954; Distefano, 1976).

of the Marakwet does not, as yet, exist. There has been no systematic attempt to collect and collate oral testimonies, as has been done so successfully
for the Luo and the Abaluyia (Ogot, 1967; Were, 1968). It is clear that a wealth
of material exists and that there is an urgent need to collect information on
clan histories, on contact with neighboring groups, and on raids, climatic ca-
lamities, population movements and origin myths.[12] Until this work is done
it is not possible to suggest what contact the Marakwet sections had with
each other prior to their forced amalgamation by the British; nor is it possible
to know what the precolonial political and social organization of these groups
were or what form their subsistence activities took. The difficulties encoun-
tered in assessing the contemporary ethnography, in asking "Who are the
Marakwet?" are compounded by the intractable question "Who *were* the
Marakwet?"

THE SOCIAL GEOGRAPHY OF THE MARAKWET

The Marakwet, together with their neighbors the Elgeyo, form the administrative district of Elgeyo–Marakwet in the Rift Valley Province. The Marakwet number about 81,397 persons and occupy an area of approximately 1,595
sq km (Kenya Population Census, 1969: vol. 1). Within this area there is a
dramatic difference between the well-watered highlands of the Cherangani
hills and the semiarid environment of the western escarpment and the Kerio
valley. The highland area has an average rainfall of 1100–1500 mm per year,
and in this more productive environment the traditional cultivation of eleusine has been replaced by maize, supplemented by potatoes, beans, cabbage
and other vegetables. The people of the highlands have access to forest and
high-altitude grassland, and the extra grazing which this provides encourages
the keeping of cattle. The western escarpment and the Kerio valley have an
average rainfall of 600–700 mm per year, and this semiarid environment, with
its acacia and thorn scrub, is in dramatic contrast to the lush green of the
fertile highlands. The limited rainfall of the valley area falls within one main
season of six months, and, although rain-fed agriculture is possible, there is
extensive reliance (particularly in the north) on irrigation (Hennings, 1941;
Huxley, 1959; Soper, 1983; Ssennyonga, 1983). The main crops are sorghum
and finger millet, but cassava – which was introduced in the late 1940s – is
also extensively produced (Critchley, 1983: 2).[13] Other crops, including

---

[12]Kipkorir has done some work on clan histories and on the so-called "Misri legends." This work
has yet to be published and the position remains unclear. Among the Endo, I found that recollection of the Misri legends was poor and that some young men knew of them from school text-
books rather than from their elders.

[13]These two cereals are particularly well suited to the area: sorghum is drought-tolerant, and finger
millet has the advantage of pest-free storage (Critchley, 1983: 19). Each family in Endo has
approximately 1–2 acres of maize and ½–1 acre of finger millet or sorghum.

maize, bananas, mangoes, groundnuts, chili peppers, and cotton are grown, and in recent years maize has become increasingly popular. The success of various crop types depends on the availability of water – a problem which is exacerbated by the unpredictable nature of rainfall. The arid environment of the valley is not suitable for keeping cattle, and tsetse-fly and mosquitoes are an additional problem. Consequently, cattle are rare and most families own a small herd (20–25) of goats or a mixed herd of goats and sheep. The ecological differences between the highland and valley areas are paralleled by differential access to other kinds of resources, such as communications, market, education, wage labor, and government money. This point is developed later in the discussion of social change.

The Sections of the Tribe

Until the term "Kalenjin" emerged in the 1940s the Kalenjin tribes were known collectively as "the Nandi-speaking peoples." This latter term was a colonial invention and was a formal recognition of the common traditions, culture and dialects of these otherwise disparate tribes (Kipkorir, 1973: 72). The identification of similarities has encouraged a synthetic approach to the study of the Kalenjin, which tends to emphasize homogeneity at the expense of historical complexity. I have therefore referred quite extensively to the published material on other Kalenjin tribes, in order to show in what ways the Marakwet are similar to, and in what ways they differ from, other Kalenjin groups. I have already said that the Marakwet originally consisted of five sections: Almo, Cherangani, Endo, Kiptani, and Markweta (see Figure 2). It is uncertain what sociopolitical function these sections had, if any, in precolonial times. Kipkorir seems to suggest that they were territorial units with a military function, but I think that he may have been unduly influenced in his interpretation by the work of other scholars writing on the Kalenjin. Apart from oral accounts which speak of inter-section feuding, and a single occasion when three of the Marakwet sections are known to have combined to repel an aggressor, there is no evidence that the sections ever had a military organization or function (Kipkorir, 1973: 35). However, it is certain that other Kalenjin tribes did have a system of territorial, military units, though the exact nature and composition of such units is often obscured by English terms (e.g., shire) used either to translate the indigenous term or, where no indigenous term existed, merely to describe the unit. Huntingford says that the largest territorial unit among the Nandi was the *emet*, which he translates as "county," and which he says was purely a geographical division with no political function (Huntingford, 1953: 6). The *emet* was divided into a number of *pororyet;* this term "originally denoted a group of people who formed a fighting unit. . . . In this sense it may be translated 'regiment'. Later the term was extended to cover the land on which the members of the regiment lived" (Huntingford,

1953: 8). Goldschmidt notes a similar organization for the Sebei; he says that the tribe was originally three tribes, which were subdivided into *pororyet* (Goldschmidt, 1976: 44). These *pororyet* were geographical units with a council (*kok* or *kokwet*) and a definite military function (Goldschmidt, 1976: 63). Peristiany has yet another classification; he says the Kipsigis were divided into four emet or "provinces," which were independent judicial and military units (Peristiany, 1939: 2–3). These "provinces" were divided into "shires." A "shire" was a territorial unit consisting of a group of villages for which there was no Kipsigis term, in spite of the fact that these units apparently possessed separate civil, military, and religious leaders (Peristiany, 1939: 176)! Beech notes that the Pokot were divided into eight territorial sections, but tells us nothing about their function, military or otherwise (Beech, 1911: 1).

It is clear from this brief summary that the internal organization of the different Kalenjin groups is not necessarily comparable, and that units with similar names do not necessarily have similar forms or functions: Huntingford's *emet* is a nonpolitical, geographical division, while Peristiany's *emet* is a territorial unit with judicial and military functions. I would argue that the linguistic and cultural similarities which have always been apparent among the different tribes of the Kalenjin group have tended to confuse researchers and observers into looking for congruence where none exists. It stems from a colonial obsession with order and political accountability. Thus the colonial records state that Marakwet country was divided into seven sections, each of which had a separate body of warriors who undertook military activities (Eldama Ravine Political Record Book, 1928). Apart from the fact that this report confuses section names with clan names and thus makes it impossible to tell what sort of group, if any, undertook these military activities. There is also a distinct possibility that the Colonial Officer in question is merely trying to understand the organization of the Marakwet in terms of a model which is already familiar to him from work done on other East African tribes. From the earliest days of the colonial administration the Marakwet were likened in their social organization to the Nandi (Marakwet Annual Report, 1914/15). My own information, collected in Endo, suggest that there were five tribal sections (not comparable to those listed in the colonial records): Endo (from Tot to Chesegon), Mogoro (from Tot to Chesongoch), Sengwer (Cherangani location), Kiptani (south of Aror, on the border of the Marakwet and the Keyo), and Borokot (Chesoi area) (see Figure 2). These sections appear to have been territorial units with defined boundaries which used to be known to all adult Marakwet but are now somewhat blurred because they have been long superseded by the present administrative boundaries. According to informants, these sections were not military units, nor did they combine for ritual or judicial purposes. The inhabitants of each section were recognized by outsiders on the basis of certain, section-specific, cultural practices. For example, the Endo had mud hairstyles and wore lip plugs; the Mogoro were reputed to chew dry skin (*mogor*); while the Markweta dug their irrigation channels at night and were thus always muddy (*markwat*). From my information, it would appear that the original Marakwet sections were autonomous, regional groups, whose culturally defined characteristics were a recognition of important, but not radical, differences. While the geographical boundaries of the groups were known, it seems that "border" communities on either side were often indistinguishable from each other[14] and that people could change their residence from one section to another. The distinctive nature of the sections and their individual autonomy is reinforced by the fact that, according to the Endo, there is no occasion when the sections combine for ritual or judicial purposes.[15] The largest judicial unit is the individual section, and the only time a council (*kokwo*) of the whole section will be called is when a decision concerning homocide payments has to be made. This council is called the *kokwo met*, and it consists of all the elders of the section. The council has no formal structure and no existence outside the particular case it is called to decide.

Divisions within the Sections

Among the Marakwet each section is divided up into a number of *kor* or "villages." These villages are geographically and socially defined entities, whose boundaries are always delineated by physical features such as streams, trees, or rocks.[16] Among the valley Marakwet, each village contains an area on the escarpment side (*lagam*), a portion of land between the foot of the escarpment and the Kerio river (*keyo*) and a portion of land on the top of the escarpment (*masop*). This three-zone pattern is typical of the valley ecology and means that the form of all the valley villages is essentially the same. In all parts of Marakwet the term *kor* typically denotes both a residential area and an area of associated land from which its members gain their livelihood. Among the Marakwet, the link between the social unit and the land it occupies is very strong. The communal nature of land holding (although individuals inherit usufruct rights to specific portions of land) has to be seen in the context of

---

[14] It is interesting that sections should choose to differentiate between themselves by drawing attention to physical or "cultural" attributes. One remarkable feature is that it was apparently possible to become "Endo" by adopting the mud hairstyle. Hodder (1979) has discussed this sort of cross-boundary interaction between groups, but I think that further research based on the insights gleaned from the contemporary analyses of subcultures might prove rewarding (see Hebdige, 1979).

[15] It is also clear from oral testimonies that the sections of the Marakwet occasionally fought against each other—usually over cattle—as well as against neighboring groups like the Pokot and the Tugen. This would also suggest a degree of autonomy between the sections.

[16] Huntingford also notes the importance of physical and natural features in the naming of *koret*, but he does not discuss the use of such features as boundary markers (Huntingford, 1953: 14).

the deeply affective bond which the Marakwet perceive between the clan and its land. Thus, the *kor* and the land it occupies are, for the Marakwet, quite inseparable.

Other Kalenjin groups appear to be divided into units which might be comparable to the Marakwet *kor*. Peristiany explained that among the Kipsigis a few adjacent households formed a *temet* which was a distinct social unit, and several temet formed a *kokwet* or village (Peristiany, 1939: 177). These villages had headmen (*kiruogindet*), who performed judicial, economic and military functions (Peristiany, 1939: 176). Huntingford states that the basic territorial unit among the Nandi was the *koret* or parish and that this unit was based not on clan affiliation, but on "social" and age-set links (Huntingford, 1953: 17). The council of the *koret* was called the *kokwet* and its usual meeting place was outside under a shady tree (Huntingford, 1953: 23). Goldschmidt stresses that among the Sebei the *pororyet* was divided into smaller, spatially defined social units called *santa* and that these units were once identical with clan groupings (Goldschmidt, 1976: 71). However, the group whose organization would appear to be closest to that of the Marakwet is the Pokot. Conant refers to a unit of physical and social space called a *korok*, where each *korok* contains representatives of three or four lineages or sections of patriclans. Each *korok* has a *kokwa* or council, composed of the heads of all the independent households, and this council plays a role in organizing communal labor in the *korok* (Conant, 1965: 431). In his discussion of Pokot social and territorial organization, Peristiany refers to both villages and federations of villages, but it is unclear how these units are related to Conant's *korok* (Peristiany, 1954: 18–19). Comparison with the Marakwet material would suggest that Conant's *korok* is similar to the Marakwet *kor*, and that Peristiany's federation would be a village or *kor* among the Marakwet, while his village is what I refer to as a clan or lineage area within a *kor*.

What makes the Marakwet *kor* and the Pokot *korok* different from the residential units found among the Nandi and the Kipsigis is that they are identified with localized kin groups, both clans and lineages. Peristiany says that among the Kipsigis "there is not a trace of the clan as a geographical unit" (Peristiany, 1939: 121), and Huntingford notes that the Nandi clans are geographically dispersed (Huntingford, 1953: 21). The clan plays a very different role among the Marakwet. Kipkorir is the only scholar to have discussed the Marakwet clan, and the following quotation contains the substance of his remarks on their organization and function:

> Marakwet society is divided into thirteen, patrilineal clans, each of which is divided into two or more exogamic sections distinguished by totems. The clans cut across the territorial groups and many are represented also in other Kalenjin tribal groups. . . . Normally, residence was in totemic sections, scattered widely through Marakwet and often having, as nearest neighbours, settlements of other clans. (Kipkorir, 1973: 6)[17]

Kipkorir's description is substantially correct, but it does not discuss adequately the relationship between the clan (*aret*) and the residential unit (*kor*), which is an integral part of any attempt to understand the social and geographical organization of the Marakwet. The Marakwet *kor* or village is always composed of one or more exogamic clan sections; in cases where there is more than one section, the sections will not be subsections of the same clan. The clan as an overarching, geographical unit is not exogamous, for members of one totemic subsection may marry members of another. Subsections are normally exogamic, but the principles of kinship in Marakwet society are cross-cut by links which are established through coresidence. Thus, it is perfectly possible for a man to marry someone who is of the same totemic subsection of their common clan, provided that the two partners do not live in the same village or kor. However, the Marakwet do say that for this to happen the two parts of the subsection must have been resident in different villages for ten generations. This illustrates one of the fundamental features of Marakwet social organization, which is that "rules" and "regulations" governing the definition of social (and kin) groups and their interrelation do not have a fixed prescriptive form. The definition of the minimal exogamic group is not given by rules governing the structural segmentation of clan groups, but is given only by the parameters of the context in which such a definition would be both appropriate and necessary. It is for this reason that the clan as an overarching, amorphous entity has no meaning for the Marakwet, for there is no context in which it ever becomes a socially, politically, or ritually relevant grouping. As against Kipkorir, I would argue that the only relevant clan grouping for the Marakwet is the clan section; the residential group of agnatic males who trace their descent to a single founder. The names of such groups are formed by prefixing the syllable *kab* or *kap* to the founder's name. Throughout the text I use the term "clan" to refer to the residential clan sections I have just described and not to the overarching, geographical entity described by Kipkorir.

Each Marakwet village or *kor* is composed of one or more of these residential clan units, and within the village each clan has its particular clan area. The relationship between the social group and its geographical location is particularly strong. Evidence for this is given in the way Marakwet make enquiries of strangers. Kipkorir gives precedence to the exchange of clan affiliations between strangers (Kipkorir, 1973: 6), but from my experience the first question asked of a stranger is always *ichono kornee,* "from which village do you come?" Only then is it relevant to ask for the clan name, and, contrary to what Kipkorir says, the reply does not include the name of the main clan, then the name of the totemic section and so on. On the contrary the

---

[17] Marakwet clans are totemic, but there are few restrictions on killing and eating totemic animals. It is said that if a man kills his *tiongen* (totemic animal) then he must apologize to it. I have even heard of people apologizing and then killing the animal!

reply will always be, "I am of Kabisioi" or "I am of Kapsiren"; in other words the respondent gives the name of the residential clan group. Only if people from distant parts of the country meet will it be necessary to ask for the totemic affiliation of the residential group. In all other contexts this will be known once the name of the group is given.

All residential clan groups are divided into lineages (*kabor*, literally "of father") whose members can trace their relationship to a common ancestor. The genealogical depth of clans and lineages is no more than four or five generations. Thus, requests for genealogies usually produce only four generations of ancestors between the "founding father" and the present-day members of the lineage. This helps to sustain the immediacy of links with the past and with the founder of the clan. It is said either that clans are divided into lineages because the "founding father" had many sons or that each lineage is descended from the sons of different wives. Within the village each lineage has a designated lineage area, but not all members of the lineage will be resident there. This is particularly apparent in villages where there is more than one residential clan group, because these groups are permitted to intermarry, and, since residence is both neolocal and virilocal, a man may choose to live near his wife's brothers. Age-mates often wish to live close to each other, and thus a man may leave his lineage area to go and live in that of an age-mate. I have also recorded similar residential shifts as the result of stock relationships between men, and as a result of young men moving to live with their mother's brothers.

The village, the residential clan group and the lineage are all cooperative groups, and decisions concerning matters of mutual interest are made by groups of male elders. Peristiany and Huntingford speak of a council of the *koret* called a *kokwet* which appears to be a formalized body, with an appointed leader or "master of ceremonies" (Peristiany, 1939: 127; see Huntingford, above). From my experience with the Marakwet, I wonder if these two scholars have not over-formalized the *kokwet* and the role of its so-called "leader." Among the Marakwet, a *kok* is a group of men called together to discuss matters and settle disputes. The composition of the group depends entirely on the matter in hand and is another example of the contextual definition and function of social groups among the Marakwet. If a *kok* is called to settle marital or other lineage disputes then it will consist of all circumcized men of the lineage. If the matter is one of water rights or stock trespass, then all the circumcised men of the clan will be called. If it is a village matter, then all the men of the village will attend. The type of *kok* is designated by its name, which is always derived from the matter under discussion and not from the nature of its composition. It is only possible to say that there is a lineage *kok*, a clan *kok* and a village *kok*, insofar as there are matters which are of concern to the lineage, the clan or the village. There is, however, a sense in which *kokwet* as decision-making groups form a hierarchy, so that if a lineage *kok* cannot make a decision a clan *kok* will be called to discuss the matter and so on. However, this hierarchical relationship is contextual and in no way implies a permanent structural ranking.

The Marakwet say that the *kok* expresses the strength of social relationships between men and symbolizes the unity of the social group. Prior to colonial times, the Marakwet had no chiefs. There were, however, men called *kiruwokin,* who were orators of renown and whose advice and knowledge were respected in the *kok.* A man still gains much prestige if he talks well in *kok* and if his advice is seen to be sound. But, the ideal of Marakwet life is that all elders (*boyot*) are equal and none has authority over others. In the past, this ideal seems largely to have been the reality, although there were always men of prestige whose personal qualities had allowed them to prosper in wealth and in influence. Nowadays the ideal of equality is under considerable pressure from the alternative prestige structures which wage employment and Western goods have created.

In this brief introduction I have tried to give some sense of Marakwet sociopolitical geography and social organization. In the next chapter I turn to the people of Endo and to the village of Sibou which formed the locus of my study. It is hoped that by moving from a general ethnographic account to a focus on the organization of Sibou village, we can begin to construct a sense of the lived space of the Endo.

CHAPTER 3

Sibou Village

~~*T*~~

> *Marakwet country, starting thirty miles north of Tambach, is one of the*
> *most secluded corners of Kenya. Beyond the old Government station of*
> *Marakwet (Kapsowar) there are no motor roads at all.*
> — R. O. HENNINGS, 1951: 201

Thus did Hennings begin a picturesque description of Endo location and its people. The isolation and seclusion which so impressed the young English-man in the 1950s remained characteristic of the area until the 1970s. In the last decade change has been extremely rapid, and the bewildering speed with which it proceeds creates an impression of making up for lost time. The aim of this chapter is to provide some background to the history of the area; to place Sibou village in its context; and then to discuss the organization of families, compounds, and houses within a section of the village.

THE HISTORY AND THE SETTING

The Cherangani hills, which define the western edge of the Kerio valley, rise to a height of 3,500 m. The eastern side of the range slopes steeply down to the floor of the valley, and most of the Endo settlements are to be found between 1,000 and 2,200 m on the lower slopes of the escarpment. The vil-lage chosen for this study was Sibou village, in the Endo location of Elgeyo-Marakwet District. Sibou is an area of approximately 4.5 sq km and covers the sides of a "bowl"-shaped hill at the foot of the escarpment, from which it takes its name.

The village of Sibou occupies a position on the escarpment just above the modern settlement of Tot (see Figure 3). Tot, like a number of other small settlements, lies on the one road which runs north–south along the floor of

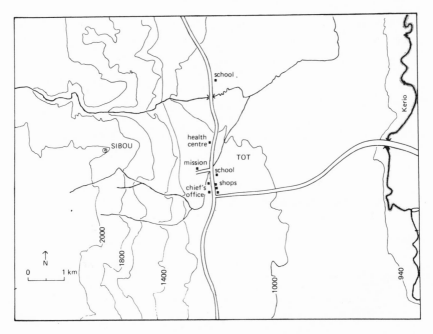

FIGURE 3. The location of Sibou village.

the Kerio valley. This road, which for most of its length stays close to the foot of the escarpment, existed in precolonial times; oral traditions describe it as the trade route through the valley, a claim which is supported by the Marakwet name, *aarap koton,* road of succour (Kipkorir, 1983: 5). During coloni- al times, a road which coincided, more or less, with the traditional commer- cial route was constructed along the length of the valley floor. This road was started in 1913 using forced labor, and finally completed in 1936 (Marakwet Annual Reports, 1913, 1936). The route was primarily intended for adminis- trative and security purposes, and the earliest settlements to grow up along- side it were for administrative convenience rather than commercial enterprise.

The settlement of Tot dates from *c.* 1949 and apparently began as a col- lection point for the taxes from Endo and Mokorro locations.[1] The chief's office (now the police station) and a lock-up were the first buildings to be constructed and the rest of the settlement grew up around them. Two tea- houses and a shop were built in 1950, and in 1953 a small primary school was started. In 1951, the colonial government tried to establish a bridge over

---

[1] The Marakwet District Handing Over Report for 1950 mentions the existence of a lock-up at Tot and the need for more buildings. Other details on the history and development of Tot were collected from informants.

the Kerio river at Tot. Early attempts were frustrated, but the bridge was eventually completed in 1953. This provided the only road link in the north between the east and west sides of the valley and further encouraged the growth of the settlement. In 1959, a government health center was established at Tot and in the same year the Chesoi–Chesongoch road down the escarpment was completed (Kipkorir, 1983: 8). This road joined Kapsowar to Endo and marked the establishment of a major communication link between the valley and the highlands. At the present time, Tot is the largest center on the western side of the valley between Tambach and Chesegon. It has a police station, a health center, two schools and the offices of the education, health and agricultural ministries for the locations of Endo and Mokorro. In short, it is a growing administrative center, which is rapidly developing certain commercial and service interests. But, in spite of increasing government interest in the area, both Tot and the whole of Endo location remain somewhat cut off from the more developed areas of the highlands and the southern part of the Kerio valley. This is, in large part, due to the continuing problem of communication; neither the road along the valley floor nor the Chesoi–Chesongoch road is passable in all weathers. Consequently, there is no regular system of transport, and this makes the movement of people and goods very difficult and arduous. The northern part of the valley is still considered remote and underdeveloped: The way of life is still traditional, the government presence is small, and the permanent Catholic mission was only installed in the mid-1970s. The history of this area is very different from that of the highland Marakwet areas (Moore, 1985). Nevertheless, change is obvious, and the settlement of Tot, with its government officers, schools and shops, has had a considerable influence on the neighboring escarpment villages.

The modern center of Tot actually occupies land which belonged to the people of Sibou, and the village itself is contiguous with the modern settlement. Other villages in the area have undoubtedly been influenced by Tot center, but it is Sibou that has been most strongly affected by the influx of government officers, school teachers, army personnel, and traders who are impatient with the traditional way of life, demand certain facilities, wear "Westernized" clothes, eat slightly different food, and require a certain "standard" of accommodation. These differences and demands are obvious to people in villages all along the escarpment, but for the inhabitants of Sibou they are a pressing, everyday reality.

The village of Sibou rises behind Tot (Plate II), on the steep slope of the escarpment. There is no sense of a nucleated settlement; approximately three hundred homesteads cover an area of 4.5 sq km. Sibou is typical of other villages in the area, where residence is almost exclusively confined to the escarpment side (*lagam*). The boundaries of the villages are marked by natural features: stones, trees, and water courses. To the untutored eye, the whole escarpment seems to be one great village. Village boundaries are contiguous:

PLATE II. A view of Sibou village from Tot center.

On either side of a dry stream bed, households 100 m apart are in different villages, often with different allegiances and different interests. Firmly bounded communities live literally side by side.

The three-zone pattern of land use is what gives the "valley" villages their distinctive topography and sense of place. The valley floor (*keyo*) is the zone of economic activities: agriculture, grazing, bee-keeping, hunting and gathering, and fuel collection. Above it, the escarpment (*lagam*) is the residential area, where houses are built, grain is stored, and ceremonial and political activities take place. The highland area above the houses (*masop*) provides timber, game, and crops suitable to the cooler climate. The people of the valley live in a "sloping world," which powerfully constructs their sense of place.

THE ORGANIZATION OF THE VILLAGE

Clans and Lineages

As noted in the previous chapter, all Marakwet villages comprise one or more patrilineal clan groups. The Endo say that the exact composition of each village is a matter of historical accident: some villages contain two or three clan groups, each with several lineages, while others comprise a single clan or even a single lineage. Sibou village is made up of four different clan groups: the *Kabisioi*, the *Siaban*, the *Kapsiren*, and the *Kapchepsom*. The clan histories of the Endo have never been studied, and a small, but systematic, collection of oral traditions from Sibou produced remarkably contradictory and piecemeal accounts. One certain feature is that all the clans claim to have arrived in their present location from elsewhere: the *Kabisioi* and *Kapchepsom* from Baringo, the *Siaban* from Kapsowar, and the *Kapsiren* from Kitale. From information I collected in Sibou and elsewhere, it would appear that many Marakwet groups claim that they originally came from *Misre* (Egypt), followed the Nile south to the area of Lake Victoria, and then moved eastward into what is now the Nyanza Province of Kenya. Apparently, various groups split off at various times during this journey, but many clan histories refer to considerable movement around western Kenya before final settlement. It seems clear that the clan histories I collected from Sibou refer to this final stage of movement, but the actual origins of the clans and the details of their coming remain obscure.

A number of Endo stories link clan histories with the digging of major irrigation furrows. These furrows are impressive feats of engineering which have led a number of scholars to speculate about the date and manner of their construction (Hennings, 1941; Huxley, 1959; Sutton 1976; Soper, 1983). Sibou village has three such farrows, but it is unclear whether they predate the arrival of Marakwet people in the area, or whether the people of Sibou constructed the furrows themselves. I was told by some informants that the furrows were already in existence when the forefathers of the present clans arrived and that they found one old man living in the village who explained to the "newcomers" how the furrows worked.[2] However, other informants expressed a contrary view, and claimed that the clans of Sibou were themselves responsible for digging the furrows. This is an account of the latter type:

> The three clans – *Kabisioi, Siaban, and Kapsiren* – first constructed one furrow because they were short of labor. *Kapchepsom* found these people resting near the "mission." He greeted the Siaban man: "Hello Uncle" (*mamaa*). He then greeted the *Kapsiren* man in the same way. He wanted to greet *Kabisioi,* but *Kabisioi* refused.
>
> *Kapchepsom* was carrying a child on his back. He asked the way to the highlands. They directed him. *Kabisioi* then asked *Siaban* and *Kapsiren:* "How come this boy is your nephew?" They replied that they did not know. *Kabisioi* then said: "Why did you greet him?"
>
> *Kapchepsom* went to the highlands and then back to Baringo, where he stayed for two years. Then he returned. He met the others again, a few yards further on with their furrow. *Kabisioi* was worried that *Kapchepsom* might wish him harm for his previous failure to greet him. So he

---

[2] Hennings (1951) recorded a similar story. It is also interesting to note that stories varied regardless of the clan affiliation of the informant.

ran away and started his own furrow. *Kapchepsom* decided to join the other two, so that there were three building the furrow as before. After some time, *Kabisioi* came and told *Kapchepsom* to go away. When *Kapchepsom* heard this he called the *boyot* (elders). The *boyot* asked *Kabisioi*: "How many was *Kapchepsom* when he came?" "One." "How many now?" "More than one hundred." "It is therefore impossible for *Kapchepsom* people to go back to Baringo. There may be no land for them in Baringo. Since you let him replace you when you ran away, they can stay."

So three clans still share the same furrow – *Kapchepsom, Siaban* and *Kapsiren. Kabisioi* has his own furrow. *Kapsiren* also started his own furrow. So now there are three furrows. As a result, *Kapsiren* have rights to a lot of water in Sibou. The head of the main furrow is the *Siaban. Kapchepsom* have no land in the valley, just a small portion at the foot of the escarpment, beyond the Health Centre. This is because they came late. They do not have any land at *masop*. They beg or work for other people. They help people of other clans who have married their daughters and sons. There are about a hundred of them today.

The value of this account, and of others like it, lies not in its historical accuracy, but in the cultural details it conveys. Clan affiliation is extremely important in establishing rights to land and water. Among the Endo, outsiders may be allowed to settle in an area if they establish close links with an individual ("special friend") who offers them access to land and champions their cause, or if they establish access to resources through kinship.[3] This is the significance of *Kapchepsom*'s greeting, "Hello Uncle," and it is also why *Kabisioi* refuses to greet him: *Kabisioi* wants no kin link established. The Endo can be wary of offering settlement rights to outsiders, not because they are strangers, but because their children will inherit those rights.

If an outsider came to the village, he would have to stay in someone's house. If he wanted to build a house, he would have to make friends with someone in the village first, and then build on that person's land or next to that person's compound. If he wanted to have a *shamba* (field), he would be at the mercy of his friend who could give him some of his land. He would be allowed to adopt the clan name if he was intending to stay. But, it is easier to adopt a woman from outside than a man, because inheritance causes problems. The sons of the outsider would want land, so the land originally given would have to be divided among the sons. They would then be short of land.

[3] Huntingford (1953: 13) notes a similar system among the Nandi.

Men from Endo quite often make private arrangements to lease land to a relative or neighbor for one or more seasons. Sometimes the owner of the land
is given a goat or a share of the harvest in exchange. However, if an arrangement of this kind continues over a period of years it is tantamount to the
transfer of usufruct rights to the land in question. For the Endo, the principles
of occupation and use are a crucial part of the legal definition of ownership.[4]
Individual clans are said to own land because they occupied it when they
arrived in the area and have continued to occupy it and use it ever since. Social units are identified, directly and indirectly, with the areas they occupy.
The fact that rights to land may be established with use and that those rights
may be transferred through inheritance helps to explain why the storyteller
emphasizes that *Kapchepsom* has a child on his back. For *Kabisioi* to exchange
greetings with *Kapchepsom* would be to acknowledge him as sister's son, and
thus open the way to potential claims based on kin obligation, not just for
the man himself, but for his descendants as well. The fact that rights may
be extended through residence and use is underlined by the elders' final decision: "They cannot return to Baringo. There may be no land for them there."
This is just another way of saying that residence and use establish rights to
land, while absence and neglect can result in the forfeiture of those rights.

Whatever the history of clan settlement, the present-day association between individual groups and their land is strong and abiding. Within Sibou
village, each clan group has a defined territory which runs in an east–west
strip about 1 km wide, from the top of Sibou hill, down the escarpment, and
across the valley floor as far as the Kerio river (see Figure 4); each, that is,
except the *Kapchepsom* clan, who, being "latecomers," are not supposed to
have any land in the valley. In point of fact, the *Kapchepsom* have adequate
land for their needs: land is leased from affines within the village; rights to
small parcels of land have been "bought" through the exchange of stock; and
the lower slopes of the escarpment around their houses are extensively cultivated.

Within the village each clan area is also divided into segments which are
occupied by the individual lineages of the clan. Ideally every man should live
in his lineage area, and if this were the case then his closest neighbors would
obviously be members of his clan. However, as we have noted, in a village
like Sibou which has several clans there may be a considerable degree of mixing between the clans, either for historical reasons or because of affinal ties.
In addition, cooperative links (usually concerning stock or land) between age-
mates may also mean that there is a considerable degree of mixing between
lineages of the same clan. It is therefore, not always the case that individual
lineages occupy discrete geographical areas within the village.

[4] The concept of ownership among the Endo involves (1) ownership with rights of disposal;
and (2) ownership involving usufruct rights which may sometimes be transferred but are not
ultimately disposable.

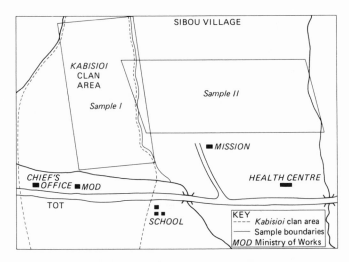

FIGURE 4. Sibou village and sample areas.

Sample Choice

In Sibou village there were two lineages where the majority of lineage members were in fact resident in their designated lineage area, and I chose one of these areas as the main sample for my study (Sibou sample I). The lineage area concerned belongs to the *Kakibelkio* lineage of the *Kabisioi* clan (see Figure 4). Within the area all the households, except one, were of the *Kabisioi* clan, but the actual breakdown of households by lineage was as follows: *Kakibelkio* 22, *Kapchemosi* 10, *Karmolei* 4, *Kacheserek* 3, *Kaberke* 2, and *Kakabisioi* 1. Of a total of 32 *Kakibelkio* households in the village (see Table 1) 22 were within the lineage area and a further 4 were to be found in an extremely high part of the village once occupied by all the members of *Kakabisioi* lineage but now deserted by most families in favor of sites nearer the valley floor. There were no *Kakibelkio* households resident outside the *Kabisioi* clan territory.

Figure 5 shows the relative positions of all the households in the *Kakibelkio* lineage area (Sibou sample I). Figures 6–8 contain genealogies of the same households. They also indicate male members of the *Kakibelkio* lineage who do not live in the area and wives of lineage members whose natal clans are resident in Sibou. Men and women from different clans within the village may marry each other, but among the three largest clans—*Kabisioi, Siaban,* and *Kapsiren*—the incidence of intermarriage is low. This is partly to do with the rules governing marriage. These rules prohibit marriage between people of different clans if they share one or more great-grandparents of the same clan. In practice, the Endo only extend this rule to the individual lineages of the clan and not to the clan itself. The result is that a man and a woman who come from different clans will be refused permission to marry if the elders

TABLE 1. Sibou Village: The Division of Households by Clan and Lineage

	Clans						
	Kabisioi		Siaban		Kapsiren		Kapchepsom
Lineages:	Kakibelkio	32	Kamaril	11	Kachesir	30	Kachepokipken	3
	Kacheserek	42	Kakatilowo	7	Kakaloput	6	Kachesokanda	23
	Kapsingwel	18	Kakipjesok	12			Kalaptany	7
	Kakabisioi	33					Karesin	18
	Kapchemosi	18						
	Kaberke	12						
	Kabangwan	16						
	Total	171		30		36		51

Note. If a man has two wives and each wife has a separate compound then they have been counted as two separate households.

can trace a previous marriage between their lineages in the last three generations. The third ascending generation (great-grandparents) is as far back as Marakwet kinship terminology differentiates between generations. In any event, Marakwet genealogies are never more than four or five generations deep, and it is certain that after the passing of the third generation there are few, if any, alive who could remember the details of previous marriages.

Figures 9–16 show the spatial relationships of households based on clan affiliation and on links between age-mates. The results are not conclusive, but it seems clear that residence relates more closely to clan and lineage associations than it does to links between age-mates and stock partners. Links of the latter kind were evident in residence patterns collected from other parts of the village, and were also attested by informants, although they are not particularly evident in Sibou sample I. One noticeable exception is household 8:

Household 8 is the compound of a young man called David, of *Kapchepsom* clan. He built his house in 1976 and was married in 1980 to a woman from *Kapsiren* clan. His residence in the *Kabisioi* clan area is the result of marriage links established in the previous generation. His mother (household 9) came from the *Siaban* clan and married a *Kabisioi* man. When her husband died she became the second wife of a man from the *Kapchepsom* clan and moved to the *Kapchepsom* side of the village. When her second husband died, she moved back to the *Kabisioi* area to be close to the sons from her previous marriage (households 11, 12, and 1). When she returned, she brought her young son (David) with her because he was only four years old. David was circumcized with his contemporaries from the *Kabisioi* clan and, through his brothers, has established rights to residence and land in the *Kabisioi* area.

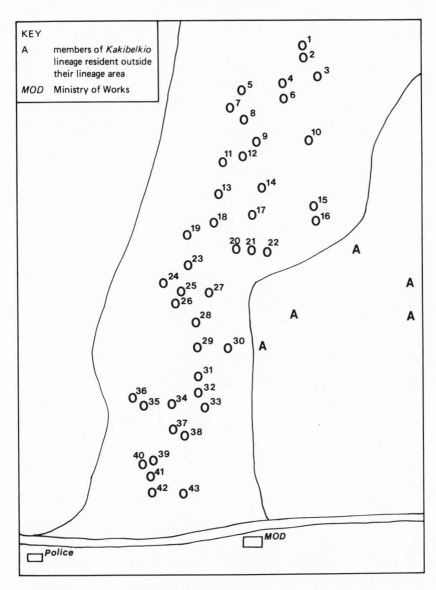

FIGURE 5. Households in Sibou sample I.

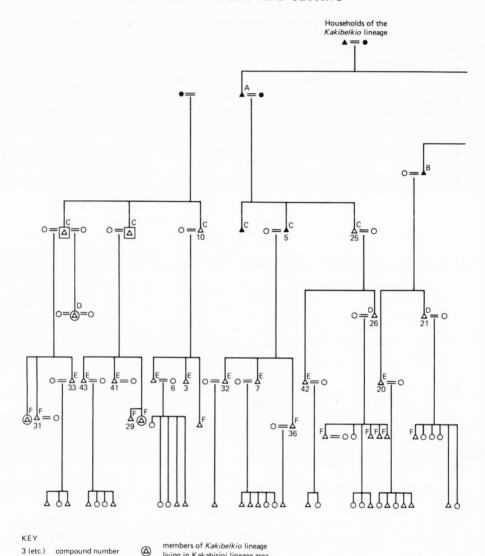

KEY

3 (etc.)	compound number
A	*Chumo* age-set
B	*Sawe* age-set
C	*Korongoro* age-set
D	*Kaberur* age-set
E	*Kaplelach* age-set
F	*Kimnygeu* age-set

members of *Kakibelkio* lineage living in Kakabisioi lineage area

members of *Kakibelkio* lineage living in Sibou Masop

FIGURE 6. Genealogies of *Kakibelkio* and *Kakabisioi* households.

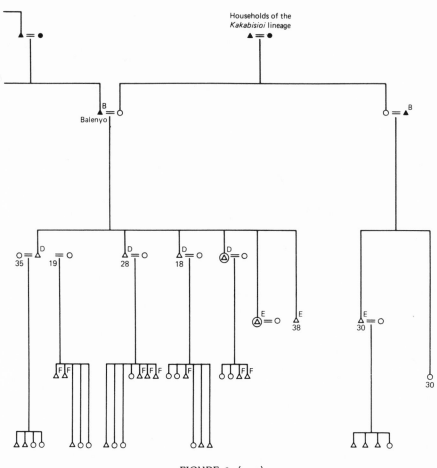

FIGURE 6. (*cont.*)

This story of "village intermarriage" is not typical, but it does illustrate some of the factors which may influence decisions concerning residence. However, it is worth pointing out that the incidence of village intermarriage for people of the *Kapchepsom* clan is high–about 20% of marriageable youth in 1980. This figure reflects the strategic importance for the *Kapchepsom* of acquiring additional rights to land and other resources within the village.

The decision to base my sample on the *Kakibelkio* lineage provided me with both a defined social unit and a discrete geographical entity, within the larger sociogeographical unit of the village. In addition, since lineage areas, like clan areas, are strips of land which run down through the village, it also

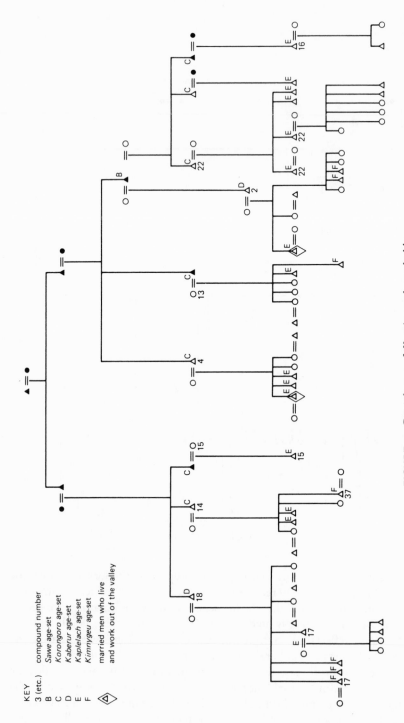

KEY

3 (etc.) compound number
B   *Sawe* age-set
C   *Korongoro* age-set
D   *Kaberur* age-set
E   *Kaplelach* age-set
F   *Kimnygeu* age-set
          married men who live
          and work out of the valley

FIGURE 7. Genealogies of *Kapchemosi* households.

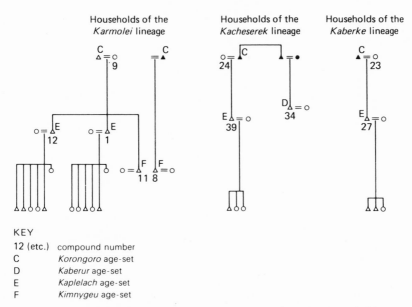

FIGURE 8. Genealogies of *Karmolei, Kacheserek,* and *Kaberke* households.

provided me with a vertical transect through the village. A second sample of 40 houses was also taken by following a horizontal, north–south transect (.5 km wide) through the village (Sibou sample II). This was designed to act as a check for variables which might crosscut lineage and/or clan areas.

BUILT SPACE

In the dry season, the scattered compounds of the Endo are indistinguishable from the rocky slope of the escarpment. The wooden fences and thatched roofs merge into a single color with the weathered landscape. But, however undistinguished, the importance of these compounds cannot be overestimated: houses and their associated structures are the only permanent buildings. Apart from the great irrigation furrows and the cultivated fields which they feed, the construction of houses and compounds is the only way in which the Endo transform their natural environment. There are no men's meeting-houses, no shrines, no public places for the consumption of liquor and food, no physically constructed space outside the family home. The nature of village organization is an interlocking set of social units which are also territorial units. At every moment, the life of the village focuses down onto the household, and that of the household expands out to meet the world of the village: a world where social relations are also spatial relations.

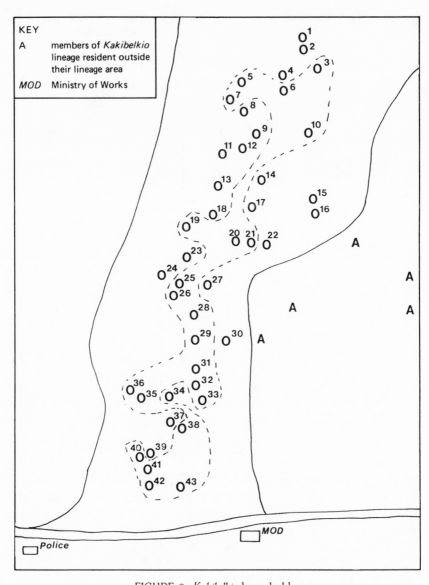

FIGURE 9. *Kakibelkio* households.

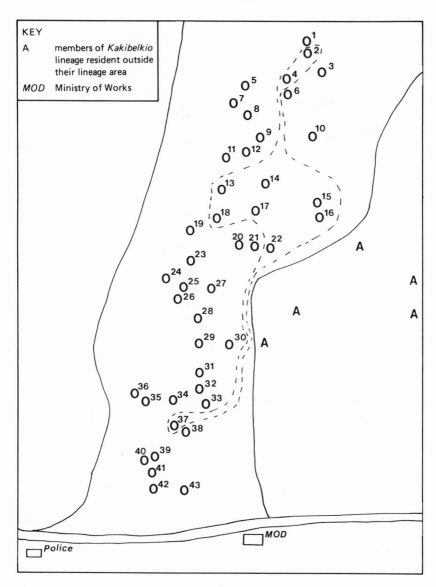

FIGURE 10. *Kapchemosi* households.

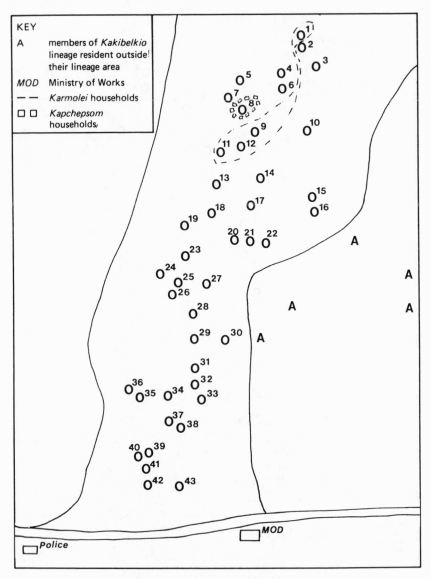

FIGURE 11. *Karmolei* and *Kapchepsom* households.

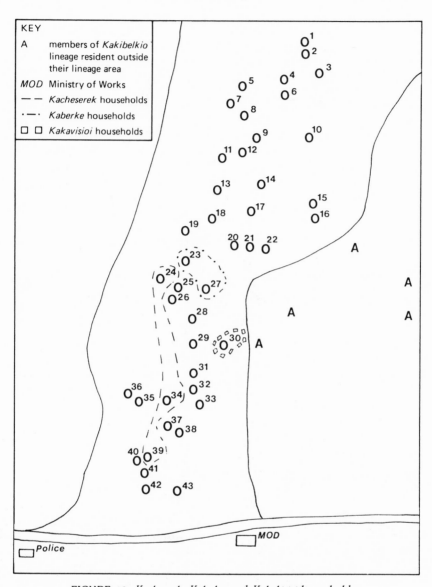

FIGURE 12. *Kacheserek, Kaberke,* and *Kakabisioi* households.

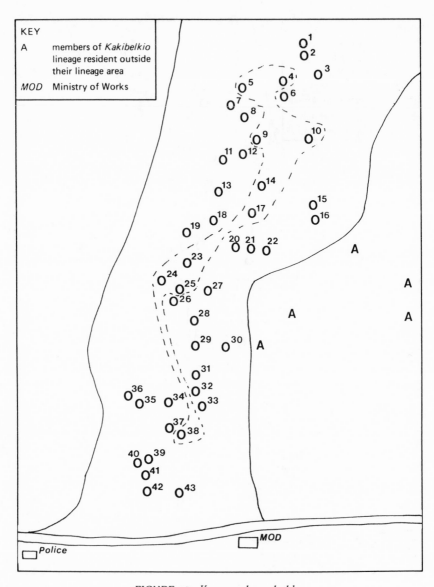

FIGURE 13. *Korongoro* households.

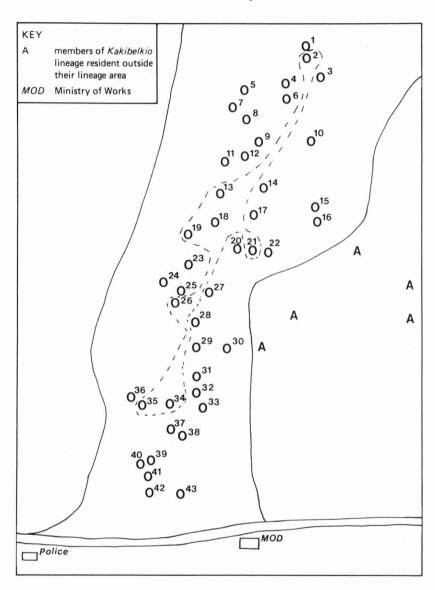

FIGURE 14. *Kaberur* households.

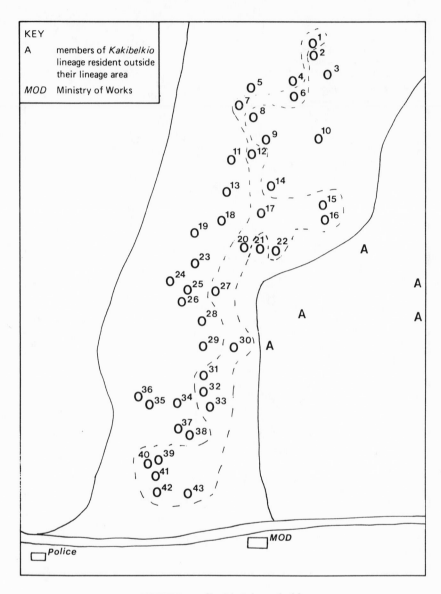

FIGURE 15. *Kaplelach* households.

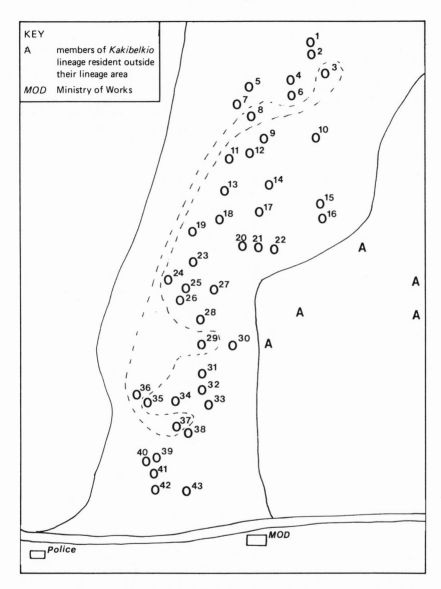

FIGURE 16. *Kimnygeu* households.

Compounds and Houses

The Cherangani escarpment runs north–south, and the Endo insist that a house (*go* or *ko*) must never face out over the valley: it must never face east. As a result all houses face either north or south, along the line of the escarpment (see Figure 17 and Plate II). Each individual compound (*birir*) consists of a levelled platform with a stone revetment (*telek*) cut into the side of the slope. Compounds normally contain one or more houses, in addition to various other structures (see below). The distinctive shape of the Endo compound, with its houses facing each other along a north–south axis, is largely determined by the topography of the Cherangani escarpment itself. This consistency of orientation and form facilitates comparison between spatial units, since the layout of all compounds follows a basic pattern.

House Types

The houses of the Endo are subcircular, with a single entrance and sometimes a window. The walls are between 1.5 and 1.8 m high, and the roof, which may be supported using a variety of techniques, is thatched with grass. There are three distinct house types: (1) wattle and daub (*kokom*) (see Plate II), (2) post and daub (*kimagen*) (see Plate III), (3) mud and stone (*kobokoron*) (see Plate

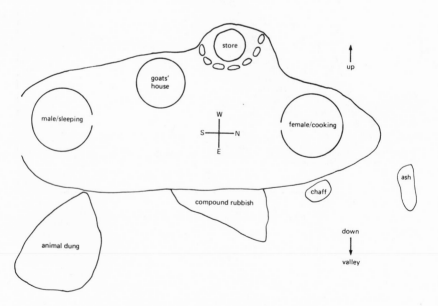

FIGURE 17. A typical Endo compound.

PLATE III. A compound from Sibou sample I, illustrating the distinctive shape of an Endo compound with its houses facing each other along a north–south axis.

IV). All three types of house are still built, but mud and stone houses are becoming more popular now that the majority of villagers live nearer to the valley floor (see Chapter 8). Among the Kerio valley Marakwet as a whole, post and daub houses are rare; they are mostly to be found in the highlands. Wattle and daub houses are preferred by older people and the Endo themselves speak of these houses as being more "traditional." Since older people and some more "traditional" families have been slower to move nearer the valley, the higher up the escarpment one proceeds the larger the number of wattle and daub houses becomes in relation to the number of mud and stone ones. Of houses sampled in the lower part of Sibou village, 63 were stone and mud and 6 were wattle and daub. In the upper reaches of the village, where there is less modern influence, all 39 houses sampled were of wattle and daub construction.

The internal arrangements of all three types of house are similar; Figure 18 is a standardized example of the interior of an Endo house. There are variations with regard to the presence or absence of certain structural features and certain types of artifacts, and these will be discussed in Chapter 8. However, the underlying principles of organization are invariant and are based on the division of the house into three areas: *kowerir* (area of bed), *kapkoschio* (area for cooking), and *kuti ya tobot* (area beneath the entrance to the roof store). The location of these areas is the same in all houses, because the division of space within each house is constructed according to the following: the position of

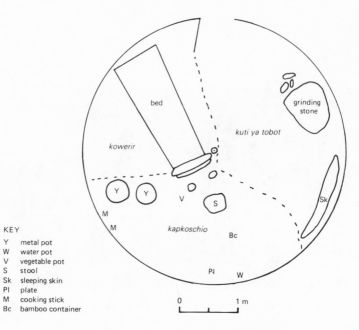

KEY

Y   metal pot
W   water pot
V   vegetable pot
S   stool
Sk sleeping skin
Pl plate
M   cooking stick
Bc bamboo container

FIGURE 18. The interior of a traditional Endo house.

PLATE IV. A wattle and daub house from Sibou village.

the bed, the position of the fireplace, and the entrance to the roof store. The bed must always be behind the door: this area is considered the most private space within the house. The fireplace must be just behind and to one side of the center post. And since the entrance to the roof store may never be over the cooking or deeping area, it is always on the opposite side of the house from the bed (Figure 18). In short, although most Endo houses are subcircular, the internal divisions are organized according to a system of cardinal points, all of which have their relative, but invariant, positions with regard to one another (Figure 19). These relative positions are maintained even when certain figures are missing (e.g., center post) or displaced (e.g., fireplace).[5] The houses in an Endo compound always face each other (Figure 20). If a man builds a house for a second wife, an elderly relative, or a younger brother, then those houses will either be provided with a site platform adjacent to the main compound or will be placed behind one of the existing houses (Figure 21). This is, the Endo say, because the door of a house must never face out over the valley.

In the past, in a compound of two houses one house would have been for the man and the other for his wife (Figure 22). Nowadays some Endo

Cooking

Sleeping   Center Post   Store

Door

FIGURE 19. The cardinal points of the house.

FIGURE 20. Position of houses in the compound.

FIGURE 21. Position of additional houses.

[5] Nowadays not all houses have fireplaces, especially if they are used solely for sleeping/entertaining. Similarly, the number of houses with center posts is decreasing: see Chapter 8.

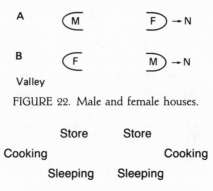

FIGURE 22. Male and female houses.

Store   Store

Cooking   Cooking

Sleeping   Sleeping

FIGURE 23. Orientation of houses.

families prefer to express this division as one house for cooking and the other for sleeping/entertaining. In the case of the Endo, even when houses are differentiated in this functional manner they are still thought to have a gender affiliation, partly because of the marked identification of a woman with her hearth, home and cooking activities. However, the Endo do not insist that the "male" or "female" house should have a particular position in the compound, thus both positions shown in Figure 22 are equally possible. But, they do specify that the doors of houses should be hinged on the valley side, a fact which then dictates the organization of space within the house, because the bed, on which everything else depends, must be behind the door (Figure 23).

All compounds contain at least one house, but not all compounds have stores and/or a goat house. The growth and decline cycle of each compound is allied to the life cycle of the domestic unit which occupies it, and the position and number of individual components (houses, stores, etc.) alters as the domestic group changes and develops.

Stores

The compound of a married man will usually contain one or more stores (*kapchogo*); they may be of wattle and daub or stone and mud construction (Plate V). They are always elevated on stone stilts (approximately 30 cm high) and have a thatched roof. Entrance to the store is gained through a small (50 × 30 cm) door halfway up the side. The Endo claim that in the past each family had at least two stores, one for the husband and one for the wife (additional wives having additional stores). This is still the case in some families, but it is more common in Sibou village to find stores differentiated by use. For example, one may be for storing maize and the other for eleusine and finger millet. One store may even be used for cassava, bananas, and other

PLATE V. A store associated with the house illustrated in Plate IV.

foodstuffs. When food is short and the stores are empty, they are often used to keep blankets, tools, clothes, plastic jerry cans, nails, and the like. However, many families only have one store. There is a variety of reasons for this, but the cost of building is an important factor. In cases where there is only one store, eleusine or finger millet may be kept in the roof store (*tobot*) inside the house, but a man's grain and that of his wife will still be kept separate within the storage area.

Whatever factors may influence how many stores a family builds and what they store in them, the positioning of these structures within the compound remains constant.[6] Stores must always be placed to the back of the compound (i.e., on its upper side: see Figure 17) and in a central position. They are often enclosed by the fence which surrounds the goats' house (*kano*).

Goat Houses

Not all compounds have a "house" for goats and/or sheep, and there are a number of reasons for this. For example, a young married man may still be keeping his animals with those of his father or brother; or a man may decide to build a separate *kano* down on the valley floor, where water and grazing

---

[6] This is a crucial point, since what is stored is separated from and opposed to that which is discarded: see Goldschmidt, 1976: 78, and Chapter 6.

PLATE VI. A view of a *kano* (goats' house) and store, showing the position of the store in the upper (back) part of the compound.

are within easy reach; animals may even live in a disused family house, or they may be so few in number that they quarter for the night in one of the houses still used by the family itself.

When a separate structure does exist it usually comprises a free-standing, circular shelter with a thatched roof. Normally this structure has 12–20 support posts, but no walls. Sometimes it will contain a center post with a fireplace. Men frequently sleep in their *kanos,* particularly if they are at a remove from the main compound. A *kano* will always be found in the back, center of a compound (see Figure 17 and Plate VI). A small area around it may be fenced, or the whole compound may be enclosed; this is a matter of preference.

The compounds of the Endo have a consistent shape and form. They exist as bounded spatial units with a defined sense of domestic place. Nevertheless, this perceived regularity of form masks a considerable variation in the number and type of structures within each compound and in the way different members of the social unit experience this "family" space. In the following chapters, I discuss how "ideal" space relates to "lived" space; how domestic space is understood in terms of a wider space/time continuum; and why different people experience space in different ways.

CHAPTER 4

Space, Time, and Gender

⟨C⟩

Any discussion of the organization of space would be incomplete without some indication of how spatial categories and orientations are linked to the ordering of social experience. In such a discussion it is essential to acknowledge the mutuality of space and time. The importance of village life lies in its "architectonic" integration of the social, symbolic, and economic experiences of the Endo. The daily relationships in household, village, and field extend spatially and temporally toward the historical and topographical links established between clan, land, and ancestors. There are, perhaps, many ways of synthesizing Endo experiences of space/time, but the perspective which the Endo themselves take most often is based on the pivotal relationship between men and women. It is difficult to demonstrate the degree of interpenetration between the daily experiences of personal and domestic space, the biographical experiences of changing social relations, and the wider space/time continuum which forms the boundaries of both the real and the imagined worlds. This difficulty is partly related to the nature of the social and conceptual topography of the Endo, which cannot be said to form an obvious cosmology or regularized system of knowledge. The nature of Endo knowledge is contingent and context dependent. Attitudes to knowing are constructed around a spatiotemporal definition of where and when it is appropriate "to know." Knowledge is both present and absent: it is always there, but never all there at once. We shall see in Part II how these qualities of presence and absence inform the analysis of symbolic forms.

SPACE AND TIME

The Marakwet place a great deal of emphasis on the importance of space in ordering social perceptions and experience. Their vocabulary and syntax made constant reference to the physical and conceptual positions of persons, events and objects. The villages of the Endo are built on the slope of the Cherangani escarpment, and daily movement from the residential area or village to the fields on the valley floor is a constant process of moving up and down. Relative location on the slope, the very axis of daily life, is always specified. *Doka* (up) and *bore* (down) are the terms used to describe movement up and down from the valley floor, the upper and lower halves of the human body, the village as distinct from the fields, and the area where ceremonies are performed as opposed to that of the bush. The heavens and the earth are distinguished, like the upper and lower regions of the house, by the terms *him* (up) and *nwun* (down). Both sets of terms are translated by the English up and down, but they form quite distinct axes (see Figure 24). The relation of the human body to the land of the village and fields, which is a statement of belonging and residence, is further extended by the use of certain linguistic terms to demarcate cultivated areas (see Figure 25).

These demarcations are physically unmarked, but are defined conceptually by a set of terms which refer to the fields furthest from the village as *bar kel* (land of foot), the fields nearest to the village as *bar mat* (land of head), and the fields in between as *bar quem* (land of middle). The terms *mat, quem,* and

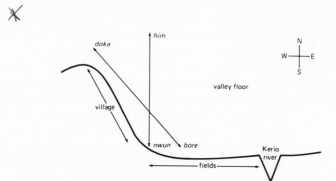

FIGURE 24. The axes of orientation.

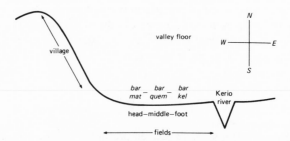

FIGURE 25. The divisions of the fields.

kel refer to the head, waist, and legs (including the feet) of the human body. The use of the human body as an axis of orientation in the physical world has been noted in a number of societies, but it is significant that in the case of the Endo the axis it represents is not the conventional one of sky/earth.

The principal orientation up/down is further complicated by the use the Endo make of the terms *tai* and *let*. *Tai* means "right" or "right-sided"; it also means "in front" or "ahead." My research assistant was a formidable walker, and as I moved about the valley in her wake, I was frequently asked *mi ano,* "Where is she?" My inevitable reply was *mi tai,* "She's in front." In contrast, *let* means "left" or "behind." I have always imagined my research assistant endlessly replying: *mi let, mi let,* "She's behind." And left behind I often was in the early stages of my work, but it was an excellent introduction to the mutually defining processes of orientation and interpretation.

The words *tai* and *let* are also related to movement up and down the floor of the valley from north to south. The southern part of the valley is referred to as *to tai,* the right or upper part; while the northern part is *to let,* the left or lower part. This orientation reflects the natural slope of the valley and of the Kerio river which flows northward (downward) toward Lake Turkana. However, the Endo make a fairly conventional association between right and up, and left and down. Several old men pointed out to me that if a man stands on the edge of the escarpment, looking out over the valley and facing the rising sun, then his right hand is to the south, and his left hand to the north. Facing out over the valley has a special power for the Endo, but especially for men; it is here, on the edge of the escarpment, that they come to be circumcised as the rising sun touches their faces, and it is here that circumcised men gather, just as the sun begins to rise, to discuss and manage the affairs of the *kor* (village) (Plate VII).

Tai and *let* are essentially terms of direction and orientation, and contain, as a result, aspects of both space and time. A traveller journeying to the south of the valley might say *aweti to tai,* "I'm going south (upward)." The quality of movement implied in the phrase is reflected in the association between *tai* and *let* and the movement of the sun. The Marakwet call the sun *asis* and associate it most explicitly with men. Women, by contrast, are associated with the moon (*arawa*). The sun has a permanence in Marakwet thought which the moon does not. The sun rises powerfully every day and is said to be "always coming"; while the moon waxes and wanes, comes and goes, just like the women who come and go from the residential clan unit. Endo men make an explicit connection between the permanence of the sun and of men, in contrast to the impermanence of the moon and of women. (Women have a somewhat different view, which is discussed in Part III.) The moon is said to be on the left of the sun, behind it, just as the woman is on the left of the man. As the sun rises throughout the year it shifts its position on the eastern horizon, moving between the tropics of Capricorn and Cancer.

PLATE VII. A men's meeting place in Sibou, showing its typically precipitous location on the edge of the escarpment, overlooking the valley.

The Marakwet refer to the tropics as "houses"; Capricorn is the southern or right house, while Cancer is the northern or left house. Thus the movement of the sun is perceived as a movement from right to left.

The association of the terms *tai* and *let* with the movement of the sun and therefore with the passing of the seasons helps to explain why the Endo use the same terms to distinguish time past and time future. *Tai* is time past: the beginning or starting point, the right side from which the sun and all other good things "come," while *let* is time future: the finishing point, the left side to which the sun moves on. This assemblage of ideas is not at all far fetched for the Endo. The passing of the agricultural year is quite naturally linked to the cycling of age sets and the passing of the generations. The association of ancestors – past generations – with the right side completes the circle. As far as the Endo are concerned, there is no contradiction in a term (*tai*) which simultaneously means past in time and forward or in front in space. Ancestors, being past in time, can naturally be said to precede in a spatial sense.

Tai	*Let*
Front	Behind
Right	Left
Past	Future
Coming	Going
Ancestors	Unborn

The Endo involved in this inquiry did not use the concept of time as it might be understood in a Western sense. Without a linear sense of time and a defined system of calibration, the past and the future have no fixed state. Genealogical time is different from historical time, from agricultural time and from social time. It is clear that these senses of time are all linked, but they are not synonymous. One explanation for this has to do with the cyclical and repetitive nature of ordering time. Repetition is a difficult concept and the Endo use it in a variety of ways, many of which will become apparent in the following discussions. However, one very important feature is that events and their effects may be reproduced by recreating the conditions under which they first took place. This is of crucial importance for the performance of rituals:

> We follow the ways of our grandfathers. When we go to *chebyogone* (circumcision), everything must be as before. We must do everything the same. Nothing can change, because if there are changes then the children might not heal quickly and fall sick.

The successful completion of the circumcision rituals is at least partially dependent on the recreation of the conditions under which previous rituals were successful. Repetition in this sense has a clear spatial as well as a temporal dimension. This is most easily understood by saying that all events have a defined location, both temporal and spatial. The Endo acknowledge the duality of location most explicitly. Phrases like "the time of ceremonies" and "the time of harvest" (*terterwawa*) have a strong and very immediate spatial referent. This fusion of space and time gives a particular quality to the divisions of social time and to their relationship with the wider social structure.

THE SOCIAL DIVISIONS OF TIME

Age Sets

The Marakwet as a whole share the system of cycling age sets which is considered so characteristic of many East African societies (Abrahams, 1978: 38) and which is thought to be of such antiquity among the Southern Nilotes that it is a defining feature of "Nilotic culture" (Ehret, 1971: 36). The cycle consists of eight sets (*ibinwa* or *eben*), each of which is divided into three subsets. The senior subset is known as *chongen*, and the two junior subsets are called *aiberi* (Kipkorir, 1973: 9).[1] The names and orders of the sets are illustrated in Figure 26:

---

[1] Subsets seem to be disappearing, and many Endo claim that they do not exist. I have never observed or heard of a situation where a distinction was made between men of junior and senior subsets. Allegiance, where it is expressed at all, is expressed to the age set as a whole.

Males		Females
Nyongi	1870	Chesyewa
Maina	1885	Charkine
Chumo	1900	Kipturbei
Sawe	1916	Kiptakai
Korongoro	1930	Kasinkin
Kaberur	1946	Chemeri
Kaplelach	1961	Silingwa
Kimnygeu	1975	Chebterntur

FIGURE 26. Age sets.

Every Marakwet is initiated into an age set through the ceremony of circumcision (*sonok*). Each age set is open to initiates for about fifteen years and closes when the men of the final subset have been initiated. The dates of circumcision are set by the movement of the stars, and in the past it seems that young men were initiated into a new subset every five to seven years, depending on whether there was enough food and on whether the stars were auspicious. Nowadays circumcision happens every two or three years, and the importance of subsets is declining. This has not, however, altered the length of time that an age set is open to initiates, which is still about fifteen years.

The Marakwet date events in the past by referring to the age set which was then open to initiates. This method of dating is hazardous, since the Marakwet tend to telescope all the events associated with a particular set into the period occupied by the most recent manifestation of that set. The effect is to reinforce a sense of identity between successive age sets of the same name, and this finds expression in the idea that the character of the two periods will be similar. This perceived similarity between named units is linked to other aspects of Marakwet life (naming ceremonies, reciprocal kin terms between grandparents and grandchildren, respect for ancestors, etc.) which also stress the cyclical nature of time and the replacement of those who die by a new generation. This replacement must be orderly, and the Marakwet link the length of the age-set cycle to the fact that the new set must await initiation until no old men of the same set remain alive; since the whole cycle takes approximately a hundred years to complete, this is, of course, virtually impossible (Baxter and Almagor, 1978: 5). The function of age sets in contemporary Marakwet society would appear to be related to the social ranking of the "old" and the "young." Control over productive and reproductive resources, including the necessary esoteric knowledge required for the guaranteed reproduction of "society," is invested in the "old."

Whatever the function of age sets now, it is clear that they are not, and never have been, important in the organization of political, legal, or military affairs. Among the Nandi and the Kipsigis, age sets apparently had defined military or quasipolitical functions (Peristiany, 1939: 29–32; Huntingford,

1953: 53). The Marakwet system seems closest to that described for the Pokot and the Sebei (Goldschmidt, 1976: 105; Beech, 1911: 5–6).

The Marakwet do distinguish young men from elders, but the young men are not classed into a single "category" of warriors, and are referred to collectively by their age set name and not by any separate term which could be translated *moran* or "warrior." Although the authority and seniority of the elders is recognized, there is no clear moment of transition into elderhood and there is, therefore, no ceremonial closing of an age set, nor any special ceremony which precedes the opening of a new set.[2] The transition to elderhood is achieved over many years and is related to rituals connected with marriage and a growing public recognition of personal, social, and ritual maturity.[3] Although it is not possible for a man to become an elder without passing through various structurally given changes of status, the final attainment of "elderhood" rests on the maturing of personal qualities and on personal achievement. This means that, unlike the Kipsigis, the existing "warriors" (as they are called in the literature) or initiated men make no effort to prevent the initiation of the next group, because their attention is on the future, not on the pleasures of the present (Peristiany, 1939: 31). Initiation into an age set does define, and redefine, an individual's stage in the life-cycle, but it is not a movement into a rigorously bounded category with rights, duties, constraints, and privileges.

The most outstanding feature of initiation for the Endo is that it marks the transition from childhood to full adulthood. Prior to initiation, an individual is thought to be a "child" because he or she has not yet assumed the social status and responsibilities of an adult. The transition to full adult status is a two-stage process, of which initiation is the first stage and marriage the second. Initiation legitimizes the individual's right to marry and to have children. This is a crucial point for the Endo, because mature social status is dependent upon having children. A man who has no children is not truly a man, and a barren woman is a person without purpose or worth. It is through marriage that men and women fulfill their aim to have children, and the importance of initiation is therefore related to marriage and to the assumption of full adult status which marriage brings. However, because of the different roles and rights men and women have within marriage, initiation affects them in different ways. Both men and women are initiated into named age sets; each "male" set has its structurally equivalent "female" set and the Endo say that men should marry women of equivalent sets. In practice, this rule is hardly ever enforced, and the only strong prohibition is that a man cannot marry

---

[2] The Kerio Province Annual report for 1925 records that the Elgeyo had their handing-over ceremony in March of that year, but that such ceremonies were unknown among the Marakwet.

[3] Spencer (1965) makes a similar argument for the Samburu.

a girl of his daughter's age set nor the daughter of a member of his own age set (regardless of her age set), since this would be incest.

The Endo say that women's age sets are not as important as those of men, and informants of both sexes were often unable to give all the names of the women's age sets and/or their structural order. A man is initiated into an age set and remains in that set all his life. A woman is initiated into an age set, marries and is immediately subsumed into both her husband's age set and his clan. The corporate identity which women gain during their initiation is dissipated when they move away from their natal group and marry into an unknown social unit. Thus initiation begins a theme of male permanence which distinguishes men as permanent, social individuals who have a life-long allegiance to the clan and their male peers.

The concept of male permanence versus female impermanence is one of the major ways in which the Endo "genderize" time. Genealogical time is effectively "male time." The absorption of a woman's age set into that of her husband is entirely congruent with the idea that age sets are essentially groups of male peers, in spite of the fact that women are also initiated into named sets. The cyclical nature of age set and generational time has a male quality, and in its repetitiveness it is like the sun, "always coming." ·

This quality of "coming," or repetition, is expressed in the naming ceremony for small children. When a child is born it is given a name (*kainap musar*) which signifies the time or circumstances of birth. After about a month, a small ceremony involving the senior men of the lineage (if the child is a boy) or the senior women (if the child is a girl) is performed. This ceremony (*kapkikut*) involves balancing a small gourd (*ribos,* used for drawing honey beer from its special container *loh*), on an object hammered into the ground between the center post and the fireplace in the mother's hut. The names of deceased members of the lineage of the appropriate sex are called, and, when the gourd balances, the "ancestor" (*oin*) is said to have "agreed" and the child is named after that particular person. This name is known as the *kainap kapkikut*. The naming of children after dead members of the lineage is a common practice throughout the Kalenjin peoples (Komma, 1979: 113; Goldschmidt, 1976: 243). It has particular force for the Endo, who set much store by the remembrance of names. Older people frequently express the desire that their names should be remembered and that children as yet unborn should be named after them. The value of remembrance is tied up with having children and with the continuity of the residential clan group. Children are not just the sons and daughters of particular individuals, but the offspring and the future of the group itself. However, this applies much more directly and forcibly to male children. The continuity of the agnatic clan group is achieved only through male children, and is naturally expressed as the responsibility of males. Male and female children thus stand in different relations to the clan group. The Endo acknowledge this difference, and it is expressed in the *kapkikut* ceremony through the attention given to the object on which the gourd is balanced. For boy children, a *kolomber* or iron awl is used, and for girl children a piece of the *makang,* the wooden cooking stick, is hammered in next to the fire. The Endo say quite explicitly that iron is used because it symbolizes the boy's permanent link with the clan; while the wooden object used in the case of girls symbolizes their future links with the hearth and with cooking.

This emphasis on male permanence through the concepts of replacement, repetition and "coming" represents an attempt to control the ordered reproduction of society. A concern with reproduction, and with the different relationship men and women have toward social reproduction (the clan), is evident from the varied significance attached to male and female initiation. We have already noted that men and women do not stand in the same relationship to the clan and that initiation emphasizes the permanent nature of a man's allegiance, as opposed to the impermanent nature of the woman's affiliation. The permanent nature of a man's age set allegiance is akin to his permanent clan affiliation, and if initiation makes a boy an adult it also makes him a social being with the responsibilities and rights which membership of the social group brings. But, since women are not initiated into the social group in the same way, they are not thought to acquire the same jural rights and status as men. Circumcision does mark a change of status for women, but it differs from the change which men undergo because it marks their assumption of procreative powers rather than any political–jural status. Circumcision for boys marks the assumption of full "personhood" or male individuality: no one may command an initiated man. Circumcision also entitles a man to marry. In other words, it is the beginning of his right to control land, livestock, and women. For a woman, circumcision marks the transition to fully procreative being. It is the social creation of her sexuality and fertility.[4] The most important fact of circumcision is that it legitimates a woman's right to have children. It is acknowledged that uncircumcized girls have sexual intercourse, but if they become pregnant then they must have an abortion. A child who is born to an uncircumcized girl is not allowed to live; as one old woman said, "Only women, not children can have children." Since initiation marks a woman's assumption of procreative powers, it is also a recognition of the social, and therefore male, definition of and control over those powers. A woman's procreative ability is not an inalienable right, and on her marriage a woman's rights to her own fertility pass, in part, to her husband.

Life Stages

That initiation and the age set cycle create structural differences between the "old" and the "young" is not to say that a man's authority and seniority de-

---

[4] Llewelyn-Davies (1981: 342) makes the same point for the Maasai and argues the case elegantly.

rive only from his age set "role." The structural division between old and young would be better understood as the distinction between adult and non-adult, between the social and the presocial. It is for this reason that other age-based divisions in Marakwet society emphasize the relationship of the individual to the assumption of adulthood (Figure 27).

The structural divisions these terms represent are explicitly related to whether a person is circumcized and/or whether a person is married. The divisions would appear to be very similar for both sexes, but it must be borne in mind that initiation and marriage do not mean the same thing to men and women. The crucial point is that a woman's life changes are related to her procreative status, whereas a man's relate to his jural status. This is emphasized by the term *karakor,* which some informants mentioned as the term given to a married woman until such time as she had produced four children. The fact that men and women stand in a different relation to major structural life changes is prefigured from the earliest days of childhood. The most prominent feature of the way children are treated is that they are socialized by the age of four or five into gender-specific roles. These roles are expressed in terms of a division of labor, or a series of gender-specific tasks. From the age of five, and certainly by the age of eight, boys are taught to take an interest in livestock, to carry food to their fathers in the *kano,* to herd, to scare birds from the fields, to make bows and arrows, to build fences, and, nowadays, to take an interest in school.[5] Herding is the main chore and is often shared by brothers or passes from one brother to another as the first grows older. Children are specifically taught and frequently reminded that they must be obedient, not just to their parents, but to anyone older than them. An adult will often stop a passing child and send him or her off on an errand; older boys often torment younger boys and try to make them perform small services of various kinds. The responsibility for herding is instilled into boys, and they are often beaten for losing animals or making mistakes. Such is the

Males		*Females*	
Boyon (pl. Boyot)	Elder	Chebyoson (pl. Chebyoso)	Married woman
Name of age set	Unmarried but circumcized	Cheres	Unmarried but circumcized
Karacheena	Uncircumcized boy	Jesela	Uncircumcized girl
Lakwe	Child	Lakwe	Child

FIGURE 27. Life stages.

[5] From my data it would appear that, in the case of Sibou village, many more boys than girls go to school. The problem of educating girls was early recognized by colonial officers: see Marakwet Annual Report, 1956.

fear of a father's wrath that a young boy will often fail to turn up for food or even sleep in the bush for a few days until his father has calmed down.

Girls are kept close to their mothers; from the age of five little girls may be left at home to look after younger siblings while their mothers work in the fields. Boys sometimes help in caring for younger children, but girls are more often to be seen doing this sort of work. Girls of eight and older will be asked to collect small amounts of firewood and bush vegetables, and to carry water. Most schoolgirls (children cannot attend primary school before they are seven in Kenya) collect water before they go to school in the morning and return with firewood when they come home at night. Girls are also taught to cook, sent to grind maize and asked to work in the fields from about the age of twelve.

From early childhood an individual's social development has a specific spatiotemporal dimension which is given by gender. This is not to imply sexual segregation or avoidance: the reality is the contrary. However, cooking is not the same as herding; and a future which involves marriage into a potentially "foreign" community is not the same as a lifetime of residence in the village of your forefathers. These differences may seem obvious, but they are not trivial.

Age and sex are regularly used as organizational principles in social systems. Age sets and residential clan groups are structural features of the Endo social system which combine both these principles. The primary function of age sets and clans is the physical and social reproduction of society. The key institution in this reproduction is marriage. Marriage is an extremely important feature because it links the formal system of social control and reproduction with the means by which command over resources and reproduction is achieved. Marriage and its physical location, the household, are not only the site of social reproduction; they are also the focus of interpersonal relationships. The individual's experience of life changes and differing social positions is constructed through two parallel systems, which always overlap. The first is the system based on age sets, where boys eventually become elders; this is essentially relevant to the wider social group, the village, and perhaps even the section. The second is a system based on marriage and kin relations, where children become parents and sisters become aunts. These two systems are naturally interdependent, and it is quite impossible to understand the first adequately without saying something of the second.

KINSHIP CLASSIFICATION AND USAGE

The kinship classifications of the Marakwet would appear to be of Omaha type: that is, father and father's brother are equated and mother and mother's sister are equated, while there are special terms for mother's brother and father's sister. (Similar systems have been suggested for the Tugen and the Sebei: see Kettel, 1975; Goldschmidt, 1976: 95–102.) Details of the terminology are given in Appendix 1. Here I shall merely discuss some of the important categories.

Parents. The word for "father" (*abor*) applies to the father's brothers, his age-mates, the husband of any sanga (father's sister) and the husbands of the mother's brothers' daughters. Girls and young children refer to their father as *papa*. The word for mother (*mama*) applies to the father's wives, father's brothers' wives, mother's sisters, mother's brothers' wives, and mother's brothers' daughters. Parents-in-law may also be referred to as "father" and "mother" as terms of respect.

Siblings. The most commonly used word for siblings, *kitupche,* does not differentiate between the sexes. It also applies to parallel cousins on both mother's and father's side. Since the term father extends to all the men of the lineage who are of father's generation, the term *kitupche* is also applied to the children of such men.

Full brothers and sisters have a special relationship. They share common interests, they play together as children, and sometime between the ages of twelve to fifteen they begin to attend dances and to prepare for circumcision. The bond between brothers and sisters is strong, and is reinforced by a boy's interest in his sister's bridewealth. The Endo did not always have bridewealth; a father merely exchanged his daughter for a quantity of *kipketin* (honey beer), the drinking of which signalled the founding of a cooperative link between men. The actual date of the introduction of bridewealth is unknown, but the Marakwet say they "learnt" the custom from the Elgeyo and the colonial records mention the adoption of bridewealth by the Elgeyo in 1937 (Rift Valley Province Annual Report, 1937). The amount of bridewealth paid today varies enormously. Among the highland Marakwet, bridewealth is discouraged by the Christianized members of the community, although there is considerable stress on providing a house and household equipment. A woman will expect to find a house equipped and will also expect to receive gifts, probably clothes. In Endo, a man may get six goats or two cows (this is unusual) for his daughter. Nowadays it is quite common for the father to demand money. If the young man or his family are wealthy, a father might demand up to 3,000 ks; a poor man will pay 1,000 ks; or less (16 ks = £1 = approximately $1.60). The actual amount of bridewealth is negotiated in every case, and the Endo are very explicit when they say that the amount of bridewealth depends on what the young man or his family has: "A man is not poor by choice."

The bond between brother and sister is also expressed by the fact that a sister may ask her brother for grain during famine and may solicit his support in cases of serious marital dispute. A man may also ask his sister to work in his fields if his wife is ill or in seclusion or if there is a lot of work to be done. The bond between brother and sister is strong, and its strongest expression is in the relationship children have with their mother's brother.

Uncle. Outside a man's own lineage the most important kin category is the mother's brother. The term, *mamaa,* applies to the mother's brother and by extension to all the men of the mother's clan and all the male descendants of the mother's brother. The clan of the mother's brother is called the *kamamaa* and is one of three clan groups which a man must ask to all the major ceremonies he performs. The relationship between a man and his mother's brother is one of respect, but, unlike the father–son relationship, it is not marked by tension. The mother's brother may receive part of the bridewealth from the marriage of his sister's last daughter, and he may be asked by his sister's son to contribute toward the son's bridewealth. Neither of these exchanges is obligatory, but the mother's brother is expected to give a gift to the sister's children when they are circumcized and to intervene in serious disputes concerning them. In the past, if a man committed an offense for which the penalty was death, then the mother's brothers were there to deal the first blow.[6]

Aunt. The term *sanga* is used for father's sister, but may also be applied to the married women of father's sister's clan. This term is reciprocal and therefore is also used to designate brother's son and brother's daughter.

Kinship plays its most important role in the structuring and organizing of interpersonal relationships; hence the wide extension of the classificatory terms mother and father. Apart from the relationships within the domestic and clan units, there are very few other important kin-based relationships or obligations. This is because all important relationships are translated into classificatory clan relations, with the exception of the most important affinal relationship, mother's brother (Father's sister is also a marked category because of its structural equivalence to mother's brother.) The importance of the mother's brother's/sister's son relationship is clearly illustrated by the structural relationships set up between a man's clan and certain other clans – links which are derived directly from the genealogical relationship between mother's brother and sister's son. First among this group of clans is the *kamamaa,* the clan of the mother's brother, sometimes referred to as the *kapchegoi,* "in-laws."[7] A man also has a special relationship with his father's mother's clan, the *kamama* ('of mother'); these are the people his own father calls *kamamaa* (mother's brothers). The third clan which a man must pay particular attention to is the clan of his wife's mother, the *kamama korga,* for these are the men his own children will call *kamamaa.* These three clans and his own clan are the people a man must invite to all major ceremonies and they are also the people who will expect to be present at the circumcision of his children.

The remaining kin relationships I shall discuss are those which exist

---

[6] Kipkorir (1973: 8) notes the role of the mother's brother in putting to death those found guilty of witchcraft.

[7] Goldschmidt (1976) notes the use of a similar term by the Sebei: *kapikoi,* which apparently denotes sister's husband and spouse's brother.

within, and are derived from, the marriage bond. As we have noted, the institution of marriage is the focus for three very important sets of relationships: those between a man and his wife, between spouses and their affines, and between the household and the residential patriclan. Since all these relationships are ultimately based on the relations between men and women, I shall discuss them in the wider context of gender relations and the socioeconomic roles of men and women.

WOMEN AND MEN

The Endo speak often of relations between the sexes; their ambiguity; their interwoven qualities of dependence, respect, and hostility. In public situations, it is men who speak most often of such matters, and they articulate a model of gender relations which is firmly based on male dominance. The structures of this domination are reinforced by the patriorientation of social and kin relations, by the fact that all property is supposed to be held by men, and by a series of cultural notions which depict women as thoughtless, irresponsible and in need of control: "Women are like children, they speak before they think." When men say that women are like children they are calling attention to a structural relation between the sexes which positions women as social and jural minors. This is not to say that women are actually like children, for in this age-oriented society children owe obedience to all adults and age and sex are crosscutting principles of differentiation. But, to say that women are like children is to make a metaphoric statement of considerable power. In their "childlike" state, women are perceived as inferior to men, and their inferiority both derives from and is based on their lack of social responsibility and control. This is, of course, the male view of things; the reality is somewhat different as the discussion in the following sections shows.

Marriage, Property, and Rights

The Endo conceive of marriage as a joint project in which men and women work together to produce foodstuffs, to maintain their herds, and to rear their children. The complementarity of male and female roles is expressed in what the Endo say men and women should contribute to marriage. A man is expected to provide land and livestock with which to support his family, and in return a woman is expected to contribute her agricultural and domestic labor and to produce children. Through marriage men and women acquire rights in each other, and in so doing they also acquire rights to land, livestock, and children.

A man only gains full ownership rights in land and livestock when he marries. Until that time such resources remain under the control of his father.

Boys acquire their first animals through promises made during circumcision; in this way a boy may acquire rights to one or two female goats. During the intervening five to eight years between circumcision and marriage, a man will try through various means – raiding, purchase, reward – to build up his herd. When a man marries, his father will normally tell him which animals he can expect to inherit. However, there is considerable variation in the ways fathers distribute their land and stock and it is always the father who decides when this distribution will actually take place. Thus, while a man will usually be provided with one or two animals to make initial bridewealth payments, the point at which he receives his whole share of the inheritance will depend on his father.[8] Nevertheless, even if a man does not receive his full share of the stock when he marries, he will be told which animals are his and thus acquires actual rights to a known number of stock. This is very different from his premarital state, when he knows he has ultimate rights in his father's herd but he does not yet possess actual rights to particular animals. As well as being allocated stock when he marries, a man will also acquire land, and although he may have been given a small (¼ acre) *shamba* before his marriage, he will now receive enough to support an independent household. It is through marriage, therefore, that a man actually acquires land and stock, and at the same time the full property-owning status of an individual man which marks his assumption of full adulthood:

> Ownership is universally in the hands of men, despite the fact that most of the cultivation is actually done by women. (Goldschmidt, 1967: 249)

On their marriage women also acquire rights to land and to livestock, but these are usufruct and consumption rights and not the rights of full ownership. A girl is first promised a goat during circumcision, but very few women ever receive this animal; and, although the Endo say that a woman sometimes receives the "promised" animal when she marries, I have no recorded instance of this having happened. (Nowadays girls receive clothes, blankets, and money during circumcision, and this is viewed as an alternative to being promised stock.) I did record two cases where a woman received a goat from her natal home on the birth of her first child, but I could obtain no clear information on the frequency of this practice.[9] On the whole, women cannot inherit stock, but they do acquire certain secondary rights in particular animals and certain usufruct rights in their husband's herd as a result of marriage.

When a man has received permission to marry, he will go with his close

---

[8] Only goats or cattle can be used for bridewealth; it would bring great misfortune on both families if sheep were to be used in bridewealth payments.
[9] It is extremely difficult to obtain information on the movement of stock through marriage, but what is clear is that there are not formal requirements and that such matters are always extremely negotiable.

male agnates and age-mates to the home of his bride, in order to escort her
to his mother's house. On the way, the woman will stop at every stream,
and at certain trees along the route, and will not proceed until she has been
promised an animal or a piece of land. When she arrives at the homestead
she will demand further animals before she enters the gate, before she enters
her mother-in-law's house and before she agrees to eat. On the first night
of their marriage, the woman must be persuaded at every stage by the promise
of an animal. The most important of all is the animal she is promised for
actually consenting to sexual intercourse. A woman must not give in straight-
away to her husband's advances, for this would be shameful; consequently
there is considerable time for these negotiations to take place. Of all the animals
a woman is promised, she will probably receive, at most, two or three. These
three animals are usually the two she is promised by her mother-in-law for
entering the house and agreeing to eat and the one she is promised by her
husband for agreeing to have sexual intercourse. These animals form the basis
of the woman's herd and cannot be disposed of without her permission.
However, she does not have full ownership rights over these animals, which
remain an integral part of her husband's herd. Endo men frequently say that
women have animals, but that "you cannot tell them from those of the husband." In other words, the herd forms a single economic unit and the husband has ultimate right of disposal over all the animals. Nevertheless, a man
would not dispose of one of his wife's animals against her wishes, for he
could only do so at the risk of considerable marital conflict. Women are extremely proud of their animals, and in private they are very specific about
which animals belong to them and why they received them. The Endo also
perform a ceremony called *bita*. At this ceremony a woman is given secondary or subsidiary rights to a portion of her husband's herd. The animals so
allocated and their progeny will ultimately be inherited by the woman's sons,
and will also be used to encourage her own daughters-in-law to enter their
new house and eat their first food. The decision as to how many stock to
allocate rests entirely with the husband, and the final number will include
those animals already promised to the woman by her husband and mother-
in-law. Some informants say that if the woman is the first (or, nowadays,
the only) wife, there will be considerable social pressure on a man to allocate
as much as half of his herd. This allocation does not represent an economic
loss for the husband, because these animals will continue to be part of his
herd and he may use them for exchange and ritual purposes if his wife agrees.
For her part, the woman cannot dispose of these animals without her husband's permission and cannot dispose of them outside the domestic unit at
all. (This does not apply to the goat she was promised by her husband for
agreeing to have sexual intercourse, since she could sell this animal if she so
wished.) These animals are not considered to be the woman's property and
are really held in trust for her sons and her daughters-in-law.

A woman also acquires rights to land when she marries. This land is given to her by her husband and will consist of several plots in different parts of the clan area. In point of fact, each woman actually shares the cultivation of all the man's land with the man himself and with other wives, if there are any.[10] But each wife is expected to grow enough food to feed her own family on the land which is hers, and it is this land that will eventually be inherited by her sons. Although a woman's land is always spoken of as "hers," she only has usufruct rights over it; and unless a woman purchases land (impossible in Endo) she never has full ownership rights. Women frequently retain rights, through their mothers, to use land in their natal village, and this is particularly important if a woman leaves her husband and has to return home. A woman's land cannot be taken from her and it cannot be disposed of without her consent. But land – like livestock – is owned by men: a woman is really only a trustee and holds the land in trust for her sons and daughters-in-law.

Both men and women gain rights in land and livestock when they marry, but it is men who control and have ultimate rights over land, livestock, and women. Women have only limited rights to, and control over, productive resources, and such rights, including their rights over their own children, are contingent upon men. However, both men and women are bound by the marriage "contract," and, since this "contract" requires a man to supply his wife with land and livestock, his control over these resources is not absolute. Male control is constrained by the fact that women have certain rights to productive resources and will try, whenever possible, to maximize their claims. The situation produced is paradoxical: on the one hand, husband and wife are interdependent, since their individual rights to stock and land can only be realized in the context of marriage; on the other hand, that interdependence is complicated by the fact that their interests are frequently antagonistic rather than complementary. Both men and women realize that it is in their best interests to get married and work together toward establishing an independent productive and reproductive unit, but this joint enterprise is constantly threatened by the conflict inherent in their differing interests.

Men and women may be ultimately dependent on each other for access to productive resources, but men are also dependent on women in other ways. Women bring three things to a marriage: their agricultural labor, their domestic labor, and their reproductive potential. Both men and women are engaged in agriculture: Men clear, fence, and irrigate the fields and may also do the heavy digging, while women dig, sow, weed, and harvest the crops. However, in spite of this joint involvement, farming is seen as women's work, and wom-

---

[10] The incidence of polygamy is declining, partly owing to the influence of Christianity. I do not know how representative Sibou village is of the Marakwet as a whole, but the incidence in my sample was about one in eight.

en spend most of the day engaged in agricultural activities. This is in marked contrast to the men, whose agricultural involvement is limited to certain periods in the production cycle. Women are not only the producers of crops; they also retain control over what they produce. A woman's granary is her own, and no one may go into it without her permission. The food she produces is used for feeding the family, and she controls its production, distribution, and consumption. A man is, therefore, dependent on his wife as the main producer of the family's subsistence requirements, and his use of any agricultural produce is constrained both by his dependence on his wife's labor and by her control over distribution and consumption.

Men are dependent on women not only for their agricultural labor, but also for their domestic labor. In short, men need women, not only to work their land, but also to run their households, gather wild vegetables, collect firewood, carry water, prepare their food and feed their families. Adult men do not engage in domestic tasks, and although men can carry water and cook if necessity dictates, they must never remove ash from the fireplace, grind flour, or carry firewood. A man who regularly carries out domestic tasks will be ridiculed. He will be called a woman, not only because he performs "female" tasks, but also because if his wife refuses to do so it implies that he can no longer control her. A man who is controlled by his wife is no longer a man. Women are well aware that men depend on their agricultural and domestic labor, and if a husband mistreats his wife, disposes of one of her animals without her permission, or takes grain from her granary she can withhold her labor. Men are equally aware that women have power in this respect and they therefore try to avoid conflict which would lead to withdrawal of a woman's labor. It is very much to a man's disadvantage if there is no one to grind flour, feed the children, or weed the fields. Men are supposed to have complete control over the members of their household, but once again the ideology of complete male control has to be seen in the context of a woman's ability to flout that control and to press her claims. Just as a woman's rights in land and stock constrain her husband's use of his resources and challenge the ideology of men's unmediated control of productive means, so the reality of a woman's power in the domestic sphere is also in very positive contrast to the ideology of complete male dominance and control.

Reproduction

Among the Marakwet both men and women fervently desire children. Children bring a man prestige; they signify the productive potential of his household, the successful nature of his marriage, the continuation of his lineage, and the reproduction of Endo society. A wealthy man is a man who has land, cattle, and children. For a woman the birth of children is the confirmation of her sexuality, the guarantee of her social status, and the provision for her old age. Children not only relieve some of the crushing burden of agricultural labor, but, if they are sons, help to guard their mother's property rights and, if they are daughters, ease the burden of domestic labor. A man without children is a man without status; there is no one to guarantee his decent burial, and there will be no great-grandchildren to remember his name. A man who dies without children dies forever and his name is forgotten. A man with many children is a man who is blessed and whose name will be known.

Every woman is known teknonymously, as the mother of (*ma* + name of child) her oldest living child until she has grandchildren, when she is called after her oldest living grandchild (*ko* + name of child) (Kipkorir, 1973: 54–6). Men are sometimes called by their teknonymous name, but more often they are known by their "ancestor" name or by their father's name with the prefix *aarap* ("son of"). Thus, the naming of children and parents identifies the woman with her living children, while the man is associated with the ancestors of his lineage and with his father's line. As we have noted, men and women have different interests with regard to children and this reflects their different positions *vis-à-vis* the patriclan.

Endo men always imply that women are individualistic, while men are more socially responsible. This judgement is made possible through a series of associations which link the social with the male and also with the patriclan. When women acquire rights in land and stock they aim to maximize their interests to improve their own position and to provide for their children, especially the youngest son. Women have the responsibility of using what they produce to feed the family and to support their children. The disposal of what a woman produces and of what she acquires during her lifetime takes place almost entirely within the domestic unit. A man does not have the responsibility of providing for the quotidian needs of the family; the animals, the land, and the produce he acquires are used to widen his network of social interaction and obligation, to extend help to agnates and age mates, and to gain prestige through the social display and distribution of his good fortune. In other words, men deploy their resources in a wider social and political sphere, which is largely composed of those men to whom the individual is related through agnatic, affinal, and residential links. Women, on the other hand, deploy their resources in the domestic sphere and provide for the personal needs of the family. The more social deployment of a man's resources creates a heavy responsibility for him as an individual, for it is he who must provide beer and food for marriage ceremonies, goats to be slaughtered at circumcision and *bita,* beer to be drunk at the naming ceremonies of his children, and the comestibles which reward his peers for help in building a house or digging the land. A man could not provide such things alone, and he must therefore have the help of his agnates and his neighbors. However, a man must not overextend his obligations, lest he should be unable to help when asked to do so in the future; he will therefore try to provide for the smaller ceremonies (e.g., naming ceremony) using the resources of the household. For this, a man needs the cooperation of his wife, who usually gives it quite willingly, and who may be able to provide both stock and grain. Thus, part of a man's social obligation is met through the cooperation of husband and wife, and this belies the male notion of female selfishness or lack of social responsibility. Nevertheless, it is true that male and female interests do conflict, and when this happens the individual household as represented by the woman comes into conflict with the clan or lineage as represented by the man. As we have noted, the relationship between the household and the clan pivots on that between the man and the woman, but this is not to say that women are always associated with the household in invariant opposition to the man and the clan. On the contrary, there are many occasions – as the Endo freely acknowledge – when a man wishes to consider the interests of the individual household above those of the clan, and the interests of the individual are therefore in conflict with what might be termed the "social good." The conflict between young men and their fathers over inheritance and marriage exemplifies this last point. Before his marriage a young man has no real access to the land and livestock which he needs in order to pay bridewealth and take a wife. The only way he can obtain such resources is to acquire them from his father and, through his father, from the lineage or clan. A father is under considerable social pressure to help his sons and may also be under pressure from the boy's mother, but he can easily choose to deploy his resources in seeking an additional wife for himself rather than a wife for his son. In such situations, if the conflict is severe a *kok* will be called and the case will almost certainly be found in the boy's favor, but what is interesting is that such conflict is expressed in terms of individual versus social interests. In this case it is a question of the individual challenging the concept of the elders' rights to control the disposal of land, livestock, and women.

The relationship between the household and the patriclan is, like the relationship between men and women, one of ambiguous and negotiable dependency. The reproduction of the clan, and therefore of society, depends on the productive and reproductive potential of the individual household. What men speak of is the authority and tradition of the clan. What they do not articulate is the clan's dependence on the individual household. The man who wishes to perpetuate his lineage and to maximize his personal prestige and wealth is also constrained in an analogous way by his dependence on the productive and reproductive potential of women. Ultimately, the reproduction of society, like that of the family and the clan, rests on the labor and the procreative power of women. This fact challenges the ideology of complete male control, as it challenges the overriding importance of the clan and the elders. It marks the relationship between men and women – on which the relationship between household and patriclan is built – as one of ambiguity and tension. For men only control women so long as they are able to renegotiate the material basis of their domination and to recreate the symbolic value of its representation. In the following chapters I shall be concerned with how and why male authority is represented in the organization of space, and with how that representation both renegotiates the material domination on which it rests and recreates the symbolic value of its cultural construction.

PART II

CULTURAL TEXTS AND SOCIAL CHANGE

CHAPTER 5

*Of Texts
and Other Matters*

Ma-Chebet had been gone for three days. She had apparently taken her youngest child to visit her parents. Initially, the reasons for this visit were obscure, and persistent inquiries merely produced grumblings about having to look after the other children, being forced to ask for firewood, having to cook, and complaints about who was going to pick the bananas. Finally, it transpired that her father had asked for help with weeding the millet, an extremely labor-intensive task, and Kipkeyo had felt obliged to release his wife's labor.

Ma-Chebet went quite frequently to help her father with agricultural tasks and usually received grain or bananas in exchange. Such regular visits to the parental home are unusual for Endo women, who often live at some distance from their natal village. However, the general experience of moving between father and husband is one which is familiar to all women. The individual biography of every woman contains a number of temporal stages which are formed and defined by spatial movement.

Ma-Chebet was born in a village about 6 km from Sibou and attended a primary school nearby for three years. She was circumcized in her natal village and became a member of the *Tabesit* age set. During her childhood and adolescence, she lived in her father's compound, sharing a house with her mother and younger sisters. She helped in the fields and in the care of younger siblings, and she left school when her mother became ill. When she was about eighteen years old she married Kipkeyo and moved to live in the *Kabisioi* area of Sibou. At this point, she relinquished her own clan and became instead a member of the *Kabisioi* clan. Her own age set affiliation withered and she became a *Kaplelachi,* a wife of a *Kaplelach* man.

The transformation from daughter to wife is much sought after, but it is also abrupt and complete. The movement from one context to another is symptomatic of a wider change in social relations, which inserts the young woman into a particular series of relationships with household, clan, and village which she has not known before. It is clear that men and women experience the "architectonic" space of household, clan, and village in different ways. The main locus of these experiences is the household, because it is through the household that men and women are inserted into the wider relationships with clan and village.

ANALYZING SPACE

The problem in analyzing household space, therefore, is how to take account of the different experiences of men and women. The contemporary view of culture, as noted earlier, is a holistic one and gives priority to collective values which form the basis of society. These values also constitute a coherent and binding ideological system which determines social structure. The result is that conflicting interpretations of "cultural ideology" by different groups in society are played down – even though a certain role in the analysis is often given to "deviants." The ruling or dominant groups in society always present their culture both as natural and as the "culture of the whole society." The analysis of "muted groups" is an approach which attempts to dismantle this presentation and to look at conflicting interpretations and positions within society; but, on the whole, anthropology seems to have been slow to appreciate the value of the more sociological concept of subculture.[1] The dominant definitions in anthropology still seem to define culture as a *Gestalt,* as organic and unique, a way of life:

> For holistic anthropologists, culture was assumed to be coterminous with society. The holistic conception of culture therefore obscures the fact that culture is always plural: that there are subcultures and counter-cultures within any society. (Worsley, 1984: 53–4)

The plurality of culture and the existence of alternative interpretations and values are not usually emphasized in the symbolic analysis of space, or indeed in the symbolic analysis of any form of cultural representation. Such analyses frequently emphasize coherence and systemness at the expense of concepts like conflict, contradiction, and power. Both Hobart (1978) and Turton (1978) in their respective analyses of Balinese and Thai space speak of

---

[1] The most notable exception to this is the work of Victor Turner on countercultures and mechanisms for expressing dissent (Turner, 1974).

architectural symbolism as involved in making statements about social structure and in "justifying the unjustifiable." This line of argument is also evident in some of the papers in Shirley Ardener's collection *Women and Space* (Ardener, 1981). In all these cases, the organization of space is seen as representing social relationships through ideological structures. But there is no sustained inquiry as to how these ideological structures work, how their production is linked to actual social conditions and relations, or how such structures are maintained given the alternative views of social relations which they must mask. The question is always "What are the meanings encoded in the organization of space and how do they relate to social structure?" The theoretical perspective evolved in this chapter is an attempt to shift the focus of that question to: "How does the organization of space come to have meaning and how are those meanings maintained through social interaction?"

Outside the social sciences, there is a line of intellectual inquiry concerned with the relationship between culture and society, which deals exclusively with cultural representations and productions. This is the work of literary theory and criticism. The value of utilizing such work for the analysis of cultural productions other than literary texts has already been realized both in anthropology and in contemporary culture studies (Geertz, 1984; Rabinow and Sullivan, 1979; Agar, 1980; Kuhn, 1981; Wolff, 1981; Barrett, 1979). Recent developments in this field, variously labelled Marxist, deconstructionist, poststructuralist, and hermeneutic, are particularly suggestive because they retain a central concern with meaning, while at the same time linking interpretation to interests, conflict and power. The main organizing concept of these analyses, and the subject of their work is the text or text analogue. In the discussion which follows I use the idea of cultural text to suggest an analytical framework which retains this emphasis on meaning, while at the same time introducing ideas of social strategy and strategic interpretation.

Metaphor and the Meaning of Space

The symbolic anthropology of the last decade and a half has produced an increasingly sophisticated and insightful commentary on the content and function of metaphor. Fernandez (1974: 120; 1981: 434) maintains that this renewed emphasis on metaphor is the logical result of an increased interest in the operational meaning of symbols and symbol systems. A focus on human situations and activities has reformulated a concern with the constitutive power of language. The dramaturgical analysis of ritual process, derived from Burke (1966), and exemplified by Turner (1967; 1974) is a powerful example. In still further work (Fox, 1972; Rosaldo, 1975; Tambiah, 1969), writers have examined the role of metaphor and metonymy in ordering and reordering social categories and in giving affective power to those categories. Analysis of this latter kind is potentially applicable to all forms of cultural representation, and it has been particularly influential in the study of domestic architecture and space.

One of the distinguishing features of this "an-trope-ology" has been the dual emphasis on metaphor as figurative and creative, and yet also as everyday, basic, and experimental. Metaphor is conventionally understood as rhetorical and expansive. It is held to locate itself in the gap between what is said and what is meant. It proceeds from the literal to the figurative, and in so doing creates meaning. Metaphors are therefore repositories of affectivity and feeling. They permit apprehension. They make the unsayable into the comprehensible, however fleetingly. It is not difficult to grasp that linguistic metaphors should possess affective and processual qualities, but the extension of the use of metaphor beyond the written and the verbal is perhaps another matter.

> Metaphor is for most people a device of the poetic imagination and the rhetorical flourish–a matter of extraordinary rather than ordinary language. Moreover, methaphor is typically viewed as characteristic of language alone, a matter of words rather than thought or action. For this reason, most people think they can get along perfectly well without metaphor. We have found on the contrary, that metaphor is pervasive in everyday life, not just in language, but in thought and action. (Lakoff and Johnson, 1980: 3)

Lakoff and Johnson go on to argue that our whole conceptual system is structured by metaphors, which provide systematic models for whole areas of discourse. They use the example of the way in which we talk about winning or losing arguments, using the metaphorical model of "war," to show just how pervasive metaphorical models are and to emphasize that we perpetually structure one type of experience in terms of another. (Lakoff and Johnson, 1980: 5). Lakoff and Johnson are, of course, speaking of Western culture, but the same sorts of processes are at work in other cultures. The constitution of thought and action through metaphoric process, or rather the demonstration of that process, is one of the achievements of contemporary anthropology.

The main point is that understanding the world is something which takes place within a framework of metaphorical systems. Metaphors are thus models for understanding the world (Black, 1962). These models emerge in a wide variety of cultural forms, and are revealed in analysis by establishing their relevance to a coherent cultural framework, in a way which is familiar from structural and semiotic analysis. There are a number of different kinds of metaphor which may be distinguished (analogic, structural, ontological, orientational, etc.), but in their use all forms consistently appeal to a given body of knowledge–to known properties of things or to cultural values and givens of particular kinds:

> The grounds of likeness in metaphors thus involve all sorts of conventions of reference to the real world; and these could never be specified in advance by a linguis-

tic or any other theory, or by the analysis even of typical inference patterns. Metaphor consists in the implication by likeness of a certain description of the world, which is rationalized or justified by its grounds – and acceptability of these implications depends ultimatly upon the nature of the world, or if one prefers, upon the nature of our beliefs about it. (Butler, 1984: 16)

The relationship of cultural meanings, values and beliefs to the forms of their representation not only provides an experiential basis for metaphor, but also establishes its interpretative and strategic qualities as well. Both Geertz (1971) and Fernandez (1971) have discussed the strategic use of metaphor. Their concern is the product of an approach which focuses on the operational use of symbols, on the relationship between action and human meaning. Metaphor may be understood as strategic precisely because it is both event and meaning – through action meanings may be created, sustained or manipulated. However, this activity does not go on in a vacuum; actions and utterances of all kinds take place within a linguistic and cultural framework which is itself metaphorically structured. Metaphor thus provides a way of analyzing meaning and action within a single frame.

Structure and Scheme

One of the most celebrated examples of an analysis which uses metaphor to stress the interdependency of meaning and action is Bourdieu's analysis of Kabyle Cosmology and space. In his discussion of the Kabyle house Bourdieu shows how notions about men and women, light and dark, up and down, inside and outside are contrasts which derive from objective conditions – that is, divisions by age, sex, or position in the relations of production. These contrasts organize and order both the conceptual and the spatial domains of the Berber world (Bourdieu, 1973). Bourdieu thus argues that the organization of space is governed by the same sets of contrasts as those which inform the practical and discursive knowledge of social actors. He acknowledges that it is possible to analyze household space by reducing it to a few basic sets of oppositions and their transformations, while maintaining that the isolation of such structures provides an inadequate explanation because it fails to enquire into the economic and social conditions which produce those oppositions and contrasts. He contends, furthermore, that there is no understanding of the role these structures play in either social activities or social relations, except as immutable categories of logic, thought, or experience (Bourdieu, 1977). He challenges the idea that the "meaning" of a given spatial order is merely the relational (physical) position of its constituent elements, regardless of the activities of social actors and the economic and social conditions which inform these activities. In an effort to confront this problem, Bourdieu develops an account of the generative function and power of conceptual schemes, as they inform and are produced and reproduced in social practice. His main contention is that space comes to have meaning through practice. Such practice is informed by a set of conceptual schemes which are represented in the order of space, but the actual meaning given to the spatial order at any given time is dependent upon the nature of the activity concerned.

Bourdieu terms his theory a "theory of practice," because the practices of individual actors are not to be accounted for in terms of rule following, but are to be seen as the working out in social situations of sets of principles. Social practice, is not the mechanical reaction to a rule, but is instead the product of the application of "socially constituted systems of cognitive and motivating structures" to particular social situations (Bourdieu, 1977: 72). These socially constituted systems are, of course, the systems of social classification which many other researchers have identified as being represented in the organization of space; but Bourdieu's point is that these systems of social meanings are not just the products of action, but also operate as generative principles which inform action. However, he does not imply that these generative principles are merely rules of some sort, because he does not want to reduce social action to the activity of rule following. Bourdieu acknowledges that social actors may have considerable discursive knowledge (i.e., insight into their conditions and motives), but, like Wittgenstein, he is concerned to emphasize the practical character of rule following, with its implications for a theory of knowledge. He thus maintains that rules have no existence outside practices and can therefore never be fixed or given entities. Social practices owe their coherence – their regularities – to the fact that they are the product of a set of generative schemes which are only realized in practice. It is not necessary for an actor to possess mastery of such schemes on a discursive level in order to be able to apply them in practice. These schemes are implied in the knowledge of how to proceed, in the ability to participate in a social situation. Bourdieu links this practical mastery of the schemes immanent in practice to the spatial organization of the material world. He maintains that movement through constructed space (space constructed according to certain conceptual schemes and contrasts) acts as a mnemonic and helps to build up practical mastery of those same schemes (Bourdieu, 1977: 91). In other words, the conceptual schemes which inform the organization of space are also those which inform social action. In all this, Bourdieu insists that the spatial order can have no fixed meaning which exists outside social practices. It is true that the actions of individual actors are informed by the conceptual schemes which organize space, but the actual meaning given to the spatial order is in turn dependent on the meanings invoked through the actions of individuals. Thus, social practices are influenced by the relational positioning of individual elements in the spatial order, but the actual interpretation given to the ordering of those elements during any action or series of actions is dependent upon the nature of the action concerned and the conscious and unconscious intentions of the individual.

Bourdieu's analysis is complicated and densely argued, and is a magnificent example of the way metaphorical models inform action and interpretation in a given cultural context. He does not discuss the concept of metaphor in any detail, but he does introduce the notion of "universes of meaning" and "universes of practice," as a way of explaining how the organization of space comes to have different meanings in different contexts. He argues that if the meaning of the material world is reducible to a few basic contrasts, these contrasts are only faintly determining and obtain in many different universes of practice, having particular meanings within each universe. In other words, meaning is invoked through practice and is thus context dependent. However the actual meaning a given set of contrasts acquires in relation to a particular universe of practice resonates with all the meanings those contrasts, or any other pair of contrasts that is interchangeable with them, might be given in other fields of practice – that is, in different contexts. Thus, while the meaning given to the organization of space is context or "practice" dependent, it can also refer through association to those meanings which will be given in other contexts. This is a point I discuss in Chapter 7, where I give an account of the different meanings associated with the element "ash" in different contexts.

The fact that meanings invoked in one context have the ability to refer to meanings invoked in another is what enables the analysis of meaning to be combined with the analysis of the strategic intentions of social actors. Metaphoric statements always have the ability to refer to meanings outside the context of their utterance. For example, take Fernandez's illustration, "the Attorney General is a jellyfish" (Fernandez, 1971), or the statement by Endo men which one hears almost daily, "Women are like children." Both these statements take their meaning from a clash between a literal and a figurative meaning, but they also refer to a context outside their context of utterance where the qualities of jellyfish and children are realized. The strategies of individuals make use of this referring ability, and of the fact that action may be realized as both event and meaning. Thus, when a Marakwet girl smears herself with ash to avoid an arranged marriage, her action is realized as event and meaning. The obvious meaning is that she refuses, but her ability to refuse using this method depends on the negative connotations associated with the substance ash in a number of other contexts. Furthermore, there are other ways in which she could refuse, but her choice of this particular method reflects her determination to succeed, since she is aware, both consciously and unconsciously, of the power of the values associated with ash. It should be clear from this brief example that the concept of metaphor is useful as an aid in understanding how actors' intentions may be linked to the strategic use of social meanings. Actors are not unaware of the meanings and values associated with the organization of space, and they are also in a position to choose how to invoke and reinterpret those meanings through their actions. Of course, actors' interpretations are not without the constraints of convention and some method has to be employed whereby space can be analyzed in terms of its invariant physical form and in terms of the interpretations and intentions of actors. In order to try and do this I have developed the idea of space considered as a text. The advantages of this approach are that it extends the analysis of event and meaning, it provides a way of linking social action to the structures which inform that action, and it provides a theoretical framework for linking the organization of space to the material conditions of its genesis.

SPACE AS A TEXT

It is the apprehension of the complex weaving and interweaving of meaning and action that has led Geertz to move beyond the concept of metaphor and to speak of human activity as a text. His earliest use of the "textual" analogy characterized culture in the broadest sense as made up of a number of cultural texts which had to be read over the shoulder of social actors (Geertz, 1971). The analogy was extended in suggestive but undefined ways to imply that an ethnographic "reading" of such texts would involve a building-up or "thick description" of layers of meaning, interpretation, and action (Peacock, 1981; Shankman, 1984). It is interesting that, at least initially, it was the idea of ethnographic interpretation as akin to "reading" that encouraged the obvious extension of the analogy to include culture as a series of text. More recently, it would seem that Geertz has used the fulcrum of interpretation to suggest that all cultural behavior has textual characteristics—that is, it requires an interpretation or reading (Geertz, 1984). Geertz is not alone in this: the idea that human action may be considered as analogous to a text has also been proposed by Paul Ricoeur. The fact that Ricoeur gives a central role to metaphor in his work makes his discussion particularly helpful in an attempt to link the idea of a cultural text with Bourdieu's analysis of space, and so extend the analytical possibilities of both approaches.

To treat the organization of space as analogous to a text is to begin with the assumed interdependence of parts with the whole, of sense with reference, and of structure with action. This assumption permits a text to be approached in two ways; either it can be analyzed and explained in terms of its internal relations (*langue,* sense) or it may be interpreted as process, as the actualized product of social actors in a particular context (*parole,* reference). Both approaches are valid and, according to Ricoeur, both belong to the activity of reading, which must be understood as a dialectic between them (Ricoeur 1981: 152). He further equates the "internal" analysis of texts with explanation, and the investigation of their ability to refer outside themselves with interpretation. In an essay entitled "The Model of the Text: Meaningful Action Considered as a Text," Ricoeur contends that action, like texts, has a sense as well as a reference component (Ricoeur, 1981: chap. 8). In other words, it possesses an internal structure as well as an ability to project an interpretation of being in the world – that is, to refer beyond immediate action and experience.

This referential capacity is crucial to the analysis of space as a text because it implies that, as a structured totality or "work," a text cannot be reduced profitably to its constituent elements. This is in direct contradiction to structuralist analyses of space which seek to discover meaning by reducing the organization of space to its constituent elements or underlying structures. The irreducibility of the text applies to texts of all kinds. A literary text is not reducible to the meanings of its individual sentences; a spatial text cannot be brought down to the structure of its material parts; and social action cannot be understood as a mere conglomeration of events. This is because, although the text, as work, preserves the properties of its individual elements, it produces them in such a way as to demand a particular sort of interpretation. Ricoeur emphasizes the particularity of textual interpretation by stressing the distinctions between writing and speaking. The literary text, unlike discourse, is distanced from both its author and its audience. Furthermore, since neither author nor audience participates in a direct dialogue with each other, the meaning of the text is freed from the "shared reality of the speech situation" (Ricoeur, 1981: chap. 4). This emancipation, coupled with the fact that it is the meaning of what is said, rather than the event of saying, that is inscribed in a text, unfolds the possibility that the referential dimensions of texts differ from those of speech. They are said to differ precisely because they can only be disclosed through an act of interpretation. To sum up Ricoeur's point: any interpretation of a text as a work presupposes a type of understanding which cannot be reduced to, or adduced from, a structural analysis alone, because, in his own words, "to understand a text is to follow its movement from sense to reference; from what it says, to what it talks about" (Ricoeur, 1976: 87–8).

Before going on to discuss the referential dimensions of spatial texts – that is, of the organization of space considered as a text – it is necessary to say something about how exactly we are to understand space as a text and to say something further on the subject of reference in textual analysis.

Problems of Reading, Acting, and Speaking

Thus far considerable emphasis has been placed on understanding the potential meaning of space in terms of the practical activity of social actors. While this is essential in an effort to substantiate the distinction between sense and reference, between structure and activity, and between event and meaning, it leaves aside the problematic link between activity understood as physical movement in space, and activity understood as interpretation of or orientation in that same space. The organization of space both precedes and follows the action which takes place therein; it determines those activities and is, at the same time, their product. It follows from this that to understand space as a text is to conceive of the spatial order as something more than merely the physical manifestation, or product of, activities conducted in space. Spatial texts may, therefore, be said to have both a history and a future. These temporal qualities, bound into the matrix of the text, relate to Ricoeur's concept of distanciation.[2] This notion has four principle forms, the first of which is that meaning surpasses event: what is inscribed in the organization of space is not the actuality of past actions, but their meaning. This also applies to activities in space where the individual events are superseded by the significance of what is done. The second and third forms of distanciation declare that a text is, in some sense, removed from its historical and social conditions, because (1) what it signifies does not coincide with the intentions of individual authors/actors, and (2) its signification is not addressed to a particular audience. This form of distanciation also applies to spatial texts. Since the spatial order both precedes and succeeds individual actors and their activities, it follows that the significance of a spatial text cannot be identified with the intentions of individual actors, or be held to address itself to a particular individual. This emancipation of the text from its social and historical conditions opens it to "an unlimited series of readings" – that is, to a multiplicity of possible interpretations.[3] The fourth form of distanciation is related to the reference limits of the text; these, unlike those of speaking or acting, are not confined to the context of any one action or set of actions.

On the basis of Ricoeur's four forms of distanciation it can be argued that spatial and literary texts have similar properties. A literary text requires to be read; it is in the act of reading that the act of interpretation resides. In treating the organization of space as a text, the question arises as to what activity is to be considered equivalent or analogous to the act of reading. Intuitively it might seem that movements through, and action in, a spatial framework could be considered as analogous to the act of writing, since a spatial text is both devised and inscribed in consequence of the physical movement which takes place within a given environmental context. However, this would be incorrect, or at least unfaithful to what is implied when describing space as a text.[4] Individual movement through or action in a context happens in

---

[2] This is based on John Thompson's excellent introduction to Ricoeur's work (see Thompson, 1981: 13–14).

[3] Potentially, a literary text is open to anyone who can read; other types of cultural representation may be different in this respect. I may know how to move in space but I may not be able to "read" the spatial text of another culture.

[4] In the analysis of discourse it is a reasonably unproblematic task to differentiate between speaking, writing and reading. Although various authors stress the analytical similarities between these activities. Ricoeur sees speech and text as two different ways of realizing discourse; Jonathan Culler sees writing as akin to an act of critical reading, "in which the author takes up

space – that is, within an historically constituted spatial framework. Such movements also take place in consequence of and in relation to prior and future meanings – that is, to prior and future interpretations of the spatial order. As a result I would argue that individual actions, even those often repeated and reidentified as the same in their repetition, are more akin to speech utterances than to acts of writing. Movement through and action in a spatial context may be analyzed as discourse, but it is a discourse delimited precisely by the strategic intentions of the actor, by the responses of the individuals to whom the action is addressed or who become embroiled in it, and by the shared immediacy of the spatiotemporal context of the various individuals concerned. This is the level of practical discourse and practical necessity identified by Bourdieu (1977). However, discourse has two distinct aspects, or, as Ricoeur would claim, discourse may be realized in two different ways – either as speech or as text. Each is an equally legitimate mode of realization. What distinguishes the analysis of discourse as speech and literary text from the analysis of space as action and spatial text is that in the latter case both modes of realization are simultaneous. In this sense movement through and action in organized space are simultaneously analogous to both speaking and reading.

The different ways in which speech and text are realized in discourse are contained in the concept of distanciation. The most crucial form of distanciation, with regard to spatial texts, is that the text is freed from the limits of "ostensive reference" – that is, from the situational context of the speech utterance (Ricoeur, 1981: 202). The text possesses nonsituational references which outlive the immediacy of contextual reference and which offer possible representations or possible orientations in the world, and which finally proffer a symbolic dimension to understanding: a play on form, "a story we tell ourselves about ourselves." To interpret a text is to enlarge our understanding of our position in the world. A particular interpretation of a spatial text develops meanings which can then be pursued or fulfilled in other situations occurring outside the specific interpretation in question. This is a point I develop in Chapter 9, where I discuss the relationship between cultural representations and the material conditions within which they are produced and understood.

The ability of a text to refer, through the act of interpretation (which in the case of spatial texts must be understood as types of participation in the spatial world), to a "world outside itself," can be grasped, as I have already noted, through a discussion of the referential dimension of metaphor. Words – and, through analogic extension, actions – have more than one meaning, and

---

a literary past and directs it into the future" (Culler, 1980: 50). Culler's point shows how difficult it is to distinguish – at least on some levels of analysis – activities which are all grounded in the same set of conventions or conditions of meaning. This is particularly problematic in the analysis of space, where physical movement in and through space simultaneously inscribes the text (writing), acts within it (speech), and provides an interpretation of it (reading).

all these potential meanings can be collected and codified in a lexical system. However, the actual polysemic functioning of a word can only be grasped within the context of the sentence. Words have meanings in sentences and sentences will only be uttered in particular contexts. This hierarchy of contextualization also applies to social action. Actions only have meaning in relation to a host of alternative actions. The existence of alternatives can only be grasped within the context of sets of actions and these sets are only applied in, and appropriate to, specific contexts.

The context of a speech utterance functions to screen out some of the word's "surplus meaning" – that is, it produces a single meaning from a basically polysemic word. It is this screening that Ricoeur takes to be the first act of interpretation. Interpretation is necessary because, according to Ricoeur, all words are polysemic and take their actual meaning from their context of use. Polysemy thus provides the basis for the creative extension of meaning through metaphor. Metaphorical meaning can only be apprehended through interpretation – an interpretation which makes sense of the complete sentence or set of actions by limiting the basic polysemy of the metaphorical terms themselves (see Chapter 7). However, metaphorical meaning is more than merely the actualization of one of the potential meanings of a polysemic word or words. What happens is that the metaphorical utterance, "with the full connivance of its use-situation," confers upon the word an "emergent meaning" which, although contextually produced, refers to an understanding outside that context (Ricoeur, 1981: 166–71). In this way metaphor could be described as a "work in miniature," as a discourse. Ultimately it is possible to say that we construct the meaning of a text in a way very similar to that in which we make sense of a metaphorical statement.

Reading and Interpretation

So far in this chapter I have argued that meaning does not inhere in the organization of space but must be invoked. I have stressed that this invocation is the result of the practical activity of social actors in determinate social and historical relations. And I have also tried to pursue some ideas concerning metaphor and the analysis of space as a text. The aim of the discussion as a whole has been to try and understand how the organization of space comes to have meaning, and why it is possible for there to be a number of interpretations associated with any given spatial order. The problem which this discussion raises is: Why and how do particular interpretations of a spatial text become necessary or appropriate? And this problem is linked to the further difficulty of the relationship between spatial texts and their social and economic conditions. A possible approach to these problems may be found in a consideration of the text as work – that is, as a cultural representation which stands in a particular relation to both ideology and history. However, in order to analyze a spatial text as a cultural representation, a certain recentering of the subject is required. The focus of concern shifts from "What are the possible interpretations of a given text?" to "Why do particular social actors interpret space as they do?" It is precisely this shift that Bourdieu attempts. Through a focus on social actors and their activities, he undertakes to make explicit the implicit knowledge those actors deploy in responding as they do (Bourdieu, 1977). If any discussion of space as a text necessarily implies an analysis of the purposeful activity of social actors, it also demands an account of their varying interpretations of that text. It would seem to be axiomatic that any penetrating analysis of the interpretations given in and to space by social actors must acknowledge the fundamental interdependency of action and interpretation; where meaning is only established in and through social practice. This practical relation between action and understanding given in the interpretation of a spatial text may be understood as akin to reading. In other words, actual bodily movement through and action in ordered space are simultaneously both action and interpretation; they are therefore intelligible as an act of reading, where reading itself is understood as conjoined decoding and interpretation.

To see bodily movement through and activity in a spatial context as practical and interpretative action requires some comment on the term "interpretation." I am not seeking here to offer a method of interpretation, but rather to explain why people interpret the organization of space as they do. To ask about the meaning of an element within the totality of the spatial text is to ask what it does, and to understand what it does one must analyze the developing activities of the actor (reader) in relation to their temporal and spatial trajectory through ordered space. This, again, is what Bourdieu attempts, and it is a fruitful reorientation in that it moves away from a study of the semiotics of meaning and tries to make explicit the implicit knowledge of competent social actors as it is deployed in practice. However this is only one concern within the general problematic of "reading to interpret." To read is always to read in relation to other texts, in relation to the codified mode of a culture's production of meaning. Thus, while it is possible to provide interpretations of texts based on the models of observers – as in the case of semiotic analyses of modes of signification – and while it is instructive to produce interpretations on the basis of the interpretative operations embodied in the relation between practical and symbolic discourse, as Bourdieu attempts to do, there remains a third line of approach.[5]

This third approach, instead of interpreting the text *per se*, begins with

[5] Obviously reading is a rule-governed mode of behavior, and to set out the appropriate conventions for reading is an urgent task which is much complicated by the intersection of reading with the existence of specific textual forms, for example, genres, etc. However, the notion of an ideal reader should be resisted (Culler, 1981: 126–7).

an analyis of the "conditions of meaning"—that is, with the relationship between a text and its social and historical conditions. This "historical" project
has two aspects: one is a study of the relation between text and history through
the formal devices used to exploit and transmute culturally produced meanings; the other is a perspective which acknowledges the transience of any
interpretation and takes as its object of scrutiny the succession of interpretative acts (readings) through which traditions are established and meaning is
produced (Culler, 1980). It is this dual construction that links the study of
texts, as cultural representations, to the study of historical development and
changing ideological structures, which form the subject matter of Chapters
8 and 9.

To say that a spatial text is open to a multiplicity of different interpretations is to say that it is open to a series of alternative readings. A theory of
the interpretation of spatial texts would attempt to account for the range of
different readings for a given spatial frame. If it is true that there is always
more than one way of interpreting a text, it is not true that all interpretations
are equal. Cultural convention and social and historical conditions determine
the horizons of expectations within which a text becomes intelligible; they
also determine whether or not certain interpretations will be deemed appropriate. Ultimately, the potential horizons of meaning: which surround a text
are finite; the text presents a limited field of possible constructions. However,
it is always possible to confront interpretations, argue against them, or arbi-
trate between them. This process of argumentation is conducted at both a
discursive and a practical level. I wish to concern myself primarily with the
practical level, while not denying the final interdependence of both discourse
and practice. Argumentation involves conflict; frequently it also implies an
ability to marshall resources, appeal to authority or extend control in various
ways (Giddens, 1979: 88–94). It is thus axiomatic that in many situations
argumentation will involve asymmetries of varying sorts; this is most particularly the case at the level of the text, where the argument is not pursued
between two interlocutors. The problem of asymmetry is further compounded
in analyzing space, since, although understanding practical activity in space
is not the same as interpreting the totality of the spatial text, neither practice
nor text is realized, or necessarily realizable, in verbal discourse. It is therefore not entirely possible to consider the relations thus:

Practice	Spatial text
Speech	Written text

However, if the negotiability of interpretation is not conducted through the
process of verbal argumentation, then it can be understood as being pursued
at the level of representation. Physical movement through and action in space
are both, of course, types of representation (Goffman, 1971). But a spatial

text can be understood, first and foremost, as a cultural representation: a representation completely bound up with the conduct of a continual process of argumentation. To provide a reading of spatial text is to stake a claim in this process. It is, quite simply, to provide an interpretation. The ability to provide interpretations, based on prior representations, and then to deem those interpretations appropriate, is not one held equally by all members of a given group. It is this point that I wish to pursue now in a consideration of the relations between texts and their historical and social conditions of production and reproduction.

IDEOLOGY: PRODUCTION AND SIGNIFICATION[6]

I began with an assertion that, in structural/semiotic approaches to the study of space, space is frequently understood as a reflection of social categories or systems of classification. These categories are themselves only intelligible with reference to an *a priori* set of essential meanings which is culture. Culture in this sense is understood as an ideology or "world view" which consists of sets of meanings, values, and beliefs. If however, the organization of space is understood merely as a reflection of an ideology or "world view," then it becomes extremely difficult to specify how social change might occur, except as a result of changing values. I shall therefore argue in this section that spatial texts are not the expression – let alone the reflection – of ideologies, and I shall try to characterize the relationship between ideology and text as one of produced representation, in order to remove one obstacle to the understanding of social change.

To consider a spatial text in terms of the ideology which can be said to inform it is to analyze the relations between its material conditions of existence and its work as a representation which produces meaning.[7] In other words there is a concern both with modes of production and modes of signification, in the attempt to steer a *via media* between opposing views: that representation is a direct reflection of historical and social conditions, or that it is totally autonomous of such conditions. The notion of a direct, spontaneous relation between a spatial text and its historical and social conditions cannot be maintained (Eagleton, 1976). What the text signifies is not "real"/objective historical relations, but the same historical relations construed in terms of an ideological production, produced by the text's agents. In this sense history "enters" the text as ideology. This does not, however, mean that the "real" historical conditions are present in the text, albeit in disguised

---

[6] The argument in this section is based on Eagleton's work concerning the ideological production of literary texts (Eagleton, 1976).

[7] This has been done for other types of cultural representation: see, for example, Barret *et al.*, 1979.

form, and that what is required is for the analyst to reveal and dig them out. The text takes as its object – its subject for representation – not the "real," but rather certain significations/representations about the real. As discourse the text does not take social and historical relations as its immediate object, but works instead upon certain ideological forms and materials. If the text refers to history/historical conditions, it does so obliquely. The text talks about, or works over, states of affairs which are "imaginary," since their meaning lies not in their material reality but in how they help to fashion and perpetuate a particular process of representation (Eagleton, 1976). However, the relationship between text and historical conditions is not one of fantasy; the significations worked into the text are already representations of reality rather than reality itself. The text is related to material conditions as the product of certain representations (i.e., ideology) whose source and referent is ultimately, the material conditions of existence themselves. The text is a product of ideology, of the "lived" conditions of social reality. This emphasis on production is the key to the relation between a spatial text and the ideology which informs it. For ideology is not expressed, reflected or reproduced in the text; rather, it produces and is produced by the text, transforming it into a particular and irreducible representation. Eagleton argues this point with reference to literary texts:

> The categories of an ideology produce a series of ideological significations which form the immediate materials of the text; and those significations can be seen as a concrete "production" of the ideological categories. The study of the text is a study of the production of such produced categories. (Eagleton, 1976: 81)

He thus renders the relationship between text, ideology, and history:

                    Signifier
        Text   Signification
                    Signified
                                                Signified
                            Ideology
                                                Signifier

                                    History

This architectural formalization of interrelations is similar to Bourdieu's account of the relations between social practices, habitus (generative principles) and objective conditions of existence (Bourdieu, 1977: 78–87). The formulations are similar because both authors wish to clarify the relationship between product and history, where the product is itself the result of a prior production – that is, ideology. However, the circle continues, for the text is also the process whereby ideology produces the forms which produce it. Every order tends to naturalize the arbitrariness on which it is based. The text is thus displayed as a "natural" construction.

Space as Representation

The systems of classification at work in the ordering of space reproduce, through metaphoric extension and transformation, representations of such things as divisions by age, sex, or position in the relations of production. These systems of classification contribute to the reproduction of the power relations of which they are the product. They help to secure the misrecognition of the arbitrariness on which they are based. They appear natural. It is in the natural order of things that the old are superior to the young, that women are inferior to men. The text as an instrument of knowledge, referring simultaneously to the individual's position in the world and to the "natural" world outside its context, is a political instrument. It reproduces the ideological forms which produce it and which make both those forms and itself appear "natural," self-evidently true. There is no need to insist on the legitimation of a division of labor and power between the sexes which already produces and is produced by a spatial representation entirely dominated by male values (see Chapter 7, and Bourdieu, 1977).

Spatial representations express in their own logic the power relations between different groups; they are therefore active instruments in the production and reproduction of the social order. The ability to provide interpretations of a spatial text (on the level of practice) is political, because the power to impose the principles of the representation of reality – which is no more than the construction of those principles – is a political power. Bourdieu elaborates this point and shows that in the act of representation, which is the act of production, a correspondence is established between social (external) structures and mental (internal) structures. This correspondence, which produces the cosmological and political as self-evident and natural orders, is reinforced by the activities of other individuals in the group and by institutions such as space, language, and art, which constitute the ideological structures of lived reality as much as they express them.[8]

IDEOLOGY: THE PROBLEM
OF ALTERNATIVE INTERPRETATIONS

In this characterization of the relations between ideology, representation, and power the social actor disappears once more from sight and is replaced in-

---

[8] Bourdieu is quite careful not to allow this argument to become too determining, and therefore makes a distinction between doxa, orthodoxy, and heterodoxy, which he correlates with types of society on a developmental scale.

stead by structures of domination and control (societal conventions and the like), which are beyond the control of individuals, and by which they are duped. Furthermore it gives no adequate account of how competing interpretations of a spatial text might be understood to coexist, except as products of differing metaphoric extensions in particular spatiotemporal contexts of action. Both these problems can be resolved, in part, through elucidation of the fact that relations between text and ideology are not only historically mutable (i.e., mutable in historical time), but may also be differential in a synchronic or simultaneous sense.

The point I wish to stress is that ideology is not the "truth" of the text; it is not necessarily or entirely what the text is all about (cf. Eagleton, 1976). A spatial text has no intrinsic essence, just as it has no inherent meaning; the truth of the text resides in practice. It is through practice that a spatial text at once "inserts" the actor into a particular relation both with ideology and history and with the constructed representation of both which is the text itself. Since the relation between ideology and text is only invoked in practice—that is, by participation in a given spatial order—there is no question of a fixed, immutable relationship between text and ideology. Yet certain forms of relationship are, of course, more conventional or more appropriate—and it is in the interests of dominant groups to narrow, or at least control, the range of possible relationships between text and ideology (see Chapter 9). Action in a given spatial domain may be understood as the meaningful construction of a representation, albeit in relation to an already existing text; the interpretation thus produced gives rise to an ideological discourse. That is to say, it produces a moment of reflection on the ideology which informs the text, which then permits the text to contain and produce variable degrees of internal conflict and disorder.

Nonetheless, it must be said that the text only contains or permits ideological conflicts or tensions which it can itself resolve, or leave unresolved, without radically interrogating the ideology which informs it. Thus, a wide range of both conflicts and solutions may exist simultaneously in a text, which casts them from the outset into resolvable or acceptably unresolvable forms, as part of the very act of representation. It is therefore possible to understand the ideological conflicts which necessitate and/or inform the text by analyzing the solutions it proposes. This supports the characterization of the text as the product, rather than the reflection, of an ideological solution.

In this discussion I have argued that the existence of ideological conflicts and tensions within a given text helps to account for the multiplicity of potential interpretations to which that text is open. Action in any given spatial order "inserts" the individual into a particular relation both with the text (as representation) and with ideology and history. As a result, different individuals and different groups of individuals may be seen to stand in a particular relation both to the text and to its ideological and historical determinants.

This last point lays the ground for a theoretical approach which does not subscribe to the notion that social actors are completely opiated by the ideologies embodied in cultural forms. For they clearly have the reflexive ability to use a particular cultural text–in this case space–to produce a specific orientation toward a given ideology.

CONCLUSION

The approach to the study of space presented here lays considerable emphasis on space as a cultural representation, and this theme will be developed in a variety of ways in the chapters which follow. In Chapter 7 I shall show how the organization of domestic space among the Marakwet both reworks and is a reworking of conflicts and tensions which exist within the society and which arise as a result of conflict between different interest groups. In Chapters 8 and 9 I take up the problem of social change and demonstrate the way in which relations between spatial text and ideology are mutable, with respect both to historical time and to the differing positions of particular groups of individuals in the social relations of production. In Chapter 9 I discuss gender relations in Marakwet society in an attempt to demonstrate the intimate relationship which exists between the distribution of power and the production of cultural representations.

CHAPTER 6

Ash and Animal Dung: The Organization of Domestic Space among the Endo

⟡

Before any discussion of the organization of Endo space can really begin, it is necessary to examine some of the temporal features which affect the construction and use of domestic space. Household space is never static, and even without the inevitable changes which occur through historical time, there is also the fact that households and household arrangements change with biographical time. This is an attribute of domestic space which is well recognized (Goody, 1971) but is rarely discussed in the symbolic analysis of space. When Bourdieu presents an image of the Kabyle house and the world of which it is a microcosm, are we seeking an "ideal" house, a typical house, or merely a collage of common features noticed by one anthropologist? It seems most likely that what we are presented with is a combination of an "ideal" house and a typical domestic unit. Of course, these features are culturally specific. In a culture where permanent dwellings are erected and handed down from generation to generation, the reordering of space may be minimal or it may involve a process of recategorization rather than reconstruction. In the case of the Endo, the life-cycle of the individual compound corresponds to the life-cycle of the head of the compound. However, as we shall see, this is a generalization which needs some qualification.

CHANGE AND DECAY:
THE LIFE-CYCLE OF COMPOUNDS

So far I have characterized the typical Endo compound as defined by two houses which face each other across an open area. This typical compound is illustrated in Figure 28, and is not so much a representation of Endo compounds in general as of a particular stage in the compound development cycle. The life-cycle of a compound is allied to the development cycle of the domestic group which occupies it. There is, however, no easy correlation between the life stages of a particular man and the structures to be found in his compound.

Around the age of eighteen years a young man will normally ask his father to help him build a house. The decision as to where to build the house will be constrained by a number of factors, including the availability of lineage land and the position of the son in the sibling order. However most sons (excepting the youngest) build their houses separately from their father's compound. At the time a man decides to build his own house he takes the first steps toward establishing a separate domestic unit, of which he will be the head and of which his first house will be the core. A man cannot marry without a house. If a man wants to marry, a house will be speedily constructed. However, it is more often the case that a young man will build a house as a way of signifying his readiness and intention to marry. The stages which

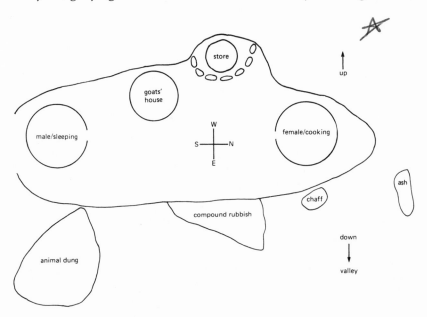

FIGURE 28. A typical Endo compound.

TABLE 2. Household Development Cycle:
Phases and Their Concomitant Structures

	1	2	3	4	5
Hut 1	*				
Hut 2	*	*	*		
Store	*	*	*		
Kano	*	*			
Hut 3		*	*		
Store 2		*	*		
Separate *kano*			*		
Hut for son			*	*	
Hut for father or mother			*	*	
Kano collapses				*	*
Store collapses				*	*
Hut 2 or 3 collapses					*
Compound ceases					*

follow from this, as they relate to the development cycle of the compound, are summarized in Table 2. The following discussion is presented as the way Endo men perceive this cycle, and should be treated as such.

Phase I (see Table 3)[1]

Every man starts with one house. After he marries he can continue to live in the one house, or he may build a second. As I have said, it is the Endo ideal that there should be one house for the man and one for the woman, but nowadays this is often translated into one house for cooking and the other for entertaining/sleeping; it is considered a sign of "modernity" to split the functions/use of houses in this way. It is therefore usual for a man who has sufficient means to build a second home as soon as possible after his marriage, and to relegate his first house to use as a kitchen. It must also be said that the pressure to build a second house increases once the woman of the household is pregnant. However there are three cases in Sibou sample I of men who, despite more than ten years of marriage, have only one house. In one case the couple is childless. In the other two cases the men claim that they have never had the means to build a second house. This should not be

[1] The development cycle of domestic groups is discussed by Meyer Fortes, who identifies three stages in the cycle: expansion, fission, and replacement. These stages are almost identical to my five-phase model set out below. This similarity is partly due to the fact that Fortes links the development of domestic groups – as I do in the case of the Endo – with a redistribution of control over productive and reproductive resources associated with a change in the jural status of the spouses (Fortes, 1971: 4–5).

TABLE 3. Composition of Compounds in Sibou Sample I

	No. of yrs. married	No. of adults	No. of children	Hut 1	Hut 2	Store 1	Kano	Hut 3	Store 2	Hut Br.	Separate kano	Hut son	Hut father or mother	Kano collapses	Store collapses	Hut collapses	Compound ceases
1	13	2	6	x	x						x						
2	27	2	4	x		x	x										
3	unm.	1	0	x													
4	30	2	0	x	x												
5	wid.	1	0	x		x								x	x		
6	15	2	5	x	x	x											
7	10	2	5	x	x						x						
8	1	2	0	x													
9	wid.	1	0	x			x										
10	30	2	2	x			x										
11	2	2	1	x													
12	15	2	6	x	x												
13	wid.	1	3	x	x										x	x	
14	wid.	1	4	x	x	x											
15	unm.	3	0	x								x					
16	5	2	2	x		x						x					
17	9	4	4	x		x	x		x	x							
18	20	2	6	x	x	x	x										
19	17	1	4	x													
20	11	2	5	x		x					x						
21	18	2	6	x	x	x											
22	15	5	7	x	x	x		x	x		x	x					
23	wid.	1	0	x				x									
24	wid.	1	4	x													x
25	wid.	1	0	x			x										
26	23	2	5	x	x	x						x					
27	7	2	3	x								x					
28	23	2	5	x	x	x											
29	unm.	1	0	x													
30	7	2	3	x	x	x	x	x									
31	1	2	0	x													
32	5	2	1	x	x	x											
33	5	2	3	x	x	x											
34	30	2	0	x													
35	18	2	5	x	x	x		x	x								
36	2	2	1	x	x												
37	unm.	1	0	x													
38	wid.	1	0	x			x										
39	8	2	3	x			x										
40	3	2	0	x	x	x				x							
41	4	2	0	x	x	x		x	x								
42	1	2	0	x	x	x											
43	6	2	4	x	x	x											

understood in an absolute sense, but in terms of a set of decision-making strategies. It seems reasonably clear that when these men have had the resources
(principally labor and money), they have always chosen – and perhaps have
sometimes been required by kinship obligations – to deploy them elsewhere.

> Loicaita is the head of household 28 (Table 3). He married in 1959 and
> lived in a house he had built in an upper part of the village, once occupied
> by all members of the Kabisioi clan, but now deserted in favor of sites
> nearer to the valley floor. During this period, he had a *kano* (goat's house)
> further down the escarpment and quite close to the modern settlement
> of Tot. In 1963 he decided to move down and build a house on the site of
> the *kano*. At that time, he had two children and his wife was pregnant
> with a third. When the family moved they dismantled their old house, but
> left the fireplace intact as is the Endo custom. They then used the materi-
> als to build their new house.
>   Between 1963 and 1980 the family all lived in a single house. In 1980,
> Loicaita decided to build a second house for his eldest son. This son works
> in a factory in western Kenya and rarely comes home. The house is not
> completed, and the family continues to live in one house. The second and
> third born, who are girls, sleep with relatives further down the escarpment.
> Loicaita has no *kano* and no plans to build another house or any other
> structure.

Loicaita is a well-respected man, and there is no obvious reason for his failure
to build a second house. He has five children, two of whom are sexually mature daughters. When questioned about the situation, he merely replied that
he would have liked a second house, but the cost of school fees for his eldest
son and the size of his lineage (Figure 6) prevented him from "having the
means." The decision not to build a second house was clearly Loicaita's and
cannot be entirely accounted for by the pressure of external factors. This is
clear from the fact that other members of his lineage mention his lack of a
second house, although no further comment is usually passed. Their concern
is minimal, but it arises because to build a second house is a sign of wealth
and maturity, both of which are qualities which are defined, in part, by marital status itself. It is marital status above all that defines the achievement of
adulthood in Endo society, and it is therefore considered slightly unusual for
a man not to divert what resources he has toward building a second house.
    The ideal of the two-house compound conforms to the ideal of achieved
adult status. Indeed the two are almost synonymous, since the layout of the
compound reflects the maturity of the domestic unit and confirms its productive capabilities (Figure 29). On his marriage a man will finally receive all
the stock and land that are due to him from his father.[2] This, like the birth
of his first child, defines his domestic unit as independently productive. Each
man is then faced with the choice of whether to build a store and/or *kano*.

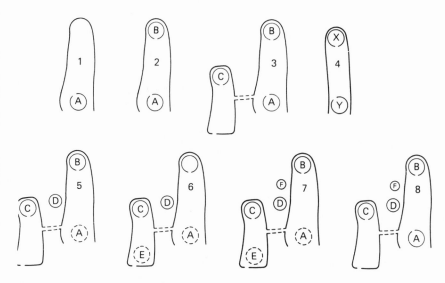

FIGURE 29. The development of a single family compound.

Neither structure is essential: A man may continue to herd his stock with that of his father, or it may be the case that the amount of grain produced by his household is still small enough to be easily stored in the house.

Phase 2

Phase 2 corresponds to a period when a man already has children. If he has not already done so, he may at this point build a second house, a store and/or *kano*. One crucial factor is that once his eldest daughter approaches the age of eight he will no longer be able to sleep in the same house as her, and this may initiate a move to build an extra house. Similarly there may by this time be a need for extra storage space. It is often the case that as the domestic unit matures husband and wife want to keep the man's grain separate from that to be used for family consumption. Also, once a man has children he will be most unlikely to keep his animals with those of his father, and he may make renewed efforts to build a separate *kano*.

Phase 2 may also coincide with a decision to take a second wife. A third house and second store may then be built for the new wife. Or, if a man has only one house, he may decide to build a second house for his new wife, and he will then move and stay with each wife alternately.

---

[2] A man does not always receive all the stock due to him when he marries, particularly if his father is still a young man. This often causes acrimonious disputes, which are usually settled by the father's brothers or at a meeting of all male agnates of the lineage (Kipkorir and Welbourn, 1973: 31).

Phase 3

Phase 3 corresponds to a period when the domestic unit is at the peak of its cycle and will thereafter begin to fragment. There is the possibility that a man may not have built a second house by the time his eldest son wants to build his own house. In this case the father may delay his son's request until after he has built an additional house for himself, or he may decide to take a second wife rather than divert his resources to his son.[3] If something of this sort does occur, then there will be increased pressure to build a separate *kano* at some distance from the main compound, for a mature son cannot sleep in his parent's compound.

Phase 3 is also the time, depending upon a man's position in the sibling order, when he may have to build a house for a widowed parent. The Endo say that the eldest son should take care of his father and the youngest should look after his mother.

Phase 4

During Phase 4 a man may have to help a younger son to build a house and/or he may, for the first born, have to take care of a widowed parent (Plate VIII). However, his eldest children will have married and moved out of the compound, and, as a result, older structures (houses, stores) in his own compound may not be repaired in response to the shrinking size of his domestic unit. During this time a man will also allocate most of his stock to his children, and there is therefore less need for a *kano*.

Phase 5

Phase 5 is a continuation of Phase 4 and sees the further decline of the individual compound. The compound will finally cease when either both spouses die or the remaining spouse moves to live with one of the children. This completes the cycle.

The above is a somewhat condensed account of the decisions which face an individual man during certain stages in his life. The stages as given are not mutually exclusive, nor will they necessarily occur in the chronological order given. The only fixed points, which are the same for all men, are that the process begins with marriage and ends with death. What a man actually decides to do in his lifetime is the result of superimposed layers of possible

---

[3] Sons often accuse fathers of diverting resources in this way, and a young man without a wage will try to sell some produce from his father's *shamba* to earn a little money to help with building a house. This deceit is a common and acknowledged one. Wage earners frequently speak of saving money in order to build first or second houses.

PLATE VIII. The compound of a mature man, showing the addition of a third house for an elderly relative.

choices – worked out in the context of certain ideal notions, socially approved or required maneuvers and particular economic and political strategies. Such things are themselves based, in part, on previous decisions taken and acted upon. In any event, it must be recognized that the choices facing each man are different and that they are particularly affected by position in the sibling order, size of inherited herd, number of children and whether or not the man in question has any earned income.

Other factors – like the ideal of separate houses for different genders and/or different functions, the desire to appear "Westernized," the prohibition on parents and children of the opposite sex sleeping in the same house – all have to be taken into account. Nevertheless, the strategies with which particular problems are faced and solved vary enormously. For example, a man with a daughter approaching puberty may build a second house for himself, take to sleeping in the *kano*, allow his daughter to sleep with friends or agree to allow her to live with relatives.[4] Consequently it is not possible to make a single generalized statement about what the Endo do. It is only possible to outline some of the choices and constraints. Table 3 shows all the compounds in Sibou sample I, the number of people resident in each one, the length of

---

[4] Households always contain people who are not members of the immediate family. This is often because young children are "lent out" as child minders or herders, and in fact this is one of the common ways in which sisters retain links with each other after marriage.

time the partners have been married and the composition of each compound. Even such a small sample gives some idea of the enormous potential for variation.

In addition to the choices outlined above, a man may also move his entire compound, at least once, during his life. Persistent misfortune – for example, where two or more people die in rapid succession or all the animals are struck down by disease – is a common reason for movement of this kind. Since 1968 several families in the sample area have moved, in order to be closer to their fields in the valley and to the modern center of Tot. Homicide and stock-raiding may also force whole lineages to shift their compounds.

Although the choices and constraints which face each individual family vary enormously, it is possible to understand the development of a particular domestic unit in terms of the unfolding of specific choices and constraints within the context of a particular individual's life. In order to illustrate this point, I shall describe the case of one man, Kipkoimet, and relate the development of his compound to the first two phases of the five-phase model given above.

CASE HISTORY

Figure 28 shows the development of one family compound over the last ten years (Compound 30, Figure 5). Compound I is the single house (B) of an unmarried man, Kipkoimet, and corresponds to Phase I of the five-phase model. By the time Kipkoimet came to build a house his own father was dead and he received help – in the form of money and labor – from his father's brother and his mother's sister's sons.[5] The support offered to Kipkoimet by his maternal cousins (mother's sister's sons) and the close links between them encouraged Kipkoimet to build his house in their lineage (*Kakibelkio*) area, rather than his own (*Kakabisioi*).

Kipkoimet married in 1972. He did not build a second house immediately, although he had intended to do so, because he did not have the resources. At this time Kipkoimet was not in a strong position. With his father dead and his elder brothers away, he had few close kin to whom he could turn, and he could not ask his maternal cousins for help again so soon. Kipkoimet's father had left very few animals, Kipkoimet himself was not employed, and, with only his wife as labor, the productivity of his fields was not great. It is hardly surprising, therefore, that he did not build either a goats' house or a store. This stage in Kipkoimet's life is still part of Phase I, and at this

---

[5] It is unusual for a man to ask his maternal cousins (mother's sister's sons) for help; this is because, given the rules of clan exogamy, it is most unlikely that a man would be living in close proximity to this category of kin. Kipkoimet's case was rather special since his mother and her sister actually married into the same clan (also unusual), although they married men of different lineages.

point it is a lack of resources that prevents him from building additional structures.

In 1974 Kipkoimet was forced to build a second house when his widowed mother came to live with him. This point corresponds to the beginning of Phase 2 as outlined above. But it is interesting to note that the existence of a widowed mother forced Kipkoimet to use his resources to build a house for her, before he could build one for himself. His mother chose his compound because her two elder sons lived outside the valley and the youngest son, who was unmarried anyway, was away at school. Kipkoimet was therefore the only "available" son and, since a mother and an adult son cannot sleep in the same house, a second house had to be build. At this point house A was for Kipkoimet's mother and house B was for the family (Compound 2).

In 1976 (Compound 3), Kipkoimet decided to build a house for himself (C). He was able to do so because he had now established a herd of sheep, his bananas were producing fruit, and his wife had established cooperative links with her neighbors which had meant an increase in grain yields. Kipkoimet was also under pressure from his wife, who wanted a second house; for to have separate houses for cooking and sleeping is a sign both of "modernity" and of status (see above). In addition, one of Kipkoimet's brothers was killed in an accident, and his son, a boy of seven years old, was sent to live with Kipkoimet. This also posed a problem, since Kipkoimet's wife and the son of the deceased brother could not, at least on a permanent basis, sleep in the same house. As a result house B became the kitchen house and the only person to sleep there was the seven-year-old boy. The rest of the family slept in house C, which was also the house used for entertaining. This is an example of how the "regulations" concerning sleeping arrangements can instigate a move to build an additional house. This sort of occurrence is very characteristic of Phase 2 because as the children get older it becomes more important that they should not sleep in the same house as the parent of the opposite sex.

Later in 1976 the village was attacked by cattle raiders on a number of occasions, and Kipkoimet and his family, along with many others, were forced to flee further up the escarpment. There he built a compound (Compound 4), with a house (X) for himself and a house (Y) for his wife. He was able to do this because the houses were of wattle and daub, and therefore cheap and quick to build, unlike the mud and stone houses Kipkoimet and his family had just abandoned. This new compound was adjacent to his mother's former compound, and in fact Kipkoimet's mother went back to live in her old house.

A year later the family was able to return to its original compound (Compound 5). House A fell into disrepair since Kipkoimet's mother did not return, having decided to remain in the upper reaches of the village for fear of further attack. At this point Kipkoimet built a *kano* (D).

In 1978, Kipkoimet had two children of his own, plus the son of his dead brother. His younger brother, William, was about to finish school and return home. Plans were made and Kipkoimet started to build him a house (E, Compound 6). As it turned out William got a scholarship to study abroad, house E was never completed, and Kipkoimet built a store (F) instead, using the materials which would otherwise have been used to complete house E. In 1980, the walls of the half-finished house E were used to help rebuild house A (Compound 8), which was then occupied by the researcher. At this time Kipkoimet had three children of his own, plus the son of his dead brother. His mother was still living in the upper reaches of the village, and his brother had not yet returned from abroad. During 1981–2 Kipkoimet built a separate kano down on the valley floor, and D then fell into disrepair. The decision to build a separate kano was based on the size of the herd and the fact that his dead brother's son would soon be too old to sleep in the same compound as Kipkoimet and his wife. The events described in this last part of the case history all correspond to Phase 2 (above).

Phase 3, which corresponds to a period when the household has reached the peak of its cycle and will thereafter begin to fragment, has not yet begun. However, such a phase is presaged by the building of a *kano* on the valley floor. The recognition that the eldest boy will soon be too old to sleep in the same compound as Kipkoimet and his wife announces the future of a new compound and a separate household.[6]

The above case history demonstrates that any discussion of the typical Endo compound must be set against the development and decline of the domestic unit. Kipkoimet's case is also an illustration of the extremely variable circumstances which may affect decisions concerning the building of houses and the ordering of the compound. It is clear from the material I have presented that it is not just a matter of a man building additional houses and structures when he has the resources to do so. Cattle raids, kin obligations, position in the sibling order, and a host of other factors, govern the available choices and will ultimately determine the size and form of the family compound.

The fact that the life-cycle of the domestic unit is the key to understanding compound organization emerges from an examination of those compounds which are not occupied by a family unit: man, woman, and children. As I have suggested, symbolic analyses of the organization of space usually depend on the combination of an "ideal" house and a typical domestic unit. There is rarely any discussion of the houses of widows or widowers, or of how a household of mother and son differs from one of husband and wife.

---

[6] It would be a mistake to imagine that Kipkoimet's case is a result of the impact of modern influences (e.g., brothers who are away at school and itinerant anthropologists!). Even in the past the factors affecting the development of compounds were extremely variable. I could have selected a more "senior" man's compound, but chose not to do so because of problems of accurate chronology and the tricks of memory and time.

Among the Endo there are differences, but these differences are variations on a theme.

Compound 13 (Table 3) is occupied by Ko-Jemutai, a widow in her fifties. She has five children, only three of whom now live at home. Since the death of her husband, the fortunes of the family have declined. One house has fallen into disrepair, along with the *kano* (goats' house). The family's goats were decimated by disease in 1980 and the remaining two animals are on "loan" to the brother of the dead man. The impermanent nature of Endo compounds means that they contract and expand in accordance with the occupiers' needs and fortunes. A widow's or widower's compound is always a former "family" compound which has contracted in size. The nonproductive nature of such households is forcefully exhibited by their air of decrepitude and disrepair, their smaller size and their lack of animals, grain, and children.

Households of mother and son are extremely rare. A sexually mature son cannot sleep in the same compound as his mother, although if he is unmarried he will return to his mother's house to eat. If a widow has to leave her home, or if she feels she is getting too old to cope, she will move in with one of her married sons. At this point she becomes part of her son's household, and is therefore reincorporated into the family compound. A widower will either live alone in what was his "family" compound, or he will move to live with one of his married sons. A widower would never live with an unmarried son because there would be no woman to cook. A man living with a single daughter is inconceivable.

The main point of the argument is that compounds are always a phase in the life-cycle of households. The elderly either continue to live in their own "reduced" compounds, or they move in with a married son and become part of the son's household. There are therefore no "special" or "anomalous" compounds. This means that, while household space is continually changing and developing, there are certain principles of organization which can be apprehended in the layout of all compounds. As I have stated, these principles induce the north–south orientation of the compound, the oppositional placing of houses, the cardinal arrangement of house interiors and the different functions of certain spaces. However, the most important principles of organization are probably those which relate to the disposal of household refuse.

THE SPATIAL ORDERING OF HOUSEHOLD REFUSE

The Endo recognize three kinds of rubbish which are spatially and semantically distinct: ash (*eron*), animal dung (*segerr*), and chaff from finger millet and sorghum (*morir*). There are, of course, other types of refuse (animal bone, peel, tin cans, etc.), which we would term rubbish but the Endo would not.[7] All rubbish is disposed of immediately below the compound. The three recognized types of refuse have specific disposal positions relative to each other and to compound activities. Ash is always thrown behind the house from which it comes, and ash from different houses is never dumped together in the same place. Chaff is often placed just on the front edge of the compound, wherever the woman has found it convenient to do her winnowing. Given the layout of Endo compounds this means that it frequently lies between the ash and the animal dung. Animal dung is swept over the edge of the compound just below the animals' quarters (Figure 28).

The most common reason the Endo give for not mixing ash, animal dung, and chaff is the relationship between refuse and burial: "Not good to mix *takataka* [rubbish] because when a woman dies she should be buried where the chaff is, because her work is to dig and remove the chaff." "Old men should be buried near the goat dung." When a man dies he will be buried just outside the compound, a little way down on the right from his house. A woman will, ideally, be buried in a similar position, but just down from and to the left of her house. A man will be placed on his right side, with his right hand under his right ear; his body will lie so that his head is toward the compound and his feet toward the valley – so that, the Endo say, he "faces" the rising sun. It is thought that if a man is buried with his head toward the valley then his goats will die, or possibly other members of his family may die. Women are buried on their left side, with their left hand under their left ear.[8] Children who are uninitiated or who have not reached sexual maturity are buried "as if they were old men or old women." Young people who have been initiated or who have reached sexual maturity are buried further away (i.e., down) from the houses and further to the right or left, depending on sex (Figure 30).[9]

---

[7] Other types of household and compound refuse (peelings, tin cans, etc.) are scattered over a wide area on the lower side of the compound. No attempt is made to segregate such refuse from ash, animal dung, or chaff. In a week's survey of one compound I observed the disposal of food debris, including animal bones, and could discern no regularity in either the mode or the place of disposal.

[8] Hollis notes for the Nandi: "Very old men or women and very young children are buried in the dung-heap near the cattle kraal. The corpse is placed like ordinary people, that is to say males on the right side and females on the left with the hand supporting the head and the legs outstretched" (Hollis, 1909: 72). The relational pairs male/right and female/left are well established in connection with mortuary and other practices: see, for example, Hertz, 1960. The identification of the male with the right side and the female with the left is often explicitly linked to positioning in the marriage bed: that is, men sleep on the right-hand side. The Marakwet also make the link.

[9] The Endo say that a person only becomes truly adult after initiation; but young people who have reached sexual maturity are considered to be adult with regard (1) to the regulations concerning burial, and (2) inclusion in war or raiding parties. In the latter instance, young men who are uninitiated, but of suitable maturity, are expected to accompany their elders in case of war or conflict. However, they have first to undergo a secret purification ceremony.

Woman's hut   Man's hut

   X   X Old woman's   X   X Boy's child's
  Girl   grave   Old   grave
child's grave   man's grave

X Initiated girls' grave   Initiated boy's grave   X

FIGURE 30. Position of graves by age.

The Endo find the death of an unmarried person who has reached sexual maturity, whether initiated or not, very inauspicious. The reason why the deaths of young adults are thought to be particularly inauspicious is that they are said to have "died out of turn"–that is, without having produced children themselves. Some informants maintain that in such cases the arms and legs of the corpse will be bound and the body may be pushed over the edge of the grave, instead of being placed in the proper position. It is said that those who die young may "pull after them" others in their peer group. To die without producing children is a great misfortune. A person who dies childless is said to "die for eternity" and his/her name cannot be given to a newborn child of the lineage. It is therefore the case that those who die at the end of their lives or before they are fully adult are less "threatening" than those who die "out of turn."

The above statements may be understood as a set of ideals which, the Endo themselves maintain, govern the disposal of the dead. However the actual placing of burials in any given compound is extremely variable. This variability is, in part, explained by the fact that the Endo have no "rule," either implicit or explicit, governing the positioning of houses within the compound, so that a man's house may be on the right (i.e., the north) or on the left (i.e., the south) of the compound (see above and Figure 22). Right and left are, therefore, not absolutes, but relative principles. If a man's house is on the left (i.e. south) of the compound, then he will be buried just down from his house. When his wife dies she will be buried to the left of him, rather than being buried below her house, which would put her in the "wrong" position in relation to her husband. So that the layout in Figure 31A will be the result, rather than that in Figure 31B:

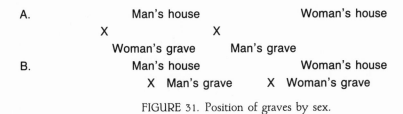

A.   Man's house   Woman's house
              X   X
                    Woman's grave   Man's grave
B.   Man's house   Woman's house
                 X   Man's grave   X   Woman's grave

FIGURE 31. Position of graves by sex.

It is also the case that the Endo rank the relevant criteria by which they make decisions concerning burial. For instance, it is apparently more important to bury a man near to his house than to bury him under the animal dung. Similarly a woman will not be buried near the chaff if this means that her grave will then be too close to another family's *kano,* a situation which would be thought to threaten its goats. Thus, it may be said that the actual positioning of each burial is the practical working out of a set of principles within a particular context (see Appendix 2).

It is through the associations established between refuse and burial that it is possible to identify a series of links which the Endo make between men and animals and between women and cooking. The emphasis of the split function of houses in the compound (cooking/sleeping), and the past and present gender associations of those functions (male/sleeping, female/cooking), is related to the rigidly maintained separation between dung and ash. In this context women are identified not only with chaff, but also with ash. (The reasons for this are discussed fully below.) It is therefore usual to find that the organization of Endo compounds relates to the association between men and animal dung and women and ash. For example, the ash placement is most commonly to be found on that side of the compound associated with the female/cooking house; while animal dung will be disposed of in the area of the compound associated with the male/sleeping hut. This does not reflect a mere functional differentiation of houses and their related activities, since animal dung, for example, will often have to be swept out of the *kano* and carried some distance, in order to be deposited in an appropriate place. Figure 32 illustrates the percentage of cases in which animal dung was actually to be found in the "male" half of the compound, and Figure 33 illustrates the incidence of spatial association between ash and the "female" side of the compound in both Sibou samples I and II. In sample I, there were ten instances where animal dung was in the "female" half of the compound; in seven of these cases there was only one house in the compound and the animals were living in that house, and in a further two cases the position of the animal dung was related to the position of the compound fence entrance; in the final case no reason could be established for the association. In sample II, there were six cases where animal dung was on the "female" side of the compound: In four of these cases the position of the animal dung was governed by the position of the fence entrance, and in each of the further two cases there was only one house in the compound and the animals were living in that house. In both samples, those compounds which I have termed "excluded compounds" are compounds without animals resident. During the period when this work was carried out, the number of compounds without animals was particularly high because a recent epidemic had decimated the sheep and goat population. In both samples, the occurrence of ash on the "male" side of the compound is lower than the occurrence of animal dung on the "female" side, but in all cases it may be accounted for by the fact that there were fires in

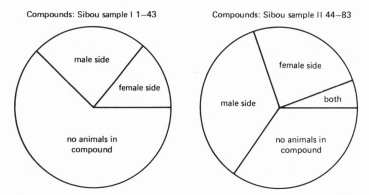

FIGURE 32. Position of animal dung in relation to the gender association of houses.

both houses in the compound and ash from different houses may not be disposed of in the same place. Figures 32 and 33, therefore, go some way to illustrate the repeated associations between ash and the area of the compound related to the female/cooking hut, and between animal dung and the part of the compound associated with the male/sleeping hut.

In the above discussion I have outlined some of the basic features of the organization of Endo compounds. I have concentrated on the major structures (houses, stores, etc.), the positioning of burials and refuse areas, and the overall shape of the compounds themselves. Other aspects of spatial organization, such as house interiors and the objects arranged and used therein, will be discussed in Chapter 8. Any discussion of the organization of domestic space among the Endo will inevitably rest heavily on an abstract notion of "the Endo compound." I have tried to show that this "idealized" compound corresponds both to a stage in the development cycle of individual compounds

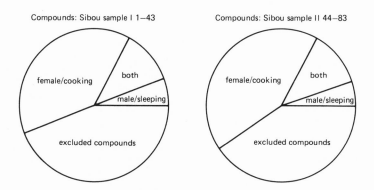

FIGURE 33. Position of ash in relation to the gender association of houses.

and to an important phase in the life-cycle of individual men. This phase, which is of varying character and duration, roughly corresponds to the period of time when the individual household is at its most productive – that is, from a point shortly after marriage, when the productivity of the unit is confirmed by the appearance of children and, in some cases, extra animals and extra stores, to the time when a man becomes a fully fledged elder and his household begins to decline in size and productivity as his own children marry and move out. During this period most compounds do, in fact, conform to the "ideal," where two houses face each other along a north–south axis and the related stores and *kano* occupy the western (upper) part of the compound. However, it is equally important to stress that this "ideal" compound is not just a physical reality for the Endo, but a formulation which represents an achieved state of maturity and productivity which is crucially linked to marital status. Thus, it is not essential that all compounds should conform to the "ideal" type. But the close link between a man's status, his married state, the size and plan of his compound and the productivity of his domestic unit is the context from within which any interpretation of the organization and use of domestic space must be drawn out and understood.

CHAPTER 7

Interpreting Space

Having looked, in the previous chapter, at the physical organization of compounds and households, we can now begin to ask, "How does the organization of space come to have meaning?" In order to answer this question it is first necessary to link the meanings given to certain elements in the spatial order to a series of conceptual schemes which can be seen to inform and sustain the Endo perception of their world. This perception only becomes comprehensible when related to the practical answers which the Endo provide to the everyday problems which confront them. In other words, to understand how the organization of space comes to have meaning it is necessary to relate that "meaning" to the economic and social realities which both produce and are produced by the ordering of domestic space. The enterprise of establishing this relation is complex, but in the case of the Endo it can best be approached through a discussion of gender relations.

I have argued that some spaces in an Endo compound are associated with men and some with women. The differentiated functions of individual houses are expressed in terms of a distinction between the activities of the sexes. This distinction is, however, very fine, and is concerned not so much with an actual division between male and female activities as with qualities of maleness and femaleness as the Endo perceive them. Thus, even when the difference between house functions is expressed as one house for sleeping/entertaining and the other for cooking, this is a distinction which can best be understood in terms of a value system which derives, in part, from differing notions about the "male" and the "female." To explain this value system, and its significance as regards the ordering of space, requires some indication of the way it is generated and expressed through the conflicts and tensions within Endo society. The Endo draw on the divisions between men and women in society and use that distinction as a symbolizing mechanism. While conflicts between male and female interests are not the only conflicts which exist, other struggles, rivalries, and antagonisms tend to be expressed through the medium of the male–female distinction. What follows is a brief characterization of relations between the sexes, in an effort to draw out the pervasive way in which the opposition between male and female is used to express other areas of conflict and tension, and to indicate the relevance of this to an understanding of the organization of space.

MEN AND WOMEN

Among the Endo the household is not only the main reproductive unit, but also the main unit of production and consumption. The Endo believe men and women to have separate roles.[1] To repeat an earlier statement: the man's job is to clear, fence, and irrigate the *shamba* (garden/field), while the job of the woman is to cook, collect firewood, and draw water. This verbalization of the nature of the division of labor masks many aspects of the differing activities of each sex, but, most importantly, within the terms of its own definition it does not reveal that women also hoe, sow, weed, and harvest the crops. A woman may be helped in the *shamba* by other women and by her older children; her husband will only help if the digging is especially heavy or if there is an acute shortage of labor. Otherwise, the only situation in which men are involved in all stages of crop production (i.e., from digging through to harvesting) is in the case of cotton. Cotton is the only cash crop, at the present time, in this part of the Kerio valley. It is therefore possible to say that while men do work in the fields (mostly clearing and irrigating), they are usually thought of as being more occupied with their herds. Many adult men actually live in their *kano* on the valley floor; such men go to their homes, if they go at all, to sleep, and spend most of the day tending the stock. Although it is also true that animals are frequently looked after by uninitiated children, or left to roam free, this very much depends on the individual family, the age of the children, and on what other work the adults have to do.[2] The fact that men may not actively spend their time actually tending their animals does not alter the identification of men with their stock, since this identification is not merely a product of the division of labor between the sexes. It is in matters relating to animals, in the kinds of activities and concerns associated with them, that a certain quality of "maleness" resides. It is in the *kano,* particularly if it is in the valley and away from the com-

---

[1] It is important to note here that the sexual division of labor is not a static, ahistorical given, and it can only be delineated in terms of specific historical conditions. The division of labor also alters as the size and composition of household units varies over the family life-cycle and the availability of familial labor power changes (Deere *et al.,* 1982: 101).

[2] Children are a crucial part of the labor force, but their tasks also tend to be assigned on the basis of gender (see Chapter 4).

pound, that a man keeps his spear, bow, and arrows. It is here that he spends much of his time in discussion with other men, making arrows and other objects, and eating roast meat or other roast foods in the company of men. In Endo, a wealthy man is a man who has land, stock, and children; but it is largely through stock that a man acquires prestige. Animals, particularly goats, have ceremonial, as well as economic, importance. For goats are the animals usually slaughtered at ceremonies; their skin provides the ceremonial clothes for circumcision, and their entrails are inspected to foretell the future.[3] As a result of their ceremonial and economic value–and because of notions of prestige which rest on the accumulation of stock–animals, and in particular goats, are uniquely tied up with the male sphere and with men's own perception of their world.

By contrast, women are identified with the crops they produce. Hence the power of a statement like, "When a woman dies she will be buried where the chaff is, because her work is to dig and remove the chaff." Endo women have considerable control over the crops they produce. In the past each woman would have had her own store. Nowadays, if cowives agree, they may pool their resources. A man normally divides his *shamba* between himself and his wife or wives.[4] He then takes on the task of clearing and irrigating the whole plot. The women cooperate in cultivating the husband's shamba and may also help each other. Every woman uses the crops she produces to support her family and to feed, or share in the feeding of, her husband. As a result, every woman controls what goes in and out of her store, for women not only control aspects of production, but also regulate consumption. In addition, if a woman has bananas, chilli peppers, or other extra food, she can sell her produce in the twice-weekly market, and the money she obtains is hers. However, it is certainly the case that men make frequent complaints about the "wasteful" way in which women spend money; in particular there is much sententious grumbling about women spending money on local beer. This last point is interesting since it begins a common theme about men's more "social" use of what is theirs, in contrast to women who are thought to consume resources of all kinds in an "individualistic" manner. For example, the harvest from the man's *shamba* will not be used to feed the family unless there is a shortage of food. The Endo say that a man keeps his grain carefully "in case of need."[5] However, men also need grain to make beer and

---

[3] Goats are the animals usually slaughtered for ceremonies. Sheep are slaughtered on special occasions, particularly when it is necessary to make something "clean" (*telil*), for example, after the birth of twins. The Endo never slaughter cattle for ritual purposes.

[4] The Endo say that when a man does divide his *shamba*, he stands facing the escarpment, with his back to the valley, and divides the *shamba* into longitudinal strips. He takes the right-hand portion for himself, his first wife takes the strip nearest to his, and the second wife takes the left-hand strip.

[5] The Endo say that the husband keeps his grain separately so that there will always be a reserve in case of famine. Beech notes from 1911 that the Endo were known to save grain for this

to sell or lend to other men as "yeast" for making beer. These "beer" transactions create and dissolve important relations of dependence and obligation. A man is, therefore, crucially dependent upon his wife (or wives), not only as reproducers (reproducing both clan and labor force), but as producers as well. But this dependence is masked, to a large extent, by a formulation which implies the woman's tendency toward individualization, as against the man's more social use of what is his. Thus, a distinction between the social and the individual begins to be mediated through, and indeed emerges from, a distinction between what is male and what is female.

The concern with a potential conflict between "social" and "individual" interests is endemic to the relationship between household and patriclan. The activities of the household and the wider sphere of sociopolitical activity find their articulation through the structure of the patriclan. The relationship between the clan and the individual households which comprise it is one of tension.[6] This is partly because the Endo recognize that the interests of the clan are not always identical to those of the household. Any conflicts, potential or actual, which arise as a result of such antagonism have to be mediated through an ideology of primary allegiance to the clan. The Endo believe that women do not feel this allegiance as keenly as men. This is, in part, a perception of the way women are peripheralized within the clan structure. As I have shown, the Endo acknowledge that even differences in the naming ceremonies for boys and girls reflect the difference in their degree of allegiance to and identification with the clan. Men are the permanent beings, while women are the temporary, the insubstantial. Such a formulation is, of course, very one-sided and effectively denies the importance of affinal links between men, the frequent incidence of men calling on the labor of their married daughters, and the very important part women, as mothers, play in the reproduction of the clan. That certain aspects of the relationship between women and the patriclan should be masked or concealed is not surprising, since such concealment itself reveals areas of ambiguous dependence and potential conflict. Ambiguity surrounding women is, in large measure, an ambiguity concerning affinal relationships of all kinds. Women come into a marriage, and therefore into the clan, bringing potential trouble with them. When conflict does

---

purpose (Beech, 1911). There are frequent food shortages and men never withhold their grain in times of hunger. However, it is a common assumption that women cannot be trusted to save grain in case of famine and the man is therefore entrusted with the care of the social good. Storing grain and making beer, both activities which are linked with men, are considered social acts. However, when women store grain or make beer they are somehow providing for consumption, rather than providing for social (sometimes expressed as ceremonial or kinship) needs.

[6] The opposition between the interests of individual households and the interests of the wider social group of which they are a part is now well documented (Sahlins, 1974: 123–30; Bourdieu, 1977: 58–71; Bloch, 1971: 101). Ortner in particular notes that the family (and hence women) represents socially fragmenting, individualistic concerns, as opposed to the integrative, universalistic concerns characteristic of the wider kin group (Ortner, 1974: 79).

occur, it is inevitably expressed as a collision between male and female interests – between the clan (which is by definition "social"), and what is not the clan (which is by definition not social but "individual").

The resulting identification of the household with the "individual," as opposed to the "social" clan, is, in part, a consequence of the strong association of women with their households. Within the exogamous patriclan, where marriage is virilocal, the only point of articulation a woman has with her "new" clan is through the household. The household is both the physical and the conceptual locus of a woman's entry into the clan of her husband. However, there are additional reasons why the household is often a focus for potential conflict. There are a number of matters, especially relating to water rights and ritual observance, where what is in the best interests of individual men, or individual households as independent units of production and consumption, is not in the best interests of the clan. An example would be the fines (usually a goat, sometimes money, sometimes a sack of cement) imposed by the clan when a man fails to turn up and give his labor in the communal task of repairing the irrigation channel. The Endo frequently point out that these fines exist to stop individuals going off to attend to personal matters (however pressing) when the livelihood of the whole clan is at stake. Here the "unsocial" action of the person involved would precisely result in the identification of household interests with the pursuit of "individual" and therefore "unsocial" concerns.

It should not be understood from what has been said that the relationship between men and women is always one of tension and conflict. Within the household men and women perform complementary roles. The division of labor delineates tasks and duties which both husband and wife undertake to form a joint project or unit for the production of foodstuffs, the maintenance of household and herds and the rearing of children. Marriage is explicitly stated to be a joint undertaking, with shared responsibilities.

To sum up: the household is the locus of potential conflict between various opposing interests and concerns. However, it should be stressed that, since it is the relationship between the sexes that forms the basis of the household unit, conflicts and tensions are frequently expressed through the opposition between male and female. Thus the male and the female are symbolized genders which can be used in a whole range of contexts to express such things as conflict, tension, and division and/or such things as complementarity, unity, and productivity. To make appeal to notions about male and female is not necessarily to refer to what men and women actually do or represent. Rather, it is to understand relationships in terms of qualities of "maleness" and "femaleness" – qualities which appeal to a structural relation in the way perceptions are ordered. The qualities of male or female are ways of thinking about the world; they both represent and are constituted through conflict and complementarity. But it is not possible to understand why this should be so, beyond the social and economic conditions of Endo existence which make this structural ordering so powerful and so appropriate.

THE INTERPRETATION OF SPACE

Ash, animal dung, and chaff are powerful symbols in Endo thought, and it is useful to examine their meaning in the context of the organization and use of domestic space. But in order to do this it is first necessary to discuss the way these substances are associated with notions about men and women in Endo society.

The Endo say that ash, animal dung, and chaff must never be mixed, and, when asked why, men commonly say that "good things should not be mixed with bad" or that "it is bitter" (*mi mwan*) to mix ash with animal dung. Ash is considered very inauspicious, and it is a commonly held belief that if ash is mixed with animal dung then the animals will die.[7] Transference of qualities through participation (e.g., physical touching or ingestion), which is analogous to metonymic transformation or transfer, is a very strong notion in Marakwet thought.[8] One informant maintained that, since ash is white, if ash were mixed with animal dung then the animals themselves would become white and could then easily be stolen by enemies. Ash is opposed to animal dung in Endo thought because of a network of contrasts which links that opposition to the division between male and female, and thereby, ultimately, to a conflict between men and women over control of production.

While marriage is acknowledged as a joint project, the idea that men control the productive capabilities of their households (including the size of herds, the harvest from the fields, and the reproductive potential of their wives) has to be viewed in the context of the considerable control women have over both their productive and reproductive resources. It is explicitly stated in Endo society that women are subordinate to men, but that they also have a considerable degree of both actual and potential power – a power which derives from their control over production, reproduction, and consumption. Within the household a woman has a large degree of autonomy, and is involved with her neighbors and kin as part of a corporate group (see Chapter 8), in the

---

[7] As far as the Endo are concerned death is the ultimate sanction. Any transgression or potential transgression of order is guarded against by the threat of death. This is particularly so in the case of ritual proscriptions, where death is always held to be the inevitable result of failure to perform the acts concerned.

[8] The relationship between metaphor and metonym is intimate, and many metaphorical movements may be understood as being generated through metonymic transfer. This point is of considerable importance in analyzing the metaphoric functions at work in the ordering of Endo space, since many metaphorical movements actually rely on metonymic connections. These connections are often contingent, but they are transformed into metaphorical expressions through lateral relations which portray chance contingencies as relations of necessity.

cultivation of crops and other foodstuffs. In many contexts the house is thought of as the woman's domain, and Endo men speak of the power women have in the home. It is always necessary to ask a woman's permission to enter her home or to remove anything from it. In yet other contexts women may be seen to exploit this "house-power" by refusing to cook, dictating the timing of meals, or going off to chat to friends and leaving the husband to prepare the food. It is therefore the case that the ideology of complete male control over the productive and reproductive potential of the household has to be understood in the context of an actual reality of male and female interdependence. Men not only depend on their wives for labor to produce the crops which feed their children and provide the grain for beer, but in addition are crucially dependent on women as reproducers, reproducing both clan and labor force.

Women are strongly identified with and linked to the home. If a women tells you she is married, she will say: "I'm in my house" (*mi go*). Within the house the area most strongly associated with the woman is the area behind the hearth, where she sits to do her cooking and where her cooking stool and other utensils are stored (*kapkos* or *kapkoschio*). Only a woman may move ash from the fireplace and take it to the *kaberon* (place of ash). Notions of the ambiguity surrounding the position of women, as perceived by men, are neatly condensed in the symbolism of ash. Through its association with the hearth and with cooking, ash has both creative and destructive aspects. Cooking and burning are processes which provide food for the living, but through these same processes things are also eaten and consumed. Ash symbolizes that consumption, while, at the same time, invoking sentiments of the woman in her home, providing for her family. This inherent ambiguity is structurally analogous to the relationship between the sexes, constituted, as it is, by relations of dependence and conflict. For the conflict between men and women over control of production stands in marked contrast to their interdependence within the joint project of marriage. Similarly, the structural ambiguity inherent in the symbolism of ash is analogous to the shifting constellation of ideas which surround both the woman, as an embodiment of the individualizing force of the household, and the man, who stands for the communal interests of the patriclan.

It is thus possible to take this series of associations one step further and say that ash and animal dung are opposed in Endo thought because they symbolize two different types of fertility. Ash, because of its association with house, hearth, and cooking, is linked to female fertility–both the socially essential productive and reproductive powers of womanhood and the threatening, potentially destructive nature of female power and sexuality. Animals, and particularly goats, represent a type of fertility which is primarily associated with men. However, this fertility has a social association, just as the fertility associated with women and ash has an individual implication. Men, through their identification with communal concerns, take much of the responsibility for initiating or carrying out certain activities and tasks which are designed to prevent misfortune or to reestablish equilibrium when misfortune has occurred. The Endo do not conceive of themselves as being in opposition to nature, nor do they believe the world to be filled with, or prey to, malevolent forces. Thus, the underlying theme of ritual is that things should be done in accordance with tradition and in a way which "manifests the proper respect." Misfortune will only occur if people make mistakes, show disrespect, or deliberately fail to do the correct thing. In the case of drought or pestilence, rituals are performed which are designed to reestablish equilibrium and make things "sweet" (*anyin*): to recreate them as they should be and have always been.

The Endo believe that the community as a whole is involved in maintaining the balance of the world, but it is men, in particular, who see themselves as the eminently social beings on whom this duty rests most heavily. The notion of fertility associated with goats has a dual quality: it refers, on the one hand, to the fertility of the herds, which is linked both with male prestige and with clan interests; on the other hand, it is associated with the fertility of the animals themselves, which demonstrates the fecundity of the natural world–a fecundity which will continue so long as "traditional" equilibrium is maintained. Thus, goats symbolize a fertility which is predominantly male and social, while ash is associated with a force which is primarily female and individual. The opposition and conflict between these two types of fertility, symbolized by goat dung and ash, encapsulates the tensions between male and female interests concerning the control of production, as it relates both to the household and to the wider social sphere.

Although the Endo say that the most important thing is not to mix ash and animal dung, they also believe that to mix ash with chaff is very inauspicious. Chaff from finger millet and sorghum is, in some senses, considered analogous to animal dung because it is also wastage. Both are substances which remain after other physical elements have been transformed into food. In the case of the opposition between ash and chaff, the latter, which is associated with the positive side of female productivity and provision, is contrasted to ash which, once again, has connotations of consumption and destruction. Chaff symbolizes an aspect of womanhood which is linked to the broader notion of natural fecundity. It is associated both with the fertility of women and with the fertility of the natural world, as expressed by the productivity of the fields and of female productive activities. In this sense chaff is associated with a "social" or socialized side of female productivity and is contrasted with the potentially threatening, and therefore less socialized, female encapsulated in the symbolism of ash. However, chaff does not just represent, in a straightforward manner, a single aspect of "femaleness"; rather, it partakes of ambiguity in the same way as other elements, like ash, do. For example, the Endo believe that chaff and animal dung should not be mixed. In this context chaff is firmly identified with the "not-male" and thereby with the "not-social." The reason for this is that, while chaff is linked with the creativity of the natural world and with the woman as provider, it is also associated with the woman as producer and with the woman's autonomous control over production—with woman as controller and provider. All these associations are shifting and reflexive. From one angle, chaff is conceptually linked to the social, through association with the fecundity of the natural world and with the woman as mother. From another point of view, chaff is linked to the autonomous woman–producer and is, therefore, associated with the nonsocial. However, such ambiguity is not in itself unidimensional. Even as chaff is associated with the autonomous woman–producer, it also retains connotations of the woman as provider and manager of the household. To the extent that this permits women to participate in qualities usually thought to be the prerogative of men, it is possible to link chaff, once again, to certain aspects of the social. But there exists no point of resolution; for, while women assert a participation in male qualities, they subvert part of the male right, the male order, and become redefined as the "not-natural," the "not-social." Such are the polysemic qualities of individual elements in the spatial order. While women are social, they are simultaneously not social. To oppose two elements is simultaneously to draw attention both to their contrasts and to their similarities.

In the previous chapter I outlined some of the main features of the spatial organization of Endo compounds. In so doing I suggested that houses, refuse areas and burials are all connected, in varying ways, to a division between what is male and what is female. I have here used this connection to draw attention to the very marked pervasiveness of the male–female distinction as a symbolizing mechanism in Endo thought. This has made possible an illustration of the multiplicity of meanings which can be invoked by reference to a particular element, like ash. The opposition between male and female—and the corresponding pairs, ash/dung, chaff/dung—are ways of thinking about the world. In this context the male–female distinction provides a kind of metaphorical filter, in which things find order and throw up images of themselves. To these images values are assigned, but these values are not fixed; for women may be associated in one context with the providing mother and in another with the potentially threatening power of the autonomous female. The male and the female are, therefore, just like other pairs of contrasts, never in fixed and permanent opposition. As symbols, they always contain their own opposites, that is, they are simultaneously what they represent and what they oppose. However, in another sense there are fixed values, and these may be understood as the values of structural relation assigned to the qualities of "maleness" and "femaleness." While women themselves may be both "social" and "unsocial"—both positively and negatively valued—the "female" quality will always have a negative connotation. This is illustrated by the fact that in a series of cultural valuations and representations, of which the organization of space is only one among many, "femaleness" is never positively valued in and for itself.[9] Furthermore, it is, without exception, aligned with other negatively valued characteristics, such as "individualism," "thoughtlessness," and "uncontrollability." Such "negative" characteristics are all transformations of each other, since their permanent structural relation to their opposites – "communality," "concern," and "control" – defines them as female. It is undeniably true that that which is associated with the "female" or the "unsocial" in one context may be associated with the "social" or the "male" in another. But that metaphorical shift is not made by positively valuing the "female" or the "unsocial"; it is achieved precisely by making what was once "female" participate in qualities normally thought of as "male."[10] There exists, therefore, a permanent structural relation between what is male and what is female. It is this fact that makes the male–female distinction such an appropriate operator for thinking about relationships in other spheres. However, it must be stressed that the power and pervasiveness of the male–female distinction in Endo thought is only comprehensible by relating that distinction to the conditions of its genesis – that is, to notions about male and female indirectly derived from the "objective conditions" of social and economic reality. It is only by relating such notions to the conflicts and tensions within Endo society that any account can be given of their importance and persistence.

In terms of the organization of space it is not enough merely to provide an account of the genesis of symbolic values; for value and meaning are not inherent in any given spatial order, but must be invoked. The organization of space is not a direct reflection of cultural codes and meanings; it is, above all, a context developed through practice – that is, through the interaction of individuals. This context, or set of relationships, may have many meanings. These meanings, as I have argued above, are in fact simultaneous, although they can never exist simultaneously in practice. The spatial organization of

[9] I am aware of current criticisms of this position; see particularly MacCormack and Strathern, 1980, and Strathern, 1981a. However, I try to go beyond a realization that what is female can sometimes also be understood as male, that what is culture is also nature. I do not dispute the shifting nature of contrastive systems of thought, or deny the ethnocentricity of particular categories of analysis (on this point, see particularly the debate on whether male–female is a transformation of culture–nature in MacCormack and Strathern, 1980: chaps. 1 and 8). Instead I am interested in why the male–female distinction does imply a structural relation, a relation which is so pervasive that it can be used to think about other contexts, where the only reason for "genderizing" the contrasted terms is to imply a hierarchical relation between them.

[10] Strathern discusses this point and notes that the Hageners make a distinction between *nyim* (prestigious) and *korpa* (rubbish), where behaving in a male way is linked to activities likely to bring prestige, and behaving in a female manner is associated with activities likely to imply worthlessness. While she points out that to behave in a prestigious way is an option open to both men and women, she does not explain the original cultural valuations (Strathern, 1981: 179–87). This is a point I discuss more fully in Chapter 9.

the material world does not define the relationship between male and female in terms of a static opposition; it is not just the physical representation of the "meaning" of that contrast. The organization of space only defines the relationship between people, things, or concepts in the specific context of a set of practices. Relationships are established and distinctions are made through the day-to-day activities of individuals, but the contrasts and relationships thus created are not immutable and may be recreated and reinterpreted in other contexts. In order to illustrate this point I shall describe some of the associations invoked by ash, in a particular context. The following incident involved two girls from Sibou village, and was observed during the early-morning cleaning of the house and compound:

> Chepkore is removing ash from the fireplace. Using a piece of flattened tin, she scoops the ashes into a wooden container and leaves the house to go to the ash placement. On the way she meets a friend, Jerop, and, in jest, she tilts the ash container toward her friend. Jerop starts backward and laughs.

This simple sequence of events appears unsurprising to a Western observer. Gestures of mock aggression, particularly involving substances considered "messy" or "dirty," are recognizable indicators of a degree of friendship and intimacy. However, this particular sequence of events can only be understood with reference to a series of associations linked with the element ash. The Endo say that only woman can remove ash from the hearth: a statement which confirms the identity of the woman with the home, hearth, and cooking. It is, however, at the same time an implicit recognition of the destructive "power" of ash – a power which derives from an association between ash and the socially and sexually destructive aspects of womanhood. Ash in its destructive capacity is harmful to men and to male interests. It would, therefore, be unthinkable for a man to remove ash from the hearth. When Chepkore "threatens" her friend with the ash, the same destructive connotation is invoked. This destructive quality is compounded by the fact that ash is also associated with sterility. This link is made by the simple fact that if a girl wishes to refuse marriage, then she will cover herself in ash. The Endo say that this act signifies her desire for the "death" and/or sterility of the proposed union. The combined force of these negative connotations causes Jerop to withdraw. Her laughter, however, is not merely her relief at a narrow escape. Ash may usually be thought of as inauspicious, but these two girls are age-mates and in the girls' circumcision house (*kapkore*) initiates are smeared with ash. This smearing explicitly draws on notions surrounding the power of female sexuality and creativity – including the fact that the girls are being prepared for marriage and motherhood. Ash, in this context, is associated with the positive aspect of female power and sexuality.

Many of the connotations, both positive and negative, which are linked with ash are invoked in this short sequence. Ash has many powerful associations, but each part of the sequence emphasizes a particular association or cluster of associations. So that, although all the "meanings" given to ash are simultaneous, they do not exist simultaneously in practice. However, it is a mistake to imagine that ash has a multiplicity of associations simply because its "meaning" is inherently ambiguous. Such ambiguity as there is is inherent in the context of use, not in the element itself. For example, in *kapkore* ash is associated with aspects of female power and sexuality, but in the boys' circumcision house (*kaptorus*) ash has other connotations. The ash from the fire in *kaptorus* can never be removed, and here ash is associated with the hearth/fire, which is the heart of the clan and resides as a permanent symbol of its fertility. This link is made possible through a series of associations which likens the genealogy of the clan to a tree; when the boys leave *kaptorus* it is said that they put certain esoteric knowledge "up the tree, for future generations." The link between ash and tree is metonymic, and it permits an identification between clan and tree which then establishes a link between ash and clan through their mutual association with fire. Thus, ash has connotations which link it to the clan, and thereby to aspects of communality and responsibility. The positive associations invoked through this particular series of connections help one to understand why the hearth (ash and fire) is linked to the institution of marriage. There are several stages in the marriage rites which involve "blessing" the fire which burns in the home. In this context, the continued vitality of the fire corresponds (the Endo make this link quite explicitly) to the fertility of the marriage union, and the productivity of the latter is indissolubly linked with the continuity of the clan itself.

The complex series of associations I have described is not the product of an inherent ambiguity, but the result of a contextual invocation of "meaning" which allows for reinterpretation in specific contexts. For example, ash may have connotations of female power and sexuality in one context and of male power and responsibility in another. This is because the ordering of space does not define the relationship between people, things, and concepts other than in the specific context of a set of practices. The relationships established in any one context are not immutable, but may be recreated and reinterpreted in other contexts.

CONCLUSION

I have shown that, as a symbol, ash has distinct polysemic qualities and can be used to represent a number of different concepts and perceptions, in a variety of contexts. However, this multivocality is not the product of an inherent ambiguity of meaning which permits constant metaphorical expansion. The "meaning" of ash cannot be reinterpreted in any particular context, just because it is so brimful of ambiguity that it at once means everything and nothing. The metaphorical extension of meaning is only possible on the basis of the recognition of a more literal meaning. This literal or primary meaning gives access to a series of secondary meanings or significations.[11] In the case of an element like ash, the literal meaning is given through a particular action in a specific context, where by the polysemy of the symbol is curbed and its meaning articulated as the product of a process of limitation. This curbing is an act of interpretation – and it is through this act of interpretation that we perceive the existence of still more meanings.[12] In other words, the ability of ash to refer across many "universes of meaning" is not the result of an inherent ambiguity of meaning, but the product of the fact that meaning is context dependent.

It remains only to link this last point to the discussion of metaphor in Chapter 5. Metaphorical movement can be seen to operate in two ways or on two simultaneous, but distinct, levels. First, metaphor moves between the contextually limited meaning of an individual element (e.g., ash) and the recognition of surplus meaning associated with that same element. Thus, as I have argued, the polysemy of individual elements of the spatial order is the consequence of particular articulations in specific contexts. Secondly, metaphoric movement may be understood as a progression from the contextually defined meaning of an element toward a referential dimension, composed of all the meanings assimilated to that element in past and future contexts of invocation. For, while the polysemy of individual elements is predicted upon a literal meaning, the historical fact that different contexts do have and do specify alternative meanings makes possible the apprehension – through the act of limitation in a particular context – of all the meanings associated with that element. Thus, to associate ash with the potentially destructive power of womanhood in a particular context is to make an interpretation. This interpretation refers to a quality of "femaleness" which is understood or apprehended precisely because in another context ash can be associated with the woman

[11] Barthes makes this point, in relation to what he calls myth. For Barthes, myth is a second-order semiotic system; it operates by taking a previously established sign and using it as a signifier. This second signifier, in conjunction with a signified concept, produces signification. Barthes claims that we are not normally able to perceive how this signification is manufactured, because the sign resulting from a previous signifier/signified relationship becomes the signifier of a further signifier/signified relationship. Signs (or rather signification) systems of this mythical or ideological kind are therefore second-order signifying systems superimposed on the first-order system. The meaning of the sign in the second-order system is not arbitrary because it is the product of an association between a signifier which already has an outline of meaning and a particular concept or idea. The meaning established in myth is ideological because it is the result of manipulating a pregiven meaning in relation to a particular idea or concept. In the second-order system it is not just a question of establishing the meaning of a sign, but also of establishing a second meaning which is dependent upon the first. This second meaning is ideological because it involves the reordering or reinterpretation of the original meaning (Barthes, 1973: 111-37).

[12] Turner (1975: 151-3) discusses the contextual limitation of the meanings of symbols and links this temporal restriction to their polysemic power.

as mother and provider. Consequently the referential dimension of meaning is given in the contextual limitation of polysemic qualities.

Metaphor therefore conjoins the polysemic qualities of individual elements with the meaning or referential dimension of the total spatial frame. It does this by bringing into play several dimensions of meaning simultaneously— even though these dimensions are nothing other than the meanings given to specific elements in particular historical contexts. The meaning of any spatial order is therefore indissolubly linked with the practical, historical interpretations given to it by individual actors in specific contexts. It is for this reason that a semiotic analysis of space as a cultural code is insufficient, because such an analysis inevitably brackets out the practical activities and interpretations of historically situated actors. An investigation of metaphor, on the other hand, permits the analysis of meaning and action within a single frame of reference, where both meaning and action belong to the actor, rather than meaning being the possession of the analyst or observer.

The return to the meanings and actions of historically situated individuals leads toward an understanding of metaphor as strategy. To invoke a particular set of meanings in a specific context is to implement a strategy. This is not to suggest that these strategies are always conscious, or that actors are necessarily aware of all or any of their potential consequences. To invoke meaning is to make an interpretation, and this interpretation in turn makes reference to an orientation in the world. This is possible because actors, through their actions, undertake a reading—that is, make an interpretation—of the spatial order. This reading, or interpretation, both produces and is the product of a particular articulation of the past, present, and future meanings of individual elements. This contextual articulation is really no more than a metaphorical play on form, which both constitutes the individual in the world and represents that world. Thus, the organization of space is a cultural representation—and it is through this representation that the individual constructs both herself/himself and her/his image of the world. Representations are therefore interpretations, and interpretations are ideological—that is, they redescribe reality. The organization of space among the Endo can be conceived of as a text; as such, it "talks about" or "works over" states of affairs which are imaginary. These states of affairs are imaginary in that their meaning lies not in their material reality, but in how they help to fashion and perpetuate a particular process of representation. Conflicts and tensions between the sexes in Endo society produce a series of concerns which become the subject of the spatial text. The organization of space presents relations between elements and concepts in a particular and contextually shifting manner, and thus provides a representation of those concerns. This representation is both product and producer. As a result, the organization of space is not just a reflection of a set of social and economic relations; rather, it is a product, through practice of individuals' images of those relations.

CHAPTER 8

Wages and Westernization: The Changing Spaces of the Endo

⌒

The world of the Endo is changing. Over the last ten years, the community has been brought into more direct contact with the modern nation-state of Kenya. The results of this contact have been various and uneven. Some changes are more easily observed than others, some seem predictable. One change – obvious both in its predictability and in its observability – is the replacement of round houses by square houses. This particular "innovation" in domestic architecture has been associated, since colonial times, with a process of "modernization" or "Westernization" – however these terms may be defined. In this chapter, I want to look at the changing spaces of the Endo, and to discuss how changes in the organization of household space are related to changing socioeconomic circumstances. I have argued that conflicts and tensions between the sexes in Endo society produce a series of concerns which become the subject of the spatial text. In the following sections, I discuss whether or not these concerns remain significant in the organization of space, in an effort to answer a larger question about how socioeconomic conditions and cultural values and ideas work together to produce and transform cultural representations.

THE CHANGING ORGANIZATION OF SPACE

In Sibou, observable changes in the organization of domestic space would appear to be related partly to the age and occupation of the householder, and partly to the distance of the house from Tot and hence from the valley floor.

The Endo themselves make an explicit link between the traditional way of life and the position of compounds on the escarpment (see Plate IX). Since early colonial times, successive governments have tried to encourage the Endo to move down from the escarpment and live on the valley floor. In the Marakwet Annual Report for 1952, the District Commissioner commented that the people's preference for the escarpment would be "one of the biggest stumbling blocks to any future development." The Endo say that they prefer the escarpment (*lagam*) as a residential area because it is cooler than the valley, there are fewer mosquitoes, and they are protected from raiders. The present government has also been extremely anxious to encourage people to move down on to the valley floor, where latrines can be dug and vegetable gardens can be cultivated without fear of erosion. Contemporary government officers, like their colonial counterparts, identify the *lagam* with tradition and with poverty. The Endo recognize this equation, since they themselves link the escarpment with the traditional way of life, and the families who have moved down on to the valley floor are those with a stated interest in change and development. An agricultural development officer, working in Endo during the period 1977–9, had this to say on the subject:

> Unless the Marakwet move down towards the foot of the escarpment, where they can develop economically, erosion and insanitary conditions will intensify. This is one area where it is right that development should run against the grain of local conditions. . . . Hot nights and mosquitoes are a reasonable price to pay for the more sanitary conditions of living in a compound where toilets can be dug and a fruit and vegetable garden can be grown. . . . It was noticeable to me that those nearer the foot of the escarpment were generally more development conscious. I venture to suggest that the progressiveness, agriculturally and economically, of a family is inversely proportional to the altitude of the homestead. (Critchley, 1983: 25)

The inverse relation between altitude and progression is explicitly recognized by the people of Sibou and can be identified with regard to houses and the organization of space. In order to be able to check for variables which might be dependent on altitude (i.e., distance from the valley floor), I conducted a survey of all the *Kabisioi* compounds which remain above the 2,000 m contour (Sibour sample III). I chose this particular group because they inhabit an extremely high part of the village, once occupied by all the members of the *Kabisioi* clan but now deserted in favor of sites nearer the valley floor. This is also the area originally occupied by some of the households which make up sample I, and there are, therefore, strong links between the households in samples I and III. Sample III consists of 15 compounds which contain 23 houses, all of which are of the *kokom* type (Plate IX). When interviewed, compound owners gave the heat and the mosquitoes as the major reasons for not leaving this upper part of the village. As might be expected, a substantial number of these compounds are owned by older men: out of a total of 15, 10 are

PLATE IX. A traditional Endo compound high up on the escarpment.

owned by men of *korongoro* age set (approximately 55–70 years old) and only 5 are owned by men of the *kaplelach* age set (approximately 25–40 years old). It is not easy to assess why the younger men (*kaplelach*) remain in this inaccessible part of the village, but it is interesting to note that three out of the five men have their compounds immediately adjacent to those of their fathers and, indeed, gave filial obligation as one of the reasons for their immobility.

House Interiors

Figure 34 shows the interior organization of three houses which belong to men of the *korongoro* age set, none of whom are employed in wage labor. Example A is drawn from Sibou sample III and is representative of houses to be found above the 2,000 m contour. Example B comes from sample II; following the 0–5 km horizontal transect through the village, this house occupies a position in the most northerly part of Sibou, at the furthest point from the settlement of Tot. Example C is part of sample I and occupies a position on the escarpment above Tot center. The diagrams show that the organization of these houses follows a "traditional" pattern, where the spatial order is predicated upon the relative positions of the bed, the fireplace, and the entrance to the roof store.[1] Within this upper age bracket (55–70 years), variation

---

[1] When I discuss the organization of space I refer only to the floor plan and to the major structural features of the house. It should, however, be noted that Endo houses of all types contain a very large number of items which hang from the walls and roof posts, or are stuck into the

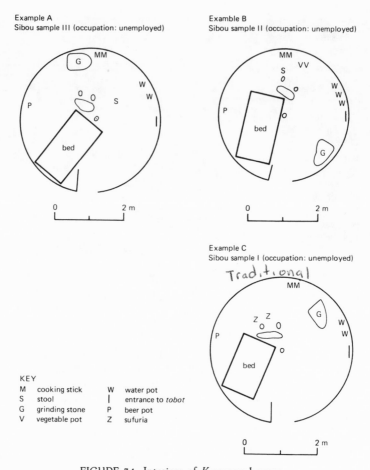

FIGURE 34. Interiors of *Korongora* houses.

with regard to distance from Tot center is minimal; this is borne out by comparing the remaining nine *korongoro* houses from sample III with the other *korongoro* households from samples I and II (nine and ten houses respectively).

---

grass of the roof or stored in the roof store. Traditionally, each house had a *sana* or *saina* (flat tray) which hung above the fire and was used for storing pots and other items and/or drying grain. I recorded the exact position of every item inside all the houses I sampled, but I could discern no particular regularity in the positioning of the artifacts and in reply to my questions informants claimed that objects were merely placed wherever it was convenient. Such responses should not go uninvestigated, but further research produced nothing which would contradict informants' statements. As a result, I have decided not to include a discussion on the positioning of individual artifacts because I do not think this would contribute substantially to my argument. Those artifacts which are included in the illustrated house plans are those which were on the floor of the house when the original drawing was made.

Figure 35 illustrates the interiors of four houses belonging to men of the *kaplelach* age-set, none of whom are employed in wage labor. Example A is drawn from sample III and is one of the five kaplelach houses from the upper part of the village; examples B and C are from sample I; while example D is from sample II and again occupies a position in the most northerly part of the village, at the furthest point from Tot. The basic organization of space

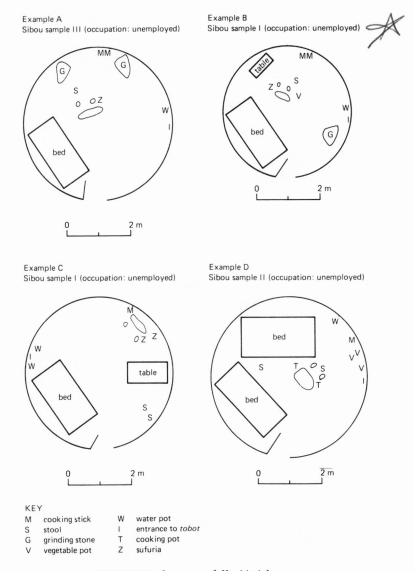

FIGURE 35. Interiors of *Kaplelach* houses.

in all four houses is similar and follows a "traditional" pattern, except that none of the houses has a center post. In home C, the removal of the center post is accompanied by the setting aside of the fireplace. The displacing of the fireplace and the removal of the center post prefigure the arrangement shown in Figure 36. Here, the owner has differentiated his houses according to function; the upper house is the kitchen and the lower house is the sleeping/entertaining area. Traditionally the spatial propinquity of the fireplace and center post was paralleled by a conceptual association which linked the home, and thereby these two structural features of the house, with the joint project of marriage. The fireplace was associated with the woman and her hearth, while the center post stood for the man as creator, supporter, and provider of the household. The fireplace has a number of different associations for the Endo, and, as I have discussed, there are contexts in which the fireplace is associated with the clan and the man's ancestors. When houses are differentiated according to function, the position/presence of the bed no longer defines the position of the fireplace. The fireplace is moved aside and the spatial and conceptual associations between fireplace and center post are broken; a break which is encouraged by government pressure to dispense with roof stores (which are, at least partially, supported by center posts) in order to improve air circulation and decrease the accumulation of smoke.[2] To differentiate houses according to function is considered a sign of modernity; and, since the fireplace and the center post are often displaced or removed in "modern" round houses, it is not surprising to discover that displacement of the fireplace and/or removal of the center post can themselves be indices of progression. Hence the situation in example C (Figure 35), where the fireplace has been moved to one side, even though this house contains a bed and is used for both cooking and sleeping. (See Plates X and XI.)

Figure 37 shows the interiors of three houses which belong to unmarried men of the *kimnygeu* age set. In example A, the bed is in a familiar position behind the door and the fireplace is set to one side at the back of the house. In example B, the spatial order is inverted: the fireplace is behind the door where the bed should be and the bed occupies that part of the house traditionally reserved for cooking activities. In example C, there is no fireplace and again the bed occupies part of the "back" of the house. The spatial organization of these houses is, therefore, very different from the more traditional pattern shown in Figure 34. In Sibou samples I and II there was a total of five houses belonging to young, unmarried men, and three of them are illustrated in Figure 37; of the remaining two, one follows the pattern of example A and the other that of example C. When studying these houses, I

---

[2] I was informed by the senior doctor at the Kapsowar Mission Hospital that the incidence of nasal cancer among the Marakwet is abnormally high and that this is thought to be the result of living in ill-ventilated and very smoky houses.

PLATE X. A traditional Endo house, with a more modern house belonging to a young man in the background.

PLATE XI. The interior of a traditional house, showing the positions of the center post, the bed, and the fireplace.

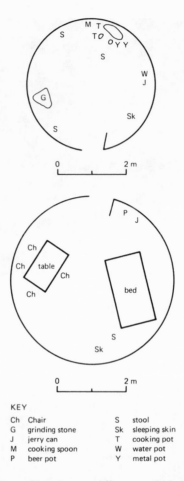

KEY

Ch	Chair	S	stool
G	grinding stone	Sk	sleeping skin
J	jerry can	T	cooking pot
M	cooking spoon	W	water pot
P	beer pot	Y	metal pot

FIGURE 36. Two houses differentiated by function.

was unable to discern any variation which would correlate with either vertical or horizontal distance from Tot center; but it is interesting to note that there are no houses belonging to men of the *kimnygeu* age set in sample III (i.e., above the 2,000 m contour).

It seems clear that the interior arrangement of these young men's houses prefigures their intention to build compounds where the houses are differentiated by function. This is borne out by information collected from *kaplelach* men, who now have houses divided on the basis of function, concerning the layout of their first house prior to their marriage. In sample I, there are six compounds where the houses are differentiated by function; all these compounds, except one, belong to men of the *kaplelach* age set. In four cases the man built a second house when he married and turned his original home into a kitchen hut. It is unsurprising to note that the fireplaces in the original houses were displaced to one side and did not need to be moved when the houses became kitchens. In the final two cases, the original house was built without a fireplace and continued as the main house, even after marriage and the subsequent construction of a second house to serve as a kitchen. The young *kimnygeu* men I interviewed declared that the position of the fireplace was of no

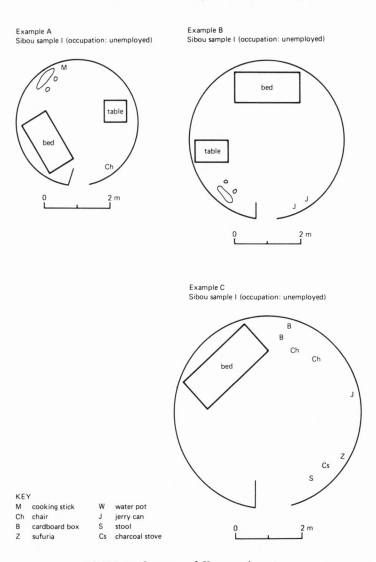

FIGURE 37. Interiors of *Kimnygeu* houses.

interest to them, except that "modern" houses do not have fireplaces in the center of the house. A fairly explicit link was established between the reordering of space and a desire to break with a more traditional way of life: "Putting the firestones here (in the center) was something our grandfathers did – some old people still do it, but we have no use for such things." The relationship between the reordering of space and the break with traditional procedures which signifies modernity is made even more explicit in the case of those compounds where the head of the household is employed. (See Plates XII, XIII, and XIV.)

WAGES AND WESTERNIZATION

Change has come more slowly to the people of Endo, than it has to other areas of Elgeyo–Marakwet District. Until the mid-1970s, poor communications and lack of government interest isolated the area to a large extent from the forces of change which were shaping modern Kenya. Nevertheless, as I have pointed out, in the last decade the people of Endo have experienced extremely rapid change. This is partly because there is now a permanent Catholic mission in the valley and partly because government interest in the area has never been higher.[3] The rapid growth of a secondary school, and the home education classes for women (provided by the Catholic mission) have all played a part in bringing the valley into closer and more forceful contact with the world outside it. It would be impossible to characterize the exact nature of this contact, but the three areas in which it is most noticeable are education, wage employment, and the influx of manufactured/modern goods. It is in terms of these three things that the Endo speak most frequently of experiencing change in their lives. The "colonial" nature of change, even in this postcolonial situation, has altered values and perceptions to produce a hierarchy: school education is valued over traditional instruction; being a teacher is more prestigious than being a farmer; wearing a dress is more dignified than wearing a skin. A certain amount of status is attached to both education and wage employment, but such opportunities are not open to everyone. Modern items, on the other hand, can be acquired by anyone who has access to the appropriate cash resources. The acquisition and display of cer-

---

[3] The Catholic Mission is the first permanent mission in the valley and was started in 1973, an extremely late date given the early penetration of missionary activity elsewhere in the country. Dr. B. Kipkorir is the head of the Institute of African Studies, Nairobi, and he and his staff have undertaken an enormous amount of ethnographic and historical work in the valley in the last three years. This activity has been partly stimulated by government interest in the area, which is also represented by the Kerio Valley Development Authority. This institution is engaged in agricultural and rural industry development and has three main centers in the valley, of which Tot will be one.

PLATE XII. A modern round house used for entertaining.

PLATE XIII. The interior of a modern round house, showing the marked difference between this house with its table and chairs, radios, pictures, books, and tablecloths, and the interior illustrated in Plate XI.

PLATE XIV. A modern store. The decoration and neat appearance are related to the status and relative wealth of the owner.

tain items is, therefore, highly desirable, since this is the only way in which most people can participate in a status system which values the "modern" over the "traditional."

Square Houses and Round Houses

The most prominent indication of modernity or progressiveness is a square house (see Plates XV and XVI). In Sibou, such houses are a recent introduction, and there are only three of them.[4] These houses are part of sample I and occupy the land at the foot of the escarpment, immediately adjacent to the modern settlement of tot (Compounds 35, 41, 42). Figure 38 illustrates these three houses and their assorted compounds. The owners of the compounds are all employed: one is a civil servant (example A), one is a council official (example B), and the third is a clerk (example C). The construction of all three houses began in 1980; they were built in mud and stone, with tin roofs and cement floors. When I left Sibou in August 1981, only one house was in use; the other two were still unfinished.

The small number of square houses in Sibou, and their comparatively re-

[4] There have been square houses in Tot since 1950, but there were none in the village itself until 1981. In the past, the only other square houses in the vicinity were the chief's house (built c. 1955) and a house for a white irrigation engineer (built in the 1950s).

PLATE XV. A square house of mud brick from Sibou sample 1A.

cent introduction is related to cost.[5] The house illustrated in Figure 38 (example A) cost over 8,000 ks (£1 = 16 ks = approximately $1.60) to build, nearly half of this sum being spent on the roof. This does not include the cost of furniture and furnishings, most of which have to be transported from the Kapsowar (highland) area. The prohibitive cost of construction has prevented several families from building square houses, and because of this there are several circular houses in Sibou sample I, where the organization and furnishings are extremely similar to those found in square houses. The compounds in Figure 38 would be included in this group, since in all three cases the square houses are recent additions; during the period of the study none of them was in full use. This group consists of eight compounds (30, 31, 32, 33, 35, 40, 41, 42) in all and includes all the compounds in Sibou where the head of the household is employed and where the houses in the compound are differentiated according to function (this group is hereafter referred to as sample Ia). There are two other men in Sibou sample I and one man in sample II who

---

[5] The government has a policy of helping its officers with housing improvements; this help usually takes the form of a loan. The owner of the house in Figure 32 (example I) is a teacher and has had help of this kind from the government. Goldschmidt notes that square houses among the Sebei are rare and are considered a sign of status. He also points out that they require considerable investment, including the cost of expert labor (Goldschmidt, 1976: 79). The availability and cost of labor are important factors in Sibou; skilled builders have only recently become available because before the Catholic mission came in 1973 there was no one to train them. Trained builders can charge heavily for their services: for example, the man who built the roof of the teacher's house charged 500 ks.

PLATE XVI. The interior of a square house: Note the particularly "Westernized" appearance and layout.

are employed; two of them work in tea houses in Tot, and the third works as a cleaner in the government health center. These three men all have compounds where the houses are differentiated according to gender, rather than according to function. Apart from the group of eight compounds in sample Ia, there are only two compounds in Sibou (one of which is illustrated in Figure 36) where the houses are differentiated according to function, but in neither case is the household head employed. These two compounds and the compounds in sample Ia occupy land at the foot of the escarpment, immediately adjacent to Tot. Since there are no compounds anywhere else in Sibou where the houses are differentiated according to function, it seems that compounds which exhibit this "modern" feature are only to be found close to Tot. However, it would also seem that only those men of the *Kakibelkio* lineage who wish to declare their allegiance to a changing way of life would choose to live so close to Tot. Other members of the lineage express a dislike for Tot and for the army and government personnel who frequent the center.

The two houses illustrated in Figure 39 are very different in their organization and content from those houses illustrated in Figures 33 and 34. These sleeping/entertaining houses have no fireplace, no center post, and no *tobot* (roof store). A string, with a sheet draped over it, divides the living from the sleeping area. The beds are modern iron beds, with mattresses, pillows, sheets, and blankets, whereas the beds in Figures 33 and 34 are traditional wooden-stick beds, covered either with goatskin or cowhide. In both houses in Figure

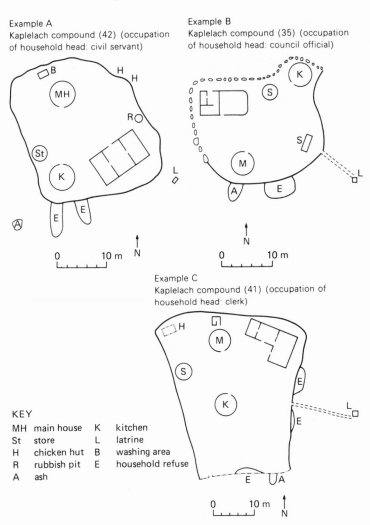

Example A
Kaplelach compound (42) (occupation
of household head: civil servant)

Example B
Kaplelach compound (35) (occupation
of household head: council official)

Example C
Kaplelach compound (41) (occupation of
household head: clerk)

KEY
MH main house   K   kitchen
St   store   L   latrine
H   chicken hut   B   washing area
R   rubbish pit   E   household refuse
A   ash

FIGURE 38. Compounds with square houses.

39, it is not only the separation of the sleeping from the entertaining area
that signals their "modernity," but also the household contents and their spatial locations. For example, in house A the sleeping area is crisscrossed by
strings used to hang clothes on; ten pairs of shoes and a pair of white wel-
lingtons are stuffed under one bed, and on the stool beside the other bed stand
two bottles of baby lotion and a bar of soap. The cardboard boxes and the
basket are full of clothes; two suitcases are piled on top of the trunk; and
a number of other small boxes contain magazines, bottles, and bits and

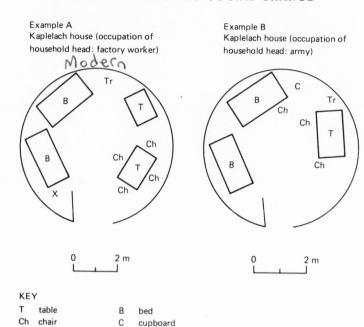

FIGURE 39. Interiors of two modern round houses.

pieces. All along the walls of the living area there are photographs, pictures from magazines, and old calendars. Table A displays seven glasses, one thermos flask, one plate, nine enamel mugs, one sieve, two spoons, one knife, and a glass sugar bowl. Table B is covered with a decorated cloth, and lying on the cloth are a comb, a torch, a radio, two books, a copy of the Bible in Kalenjin, a lamp, and two boxes of matches. Every one of the items I have mentioned marks this house out as the house of a young man who is employed.[6] This house contains and displays the status items which declare the owner's allegiance to a changing way of life. The visitor who walks into this house comes first to a table with chairs set around it – a familiar sight, even to the most eurocentric eyes – while the visitor who walks into the house illustrated in Figure 35 (example B) comes first to a grinding stone and a traditional water pot. There is nothing particularly remarkable about such differences, except that these two men are brothers and live 500 m apart.

The Endo perceive both the acquisition of certain items and the reordering of space as indices of modernity. I have discussed some of the observable changes in the ordering of house interiors and have shown that there is a certain amount of variation depending on the age and occupation of the house-

[6] This man works for the Kenya Creameries Cooperative and therefore works outside the valley.

holder. In some cases, it would also appear that there is a degree of variation which correlates with the distance of the compound from the valley floor. Figures 34, 36, and 37 show that while there are considerable differences between age groups in the ordering of space, there is a remarkable homogeneity within each age bracket. The *korongoro* (Figure 34) and *kaplelach* (Figure 35) house groups showed no discernible variation which would correlate with either vertical or horizontal distance from Tot center. The *kimnygeu* houses (Figure 37), on the other hand, showed no variation with regard to horizontal distance from Tot, but were restricted in their distribution to the lower part of the village, beneath the 2,000 m contour. This supports the Endo claim that nowadays young men want to live nearer to the valley floor. The information on square houses and on compounds where the houses are differentiated according to function suggests that those men who are employed and those who wish to "appear" modern also choose to live closer to Tot. This is supported by the fact that all the compounds with square houses and those where the houses are differentiated according to function are to be found immediately adjacent to Tot.

Household Contents

The observable variation in the organization of household interiors would suggest that age, occupation, and distance from the valley are crosscutting variables. This point can be illustrated by an analysis of household contents. Table 4 contains household inventories for the *korongoro* houses illustrated in Figure 34. These inventories are partial, and the objects chosen were selected in order to show the differential acquisition of modern items and the variable retention of one category of tradional objects (calabashes). Table 5 shows household inventories from three *kaberur* households in sample I where the household heads are unemployed. Table 6 shows the household inventories for the *kaplelach* houses B, C, and D from Figure 35. Within each category variation is minimal, but the tables show that there is apparently some variation with age. The korongoro households have fewer items in each category; this is partly because most of their children are no longer living at home and the households are therefore reduced in size, and partly because people of this age group express a lack of interest in such items as tables and chairs. While a *sufuria* (metal cooking pot) is a readily available item with an obvious and immediate use, items like tables and chairs are expensive, difficult to obtain and generally considered nonessential. I would argue that the categorization of certain items as nonessential and their high unit cost partially explain the observable differences between the *kaberur* and *kaplelach* households.

Tables 5 and 6 show that spoons and mugs are found in similar numbers in all six households, whereas the *kaberur* households lack such items as tables, chairs, and lamps, where the unit cost is high. There is nothing to suggest

TABLE 4. Household Inventories for *Korongoro* Houses

House	A	B	C
Sample no.	III	II	I
Occupation	unemp.	unemp.	unemp.
No. of children	8	5	6
Sufuria	4	2	3
Karias	1	0	0
Tea pot	0	0	0
Fork	0	0	0
Spoon	2	2	5
Knife	0	0	0
Mug	4	3	8
Plates	1	0	3
Bowls	3	2	5
Glasses	0	0	2
Bed (modern)	0	0	0
Mattresses	0	0	0
Frying pan	0	0	0
Lamp	0	0	0
Radio	0	0	0
Table	0	0	0
Chair	0	0	0
Stool	0	1	2
Mirror	0	0	1
Calabashes			
Brewing beer	2	4	0
Milk	4	3	3
Water	2	6	1
Beer	2	5	1
Honey	0	2	0
Carrying water	1	0	0

that the *kaplelach* households have any better access to cash resources than the *kaberur* households, but it would appear that there are differences in the way resources are allocated. For example, the average number of children for a *kaberur* man in sample I is 6.7 and the average number for a *kaplelach* man is 3.8. Of the eight *kaberur* men in sample 1, five have a child attending secondary school; and this means that they have to find between 1,300 and 1,800 ks per year for school fees, an almost impossible sum of money for a subsistence farmer.[7] On the other hand, none of the *kaplelach* men has children old enough to attend secondary school; their children attend the local primary school at Tot.

---

[7] Most men cannot find the money for school fees, so they ask their agnates and the mission for help, and occasionally they may even have to sell some of their stock. Women also contribute to school fees, and often the little money they get from selling foodstuffs at Tot market or from making the skin bags or jewelry for other women has to be used for school fees.

TABLE 5. Household Inventories for *Kaberur* Houses

House	18	21	2
Sample no.	I	I	I
Occupation	unemp.	unemp.	unemp.
No. of children	6	6	6
Sufuria	4	4	4
Karias	2	1	0
Tea pot	0	0	0
Fork	0	0	0
Spoon	3	6	3
Knife	0	0	0
Mug	10	6	2
Plates	3	1	0
Bowls	4	9	1
Glasses	1	1	0
Bed (modern)	0	0	0
Mattresses	0	0	0
Frying pan	0	0	0
Lamp	1	0	0
Radio	0	0	0
Table	0	0	0
Chair	0	0	0
Stool	2	2	2
Mirror	1	1	0
Calabashes			
Brewing beer	2	1	1
Milk	3	5	3
Water	2	1	4
Beer	2	2	4
Honey	2	1	1
Carrying water	1	0	0

Although primary education in Kenya is now free, parents do have to provide a school uniform. This is a burden for most families, but it is an extra load for those parents who are already paying for an older child to attend secondary school. School fees constitute the largest single outlay of cash that unemployed men have to make, and *kaberur* men, unlike the younger *kaplelach*, have to husband their resources in order to meet this demand. Consequently, while there is little difference between *kaberur* and *kaplelach* men as regards access to cash resources, there is a considerable difference in the demands made on those resources. For this reason unemployed *kaberur* men are less likely to acquire nonessential, high-cost items, like tables, chairs, and radios. *Kaplelach* men, on the other hand, have more flexibility with regard to the allocation of cash resources and are also under greater pressure, because of the example of their employed peers (of the eight men employed in the village, seven are *kaplelach* and only one is *kaberur*), to acquire modern items. The pressure to "keep up with Joneses," as far as resources will allow, is very considerable.

Table 7 illustrates the household inventories for three compounds where

TABLE 6. Household Inventories for *Kaplelach* Houses

House	B	C	D
Sample no.	I	I	II
Occupation	unemp.	unemp.	unemp.
No. of children	4	4	5
Sufuria	2	4	3
Karias	1	1	1
Tea pot	0	0	0
Forks	0	0	2
Spoons	3	4	3
Knife	0	0	0
Mug	4	3	8
Plates	0	0	0
Bowls	4	2	3
Glasses	0	1	1
Bed (modern)	0	0	0
Mattresses	0	0	0
Frying pan	0	0	0
Lamp	0	1	1
Radio	0	0	0
Table	2	1	1
Chair	0	0	3
Stool	1	2	1
Mirror	0	0	1
Calabashes			
Brewing beer	0	2	5
Milk	6	2	3
Water	2	2	0
Beer	1	2	1
Honey	1	2	1
Carrying water	0	2	0

the houses are differentiated according to function and the household heads are employed. Table 7 shows that in cases where the household head is employed there is a marked increase in the number of all modern items (with the exception of *sufurias* and spoons) and a corresponding decrease in the number of traditional calabashes. This illustrates two points: first, that there are certain modern items (e.g., *sufurias* and spoons) which are available to everyone, and also a corresponding class of objects (iron beds, radios, and lamps) which are available only to those people with large cash resources; secondly, that the acquisition of modern objects is paralleled by the displacement of more traditional types—modernity is not just the acquisition of modern items, but also the replacement of more traditional objects by those considered modern.

Tables 4 and 6 indicate that the number and type of household items does not vary significantly with distance from Tot or from the valley floor. Table 8 shows a clear difference between Sibou samples I and II, apparently attribut-

TABLE 7. Household Inventories for Employed Men.

House	32	33	39
Sample no.	I	I	I
Occupation	unemp.	unemp.	unemp.
No. of children	1	3	3
Sufuria	6	4	8
Karias	3	1	1
Tea pot	1	1	2
Forks	5	4	5
Spoons	12	4	9
Knife	2	0	3
Mug	10	8	14
Plates	4	4	6
Bowls	15	8	10
Glasses	9	3	6
Bed (modern)	2	1	3
Mattresses	2	1	3
Frying pan	1	1	1
Lamp	2	2	2
Radio	1	1	1
Table	2	2	2
Chair	6	4	4
Stool	2	2	2
Mirror	2	1	1
Calabashes			
Brewing beer	0	0	0
Milk	2	1	4
Water	0	0	0
Beer	1	0	0
Honey	0	0	0
Carrying water	0	0	0

able to their differential proximity to Tot center. If, however, the eight compounds from sample Ia are removed from sample I, then the figures alter. Houses in sample I still have more spoons, mugs, and bowls than those in sample II, but the difference between the samples with regard to beds, mattresses, frying pans, radios, tables, and chairs completely disappears. This suggests that the incidence of certain items in sample I is skewed by the presence of the compounds from sample Ia. However, although the incidence of certain modern items alters when these compounds are removed from sample I, the incidence of calabash types stays the same. In other words, sample I houses still have a lower incidence of traditional calabash types than the houses in sample II. This suggests that there may be some difference between the samples which would correlate with their distance from Tot, but I do not have any additional data which would satisfy me on this point. I also think it highly probable that such differences as do exist between the samples may be attributable to closer kinship links between the houses in sample I and those

TABLE 8. Household Items from Sibou Samples I and II

	Tot I		Tot II	
	No. per household	% of total households with the item	No. per household	% of total households with the item
Beds (modern)	0.4	43	0	0
Mattresses	0.4	45	0	0
Frying pan	0.2	19	0	0
Lamp	0.8	64	0.1	10
Radio	0.2	19	0	0
Mirror	0.9	80	0.2	23
Tables	0.7	35	0.1	6
Chairs	1.1	38	0.6	43
Stools	1.7	62	0.7	43
Sufurias	3.6	100	3.6	100
Mugs	6.3	100	3.5	100
Bowls	5.0	100	2.3	100
Spoons	4.4	93	2.3	93
Karias	1.9	66	0.7	63
Forks	1.3	26	0.4	26
Plates	2.1	69	2.1	90
Glasses	1.4	60	0.7	50
Knives	0.4	93	0	0
Calabashes				
Brewing beer	0.5	20	1.1	73
Water	0.8	41	2.4	100
Milk	4.0	100	6.6	100
Beer	1.0	50	2.0	86
Honey	0.5	35	0.7	63
Carrying water	0.2	19	0.9	76

in sample Ia than exist between sample II and sample Ia. This is particularly likely given that the households in sample I all belong to the *Kabisioi* clan and are related through a series of kin-based networks and obligations, while the houses in sample II are predominantly of the *Kapchepsom* and *Kapsiren* clans. It is certainly a well-established practice for less well-off members of the lineage to ask their more affluent peers for financial help and/or items needed for the house. It would, therefore, be unsurprising to find that a household had acquired certain modern items (or, indeed, had been influenced in a decision to discard more traditional ones) because of a relationship with a wealthier household. I have recorded interactions of this kind with regard to school fees and clothing, but have no quantifiable information on the movement of objects or on the transfer of cash resources which might then be used to purchase household items.

The concluding point of this section is that the age and occupation of the household head are the important variables when considering changes in the ordering of space. Distance from Tot or from the valley floor appears to correlate with certain changes in spatial order only because compound position actually correlates with age and occupation. Young men and men who are employed wish to declare their allegiance to a changing way of life – a life which is not traditional – and they therefore choose to live nearer to Tot. Occupation actually appears to be a much more crucial variable than age (see Table 7); but this is difficult to substantiate because there are not enough men who are employed from each of the different age groups. However, it is certainly the case that those families where the man is employed express a more fervent desire for change, this being reflected in their attitude toward the ordering of space and the disposal of household refuse.

HOUSEHOLD REFUSE

The residents of Tot center, the families who live in the eight compounds from sample Ia, and unmarried men are the only people who do not maintain the traditional spatial segregation of ash, animal dung, and chaff. Of these three categories, the young unmarried men are a special case because they have no animals in the compound, and they also have no wife to cook or to husk grain for them. Such young men usually eat with their mothers, although they often cook roast food with their friends. Young men who do cook for themselves are those who live at some distance from their close female kin.

Surprisingly, an absence of animals is also characteristic of the compounds from sample Ia. Of the eight men in this sample, only two have animals: One man has eight goats and four sheep and the other had fifteen goats before they died in the flu epidemic of 1980. It is interesting to note that these two men are the only men whose employment situation allows them to return weekly to their homes; the other six men in this group work outside the valley for extended periods of time. Although only two families have any stock, six of the eight families do have chickens. Chickens are considered a recent innovation! The people of Sibou say that there were no chickens in the village prior to 1968, and there are still older men and women who will not eat eggs or chicken flesh. To keep a large number of chickens is considered a sign of modernity, and their care and maintenance is thought to be the task of women rather than of men. The keeping of chickens is, therefore, not analogous to the keeping of stock.

The fact that none of the compounds in sample Ia contains any animals (even the two men who had animals did not keep them in their compounds) means that there is no necessity for a conscious policy of segregating ash from animal dung. However, two women out of this group of eight use ash and animal dung as fertilizers and scatter both substances on the plants growing around their houses. Both are aware that women who live higher up the escarpment would never do this, but they claim that such things are no longer important to them. The lack of interest in segregating refuse types and the verbal assurances that such practices are no longer important cannot be accounted for merely in terms of the absence of animals from the compound. It seems more likely that the segregation of ash and animal dung is no longer important, because animals as a sphere of male interest and prestige are no longer as important. In the highland areas, men who work away from home leave their cows with their male relatives, and cattle remain a sphere of male interest because they remain a valuable investment. This is not the case in Endo, where cattle are few and the value of small stock is negligible (80 ks for a goat). The acquisition of small stock is not to be understood in terms of mere economic worth; it is their identification with the ceremonial and status concerns of men that gives them their true value. The absence of animals is not therefore linked to insufficient economic resources, since the men in question are already wealthy enough to build square houses and acquire expensive items (e.g., radios). It seems more likely that these men do not possess stock because they do not participate in a prestige system which rests on the accumulation of stock.

I argued earlier that the traditional/modern distinction implies a hierarchy, such that the modern is valued over the traditional. In this context, it is not surprising to find that the modern prestige sphere, which rests on the acquisition and display of certain goods (including square houses), is considered superior to its traditional counterpart, which is dependent upon the accumulation of stock. This hierarchy is interestingly perpetuated in the relationship between modern education and traditional esoteric knowledge. The Endo have always recognized an intimate relationship between status and knowledge: traditionally, much of the prestige which accrued to elders rested on their access to and accumulation of esoteric knowledge. A man became an elder by passing through various structurally given changes of status, the first of which was initiation; each change of status was defined by the acquisition of further esoteric knowledge. Such knowledge implied power, since it was only known to individuals who had ritually undergone the prescribed changes of status. This system of successive states of knowledge, which was paralleled by increasing power and prestige, guaranteed the control of the elders over young men and over women. In the present situation, young men value their modern education over the traditional knowledge of their elders. They also value the acquisition of modern items over the accumulation of stock. The traditional prestige system has begun to be ruptured by the combined momentum of education and wage labor. The relationship between knowledge, prestige, and the reordering of space is contained in the reply a young man gave when I inquired as to why some people no longer bothered to separate ash from animal dung: "At *lagam* [escarpment part of the village] it is different because our fathers do not know everything." The value of traditional knowledge is undermined; young men know that no harm will befall them because they fail to segregate refuse types. However, the failure to observe the customary methods of refuse disposal does not follow unproblematically from the acquired empirical knowledge that such transgressions are harmless. On the contrary, such failures of observance have to be understood in terms of their relation to changing values and prestige structures.

The traditional reason for not mixing ash, animal dung, and chaff is the link which the Endo perceive between refuse and burial. From my inquiries it would seem that the provisions governing burial are slower to change than those governing the disposal of refuse. This view is, however, difficult to substantiate because there are (as yet) no burials associated with any of the eight compounds, where refuse is no longer segregated in a traditional manner. All eight men claimed that they would follow the traditional procedures for burial and would feel that this was important. Such statements are difficult to judge and have to remain unsubstantiated until such time as they may be observed in practice. The residents of Tot, most of whom are from Endo, do not bury their dead close to their homes. Instead, the dead are buried in the cemetery over the road from the government health center, and there are no special provisions for people of different ages and sexes (see Appendix 2 for further details on burial).

THE "SLOPING" WORLD DECLINED

Changing house types and household contents are part of a wider series of change in social and spatial relationships. As the villagers of Sibou move closer to the valley floor, the slope of their world declines. The daily rhythm of movement from the escarpment to the fields on the valley floor and back again is broken. The women of the eight households from sample Ia were always reluctant to venture up the escarpment, their orientation was to Tot, and beyond to the world outside the valley. The *lagam* is the area where ceremonies and dances take place. Between 1980 and 1981, I only once saw one of these eight women attending a ceremony in the *lagam*. It would be an oversimplification, as well as a misrepresentation, to say that "the break with tradition was complete." These women certainly performed particular ceremonies, like the naming ceremony for children, in the privacy of their own homes, but they were not to be seen at any of the major ceremonies (e.g., circumcision or marriages) in the village, and especially not at night. Changing attitudes and values had a very clear spatial representation. Refusing to participate is one of many ways to create distinctions, to rupture social networks, and to set up new contexts. The following case material illustrates the point.

CASE HISTORY

Sarah is the wife of the man who owns compound 42, illustrated in Figure 38 (example A); both husband and wife are employed. Sarah uses her salary to provide items for the house and to buy foodstuffs which she cannot grow in her own *shamba*. Since she is employed, she has no time to work in the fields. However she does cultivate a small area (¼ acre) around her house; in this garden she grows maize, lemons, green vegetables, watermelons, bananas, onions, and carrots. She has two acres of millet and half an acre of cotton in the valley; the work on these fields is done by women of her husband's lineage, and she pays them 3 ks per day. One of the young girls of her husband's lineage lives with them; this girl grinds the maize flour and does other household tasks.

Maria lives in compound 41, illustrated in Figure 38 (example C) and has two small children; her husband comes home about once every four months. Maria does not work, except to cultivate a small garden (¼ acre) around her house, where she grows maize, vegetables, onions, lemons, bananas, and paw-paws. The family has two acres of millet, one acre of maize, and one acre of cotton in the valley; the work on these fields is done by women of her husband's clan whom she pays 3 ks per day. Her husband's nephew (BS) and a young girl from the lineage live with her. The boy does any heavy cultivation work that is required and runs errands; the girl looks after the two small children and does other household tasks. Maria owns a handmill for grinding maize which stands outside her compound.[8] Women from the surrounding area go there to grind their maize and then hand over a portion to Maria in payment for the use of the machine.

Sarah and Maria are noticeably different from the rest of the women in Sibou; their appearance, their houses and their lifestyles mark them out from the majority of their neighbors. One of the most obvious ways in which this difference is made apparent and reinforced is through their failure to work with the other women in the fields. Women are strongly identified with the crops they produce, and much of their autonomy within the household is derived from their control over production and reproduction. In this exogamous society, women have to form cooperative links within the lineage when they marry into it, and the two major areas in which women help each other and cooperate together are childcare and agricultural work. Failure to work in the fields not only differentiates Sarah and Maria from the other wives in the lineage; it also cuts them off from the support system which the women as a group provide for each other, and which is frequently used by in-

---

[8] There are four other handmills in Sibou village, but they are considered the property of lineages, not individuals. There is also a watermill, which is operated by a man (see Plate XVII). He charges 15 ks per sack (90 kilos) or he takes 20 kilos of maize in lieu of payment.

PLATE XVII. A watermill on one of the irrigation channels in Sibou. This mill is run by a man as a commercial concern.

dividual women when they are in dispute with their husbands. Sarah and Maria are thus in a position of relative isolation, an isolation which is emphasized by the fact that they pay the other women of the lineage to do agricultural work for them. This payment constitutes the valorization of what should be a social relationship of reciprocal obligation. However, Sarah and Maria value their position and do not view it as one of isolation. They feel very strongly that they are different from the other women and that this difference is what constitutes their modernity. Thus a whole series of differences is articulated around the questions of labor and food. It is not by accident that the little gardening work Sarah and Maria do is mostly directed toward the production of foodstuffs which are themselves considered modern – for example, lemons, onions, and carrots. Some of these foodstuffs, like those just listed, can sometimes be bought (or bartered for) in Tot market and are, therefore, sometimes eaten by other women in the village. On the other hand, Sarah and Maria also grow – or attempt to grow – vegetables and fruits which other women have no access to, and would not necessarily wish to eat, for example, watermelons.

The refusal to engage in heavy agricultural labor for the production of food staples is a fairly conscious decision on the part of Sarah and Maria. By refusing to work in the fields they differentiate themselves from other women, and in so doing they validate both their own claims to modernity and the status of their husbands. To be different is to be nontraditional, and to be nontraditional is, by definition, to be modern. To be relieved of agricultural work involves having the cash resources to pay hired labor; it therefore follows that men who have sufficient cash resources encourage their wives not to work as an indication of their own modernity.[9] The status of the husband is dependent on his role as provider, or rather on his ability to support a nonworking wife. Thus, wages and the wife's withdrawal from agricultural labor work together as a multifaceted indication of modernity, which underpins the man's status.

However, Sarah's and Maria's positions are not entirely comparable, given that Sarah is engaged in full-time employment and has a salary of her own. An initial analysis would suggest that Maria is more dependent on her husband's salary than is Sarah. Maria has no access to cash resources except through her husband and makes no attempt to sell any of her produce in order to gain money.[10] Her standard of living is entirely derived from her husband and she uses her control of the handmill to emphasize her non-participation in traditional women's tasks and to extract a surplus (i.e., ground maize flour) from other women of the lineage whom she does not remunerate for their labor. Maria's nonworking position – she rarely works in the fields, she has help looking after her children, and she uses other women's labor in some of the tasks associated with food preparation – enhances her status and that of her husband.[11] However, it could be argued that she loses more than she gains through her "new-found leisure." Since she no longer retains control over production – her husband's wage pays for the agricultural labor – she no longer retains control over what she produces. Her economic autonomy within the joint project of marriage is undermined by her alienation from her production rights to land. Although Maria retains control over transactions associated with the handmill, she gains no economic autonomy

---

[9] A number of studies have noted that women withdraw or are withdrawn from agricultural labor as soon as the family income permits (see Epstein, 1982: 160). This phenomenon is apparently more common in Asia than Africa, where Boserup associates the seclusion of women with plough agriculture and the consequent male monopoly of a formerly female domain (Boserup, 1970: 25–7). Engels linked the origin of male dominance to the emergence of private property, and following Engels a number of feminist writers have linked private property and wage labor with the decline of women's role in subsistence production and increasing male control of female sexuality (Deere et al., 1982: 92–102; Sacks, 1974). It is sometimes argued that the withdrawal of women from agricultural labor is an attempt to emulate upper-class practices, and such an argument might have some validity for Kenya, where "white" women do not engage in agricultural labor.

[10] Maria is sometimes paid a few shillings by women who use the handmill and she does occasionally send a relative to sell some fruit in Tot market, but neither source provides a substantial or a regular income.

[11] Domestic labor is frequently underestimated or ignored, but fortunately there are now an increasing number of studies which illustrate just how much time such work involves and how important it is in any consideration of women and their changing economic status. (For a critique of the way women's economic activities have been underestimated by researchers, see Beneria, 1981.) Of all the domestic tasks, probably carrying water, collecting firewood, and

from this, merely further validation of her leisured position and her consequent dependence on her husband, since it is the existence of his wage which guarantees and demands her leisure.[12]

Sarah's position is somewhat different: She has a salary of her own and uses that money to pay women to work on the land for her.[13] This means that, since she retains control over production, she also retains control over what she produces. However, unlike that of women in more traditional positions, her apparent economic autonomy is illusory. Sarah has access to cash resources through her salary, but she has little choice concerning the allocation of those resources. It is her salary, not that of her husband, that is used to cover labor costs. Her husband feels no obligation to contribute to the cost of household production and reproduction, which remains the woman's responsibility. In addition, certain foodstuffs which have to be bought, like

---

grinding food are the most exhausting and the most time consuming. It is estimated that carrying water takes up 12% of day-time calorie usage, and up to 27% in very dry or steep areas (see Moore, 1974: 14). In an early study Richards noted that women were "sitting about hungry with millet in their granaries and relish to be found in the bush" because they were too tired to prepare the food which might involve three hours' grinding (Richards,1939: 104–5). It is therefore very important to realize what it means that Sarah and Maria should be released not only from agricultural labor, but also from a substantial part of ordinary domestic labor. It is a mark of considerable status that a man can afford to have his wife "sitting at home." And it is a double mark of status because it differentiates Sarah and Maria sharply from the other women and assures them of their nontraditional lifestyle.

[12] A number of studies have noted that development and wage labor make women more dependent on their husbands by undermining traditional systems where women had a certain amount of autonomous control over production and reproduction (VanAllen, 1974; Remy, 1975; Whiting, 1972; Dey, 1981). That Western influence should encourage a sharper division between the sexes is unsurprising given the vital connections between Western capitalism and the structure, both economic and ideological, of the Western nuclear family. Colonial governments were particularly instrumental in encouraging the increased agricultural participation of males, in order, as they saw it, to increase efficiency and stop the men being idle. In other words, these policies encouraged the replication of Western family structures, where men went out to work and women stayed at home and looked after the children. Emerging national elites also established their own families on Western models and thus inaugurated a prestige system based, in part, on the nonparticipation of women in economic and public life. The result has been an increasing tendency to view men as providers and women as dependants, within an ideology of improved economic status for the family unit (Rogers, 1980: 37–41). In the context of the emergence of private property and an increase in male control over female sexuality, it is interesting to note that men express some anxiety over women's increased leisure; I certainly found this to be the case among the relevant families (i.e., sample Ia) in Sibou. Hirschon links the increased emphasis on meticulous childcare, spotless houses, time-consuming cooking, and embroidering, etc., with an attempt to fill female leisure time and therefore leave less time for temptation (Hirschon, 1978: 82–4). In the light of this point it is interesting to note the increased emphasis on cleanliness and smart clothes among the women in sample Ia and their pride in embroidered tablecloths and similar decorative paraphernalia. Such items not only have to be made, but they have to be kept clean, and this is no easy task given the prevailing conditions of life in Sibou.

[13] It is interesting to note that the only time Sarah had to work on the land was when requested to do so by her mother-in-law. This emphasizes the importance of the mother-in-law and the influence she gains over the family once her sons marry.

wheat flour, tea, and salt, are bought by Sarah, not by her husband.[14] Her husband uses his salary to provide items for the house and to provide the necessary resources for building a square house. Sarah is expected to contribute cash to both of these projects, in addition to the basic payments she makes for the maintenance of the household. Unlike Maria, Sarah is also expected to pay for her own clothes and her own "luxuries." Thus, the husband's salary is completely at his disposal and is not used for the maintenance of the household unit. Instead, much of his salary goes on building a square house and acquiring objects which enhance his prestige, investing in the cotton cooperative, and loaning money to unemployed members of the lineage, which enables him to build up a very necessary network of support and obligation.[15] Sarah's salary, however, is completely taken up by the cost of maintaining the household and supporting her husband's projects. She is also cut off from the support system provided by other women because she has chosen to separate herself from them and further to transform her relations with them by paying for their labor.[16] As a result, both her economic and her social position are much more precarious than those of her husband. In spite of an independent salary, Sarah remains dependent on her husband because he effectively controls the allocation of her resources through a set of expectations, based on a traditional division of labor, which assign certain household responsibilities to the woman. Sarah remains an economic dependant because she cannot control the allocation of her salary or use it to improve her economic position. Her husband, on the other hand, can use his salary to advance both his economic position and his status precisely because it is the woman's labor (i.e., Sarah's salary) which maintains the household as a reproductive and productive unit. Thus, the prestige of the man, which derives in part from the acquisition and display of modern items, and in part from his wife's nonparticipation in agricultural labor, is crucially dependent on the woman's labor.

From the above discussion it is clear that Sarah and Maria are both economically dependent on their husbands, albeit for rather different reasons. The enforced economic dependence, which is not the lot of the more tradi-

---

[14] Sarah's case differs from Maria's in this respect, because her continuing control over production means that she still has to maintain her traditional responsibility for the running of the household.

[15] The network of obligation which men establish through their "generosity" provides them with support if, for example, they need to call on communal labor or if they need access to animals or honey in order to perform a certain ritual. Access to resources which are required for ritual purposes is particularly crucial for men who have invested their energies in earning a wage and acquiring Western goods rather than building up their herds and tending their beehives.

[16] The degree of isolation or collectivity in which women work outside the home has important effects on women's position in their own households (Caplan and Bujra, 1978). The more households are organizationally separate, the more women are confined and isolated from support networks and the more dependent they become on men (Harris, 1981: 66).

tional Endo woman, has a considerable impact on relations between the sexes. In Maria's case, her husband views her as an economic burden, and conflict between husband and wife arises over how much of his salary he should assign for the maintenance of the household and the support of his wife and children.[17] Sarah's husband views her as an economic asset, and conflict emerges over the control of resources and the necessity for the husband to maintain his wife's economic dependence, in spite of her independent salary.

In Chapters 6 and 7 I illustrated that some spaces in an Endo compound are associated with men and some with women. I argued that the differentiated functions of individual houses are expressed in terms of a distinction between the activities of the sexes. I explained the "genderization" of activities and space in terms of a value system which generates and is generated by conflicts and tensions within Endo society. How, then, does the changing order of space observable in Sarah's and Maria's compounds, and in the other six compounds in sample Ia, relate to relations between the sexes?

In the compounds in sample Ia, houses are differentiated according to function, and space is not "genderized" in the way which is familiar from the more traditional Endo compounds. This functional differentiation of space is accompanied by the casual mixing of refuse types and verbal assurances of a perceived and desired break with tradition. The break with tradition is most particularly expressed through the acquisition and display of certain modern items and through the building of square houses. The ordering of space within these compounds does not appear to be informed by conflict between the sexes. Rather, the wealth and progressiveness of the individual household form the focus of concern. The conspicuous display of modern items indicates the man's access to cash resources (all the men in sample Ia are employed) and thereby to an occupation which is, by definition, modern, since it is not the traditional occupation of subsistence farmer. The theme of spatial order is one of family unity and prosperity; conflicts and tension between the sexes do not appear to be represented spatially; the opposition male/social, female/individual does not seem to be a focus of concern.

IDEOLOGY AND THE INTERPRETATION OF SPACE

The changing nature of social and spatial relations clearly produces a complex situation. The lack of opposition between what is male and what is female would seem to be related to the emergence of alternative prestige system, which is reflected in the functional, rather than gender-associated, differenti-

---

[17] There are a number of studies which document women's increasing economic dependence as a result of wage labor (Tinker, 1976: 31). The change of gender relations in a developing economy such that women become more dependent on men–is connected to the relative degree of access of each gender to wages and other assets, for example, political influence.

ation of houses. It would thus appear possible to link changes in the organization of space to changing socioeconomic circumstances and the resulting decrease in tensions between the sexes. In other words, it could be argued that the traditional "genderization" of space has been replaced by a set of new distinctions which reflect both the changed nature of gender relations and the emergence of new tensions and concerns. However, even though changes in the organization of space are related to emerging values and concerns, this does not mean, as the cases of Sarah and Maria show, that tensions between the sexes do not exist; nor does it mean that men and women are no longer in conflict over the control of productive resources. Changes in the organization of space cannot be understood as merely reflecting changed social and economic conditions.

The idea that changes in the organization of space can be directly related to the breakdown of one value system and its replacement by another has little explanatory power. Space considered as a text does not take as its object real social and economic conditions, but rather certain ideological representations of the real. This is clear from an analysis of the compounds in sample Ia, where conflict between the sexes exists but is not apparently represented spatially. Part of the answer as to why this should be so is that the spatial text only talks about, or works over, states of affairs which are already representations of reality rather than reality itself.

As previously noted, the ordering of space in the compounds in sample Ia belies the existence of conflict between the sexes. Instead, there is a concern with an overt display of the wealth of the individual household. An employed man is at great pains to build a square house, fence off the compound, and provide plates, bowls, knives, forks, and glasses. The cooking area is separated from the main house; the room for entertaining is furnished with tables and chairs and decorated with cloths and other items. All in all a considerable amount of money is spent on doing, and being seen to do, three things: (1) building a square house; (2) equipping the house; and (3) providing for the family. This display of "modernism" depends upon access to cash resources: only money buys manufactured goods. In the conspicuous display of modern items, the opposition between what is traditional and what is modern is set up.

The provision of modern items for the home, and the provision of goods for the family, illustrates a man's status, and guarantees his progressiveness which is no more than an indication of his cash resources. A man's prestige is increasingly bound up with the display of status, which consists in the building of square houses and the provision of "modern" and expensive items. The woman is still so far identified with the home that, when a man provides these items, he is seen as providing for his wife and family. Their prosperity and progressiveness create and are created by his status. This is the solution which the spatial text proposes to an ideological conflict—a conflict which arises because it is the labor of the woman which ensures the production and reproduction of the household on which the man's status is crucially dependent. Ultimately, it is not just the woman who is dependent on the man, for the man is also dependent on the woman. As Sarah's case demonstrates so well, the interdependence of the sexes is concealed by an ideological representation which defines the man as the "provider" and the woman as the "provided for."

The ordering of space takes up this theme, and works over the notion of the "provider" and the "provided for." The meaning of this distinction lies not in its material reality, but in how it helps to fashion and perpetuate a particular process of representation. This process of representation is formed by the dialectical relationship between ideology and spatial text, such that their relationship may only be understood as one of produced representation. The notion of woman as the "provided for" both produces and is produced by the organization of domestic space. The relationship between an ideological form – for example, the notion of woman as "provided for" – and the spatial text is only invoked in practice. There is therefore no single or given way in which the ideological form will be present in the text. In other words, there is no fixed way of characterizing the relationship between space and ideology because it follows from the notion of spatial text as representation that ideology is not expressed or reflected in the text; rather, it produces the text. Furthermore, the relationship between text and ideology is historically mutable – that is, ideology does not always produce the text in the same way, or rather it is not always determined in the text in the same way. In the case of the more "traditional" Endo compounds, conflicts between the sexes are worked over in the ordering of space; they are not hidden from view, even though they are represented in a very particular way. In the case of the compounds in sample Ia, however, conflicts between the sexes exist, but they are masked by the ordering of space, which declares instead a definitive unity of interests. But in both cases conflicts and tensions between the sexes are ultimately revealed through the ideological construction placed upon them by and through the ordering of space.

To conclude, in the case of the Endo, I suggest that the changing order of space is not to be understood in terms of changing gender relations, or in terms of changing ideas about men and women. Instead, it must be understood in terms of the symbolic work which ideological representations (space) must do, within a given set of material conditions, to be grounded, sustained and produced as authoritative discourse. Material conditions do not determine the nature of ideological representations, for the same objective conditions may produce wildly disparate forms of discourse and vice versa. But the material conditions of social life enable the production and persistence of certain forms of representation; material conditions may not guarantee the form of such representations, but they do determine their force.

PART III

INTERPRETATION
AND REPRESENTATION

CHAPTER 9

Invisible Women

⌒

The rhythms of everyday life are constructed in ways which vary according to the age and sex of the individual. Women rise early in the morning, often before light, to rekindle the fire, feed the children, and sweep the house. Men, on the other hand, rise early or late, depending on what the day has in store. It is not uncommon to wake and find the head of the household gone to the valley to tend stock or irrigation channels, and then to meet him on his way back to attend a meeting of the *kok* at about the time the children are going down to school.

In the early morning, children are much in evidence. Small boys herd goats down to the valley and play games on their way to school. Young girls balance large tins of water on their heads, hurrying back to the compound to deposit their loads before dashing off to school. Smaller children, girls, and boys, look after their infant siblings and play together around the compound (see Plate XVIII). The early morning and late afternoon are periods of great activity in the village, as people move about their business, shout instructions to family and friends, and generally prepare themselves for whatever it is they have to do.

At this point in the day, the differing activities of men and women produce a temporary, but daily, segregation. The men are generally not in evidence; they have gone to the meeting place on the edge of the escarpment, where they spend the morning settling disputes, allocating water rights and exchanging news. All circumcized men, whether married or not, are entitled to attend the meetings of the *kok*. Elders are expected to be there, and few would even contemplate missing the occasion. Unmarried men sometimes prefer to meet with friends at a *kano* on the valley floor, where they roast meat and cassava, sharpen their arrows, and chat. Younger boys often gather on the fringes of these groups and learn how to make arrows, throw spears, and attend to animals.

PLATE XVIII. Infant nurses. Older children look after their younger siblings. It is a common sight to see small children, both male and female, carrying babies on their backs.

Around 10 A.M., the women go down to the valley. All women, old and young, married and unmarried, work in the fields. The infirm and elderly sometimes sit at home in the sun, but if they are able to move at all, they usually prefer to go down to the fields at midday, and chat with the other women. The women rest in the heat of the day, and sit in groups in the shade, exchanging news and discussing the matters of the village.

At about noon, the elders leave the *kok,* and descend into the valley. The young men have usually left earlier in the day to see to their fields and animals. The older men move slowly, either toward their work, or toward the nearest beer pot. Elders do not concern themselves with agriculture or herding. Men give up subsistence tasks much younger than women do. Sons are expected to take over the fathers' work, and to help their mothers in the fields.

The daily rhythm of life varies slightly from season to season. During slacker periods in the agricultural cycle, women are at home much more during the day. But the dry season is also the "time of ceremonies," and women are often away from home making beer, grinding grain, and generally helping with preparations. During the months from November to February, the lives of both men and women are taken up with ceremonies: principally marriage and circumcision. Ceremonies often involve travel, and this is the one period in the year when a woman may return to her natal village, to help

with the preparations and renew old acquaintances. Men and women participate equally in ceremonial life – with the exception of activities in the seclusion house – but they have rather different roles. The result is that, even when
men and women are participating in the same ceremony, the daily segregation of activities continues.

In an everyday context, this segregation is most marked in relation to
the compound. Women spend much more time in the compound than do
men. While it is men who build the houses, and maintain the structural features of the compound, it is women who are responsible for its day-to-day
running and upkeep. The marked identification of a woman with her house
is a product, at least in part, of the amount of time she actually spends there.
Men use their houses for sleeping and storage, and, more infrequently, for
entertaining. Women, on the other hand, use their houses for cooking, childbirth, childcare, entertaining, and general family maintenance. Furthermore,
all these activities are actually made up of a series or cluster of activities: cooking
involves everything from husking the grain to presenting the final product
(see Plates XIX, XX, and XXI). Compared to men, women spend a lot of
time in the compound because their responsibilities include a wide range of
activities which necessarily take place in domestic space.

A DAY IN THE LIFE OF MA-CHEBET

6:15 A.M. Ma-Chebet woke in the kitchen house, where she had been sleeping with her baby son, and her daughter aged nine. She rose,
rekindled the fire, and woke her daughter. The baby then began
to cry, so she stopped what she was doing and started to feed
him. Her daughter went over to the other house and woke her
father (Kipkeyo) and two younger brothers.

6:30 Kipkeyo rose, collected some boiled cassava from the kitchen,
let the goats out of the compound, and followed the animals
down the escarpment. The two younger boys were given boiled
cassava and milk to eat. After everyone had eaten, Ma-Chebet
sent her daughter to collect water and gave the baby to one of
the boys. She then swept the floor of the kitchen hut, throwing
the rubbish outside the door.

7:30 When the daughter returned with the water, Ma-Chebet washed
the children's faces and hands. The two younger boys complained
of being cold and stayed in the house, next to the fire.

8:00 The daughter dressed and left for school with some friends.
Ma-Chebet began to sweep the whole compound, but she had
to stop several times to nurse the baby or to admonish the
boys.

PLATE XIX. Pounding maize. Preparing maize-meal porridge, which is the staple of the Endo, is women's work. First the maize must be removed from the cob, then pounded in a *ken* and taken to be ground.

9:30   Ma-Chebet deposited the two boys with the children of her husband's brother, and took the baby with her down to the fields. She spent the morning hoeing a field, in preparation for sowing sorghum. She was helped by the daughter of her husband's elder brother and by one of her neighbors.

12 noon   The women rested and ate a little cassava. Talk was mostly of the new nurse at the Health Center, and of the lack of rain.

2 P.M.   The women started hoeing again and did some work on a field owned by Ma-Chebet's husband's brother.

4:30   The women left the field and went into the bush to look for firewood and wild vegetables. Here, they met other women from Sibou village.

PLATE XX. Cooking maize porridge. The maize flour is mixed with water and the mixture is brought to the boil. Cooking in a clay pot is a laborious process which involves experience in regulating and judging the heat of the fire, as well as an ability to judge when the food is ready.

5:30	Ma-Chebet returned to the compound, sent her daughter to collect more water, and went to fetch the boys. She then went down to the handmill owned by the *Kabisioi* lineage to grind maize for the evening meal.
6:40	Ma-Chebet returned and began preparing the evening meal. The daughter went out to visit friends.
7:30	Kipkeyo returned and played with the children.
8:00	Family ate together.
8:30	Children went to bed.
9:30	Kipkeyo went to bed.
10:30	Ma-Chebet retired.

This account of a single day gives some idea of the separation of men's and women's pursuits, and of the range of women's activities carried out in the compound (Plates XXII, XXIII, XXIV, and XXV). Kipkeyo was out all day, and did not return home at all until the evening. Ma-Chebet, on the other hand, spent a considerable amount of time actually in the compound and additional time preparing (collecting firewood and vegetables, grinding) for domestic tasks later performed there.

PLATE XXI. When the porridge is cooked it is placed in a gourd (*mongwo*) or basket container (*kitesa*) ready for eating or storage.

INVISIBILITY AND SPACE

> *One of the most intriguing problems raised for anthropologists is how the members of a single society, though sharing in a broad set of cultural assumptions, may nevertheless possess diverse interpretations of reality . . . despite certain shared concepts and understandings, people who are in constant and intimate contact with one another nevertheless entertain substantially different views of the nature of their social world and the kinds of persons who comprise it. How such separate yet coexistent interpretations of reality are made manifest and how they affect the relations between their respective adherents are questions of fundamental importance to the understanding of many societies.*
> —LAWRENCE ROSEN, 1978: 561–2

An analysis of the organization of domestic space poses a familiar, but nonetheless interesting, problem with regard to women. If it is women who are most strongly identified with the home, and women who are predominantly active in the compound, then how is it possible to account for their apparently minimal impact on the organization of space? To what extent does it make sense to claim that women are invisible in the ordering of domestic space, and/or that that space is the product of a dominant male orientation in the world? Is it possible to claim that Endo women have an alternative model of the world, and if they do, do they wish to express it?

There is a sense in which it would be possible to argue that the tradition-

PLATE XXII. The crafts of the Endo (1): A woman potter at work. Among the Endo, all potters are women. The skill does not pass from mother to daughter, but is learnt through apprenticeship.

al organization of space among the Endo is an objectification of the male view of the world. The segregation of houses, refuse, and burials makes appeal to a series of associations which are ordered according to a persistent structural hierarchy between what is "male" and what is "female" (see Chapter 7). This hierarchy implies a set of valuations such that male qualities are positively valued, in contrast to those associated with the female, which are not. Women themselves may be positively or negatively valued, but that which is "female," or partakes of a female quality, always retains a negative connotation. "Femaleness" is never positively valued in and for itself and is consistently associated with other negatively valued characteristics, such as "individualism," "thoughtlessness," and "uncontrollability." The reasons men give for the rigid separation of ash and animal dung are only intelligible within a culturally given set of symbolic meanings; there is nothing inherent in either substance which would preclude their combination, and no functional reason for burying certain categories of persons under certain types of refuse. The cultural valuations given to the "male" and the "female" relate to the construction of the meaning of sex difference within Endo society. Positively valued social qualities – clan allegiance, social responsibility, rhetorical ability, and the like – are associated with the male, and the predominant values of Endo society are articulated in terms of a male world position. Within this male-oriented culture, the male and the female are cultural categories and are

PLATE XXIII. The crafts of the Endo (2): Making a *sana*. These heavy basket "platters" hang above the fire and are used for drying food and storing cooking utensils.

PLATE XXIV. The crafts of the Endo (3): Making a *ketub*. These wooden containers are used for feeding children a mixture of milk and porridge. Woodworking and heavy basket work are done by men, who also learn their skills through apprenticeship.

PLATE XXV. The crafts of the Endo (4): Mending a calabash. Older men are involved
in a number of craft activities, which they may carry out in the compound or in the *kano*.

part of a symbolic order which constructs masculinity and femininity in particular ways.

In his discussion of muted groups, Ardener seems to suggest that subordinate groups have alternative models of the world, but that such models are
muted either because they remain unexpressed, or because they are expressed
obliquely, filtered through the dominant ideology (Ardener, 1975b: 21–3).
In the case of women, this would seem to imply the existence of an autonomous and authentic female model which exists outside, or below, the dominant
male-oriented culture. However, it seems improbable that there should be
separate male and female models.[1] There is, of course, a female perspective

---

[1] There is a certain amount of psychoanalytic work on language acquisition and its relationship
to positioning in the symbolic order (see Lacan, 1980).

or point of view which is an attempt by women to value themselves within the cultural structures which confront them, but this does not constitute an alternative model as such. Endo society is constructed in terms of a system of symbolic meanings which are shared by both sexes. Men and women share the same symbolic order. What they do not share is the same position *vis-à-vis* that order. Women's entry into the cultural order, and the position they hold as female selves within it, differ from those of men.[2] This may be best demonstrated through a discussion of Endo attitudes to language and the social use of language.

DOMINANT LANGUAGE

They say "life brutalizes." That they recognize it explains why, for all that has been said to the contrary, they remain painfully human. They are women of tremendous strengths, these women of the shadows. One of their strengths, and not the least, is their silence which outsiders have understood as submission.

—ANNE CORNELISEN, 1977: 9–10

Let the women learn in silence with all subjection. But I suffer not a woman to teach, not to usurp authority over the man, but to be in silence.

—I TIMOTHY 2: 11–12

The Endo do not assume that men and women stand in identical relation to the language which they speak. The acquisition of social responsibility is a process defined by a changing relation to language, and women's lack of such responsibility is explained in terms of their incomplete control over language. As I have said, it is common to hear men say that "women are like children, they speak before they think." This statement could never be made of a man, whatever his behavior. To be male is, by definition, to be in possession of language. This point is illustrated by the fact that the changing jural and social status of men is frequently linked to a developing control of language. Thus, it may be said of a boy who has just undergone circumcision that now that he is a man he will no longer be heard to say "childish things." A man's capacity to speak continues to improve with age, and at the *kok,* in which all adult men participate, elders are listened to with particular respect. Rhetorical ability and evidence of responsible thought are highly regarded and are an important part of a man's prestige and status. The relationship between male identity and the spoken word is very strong, and during circumcision girl initiates are warned not to flinch as this will mean that their

---

[2] Women's relationship to men changes with time, and postmenopausal women often have a considerable degree of influence.

fathers can no longer stand and speak at *kok*. Women, on the other hand, rarely attend *kok* unless they are past childbearing age.[3] Women's imperfect control over language identifies them as less than complete adults, and therefore as outside decision making and the exercise of power. If women do attend they sit apart and do not speak. If a woman is involved in a dispute, then the major part of the case will be put for her by her husband or son. In this situation a woman may speak if she wishes, but she cannot stand to speak; she must remain seated. Her seated position reflects her own status and that of her views. However, women's opinions are by no means ignored, and are often taken into account, particularly if the outcome of the case is thought to affect women, either individually or corporately. But it must be said that in the normal course of events women are rarely consulted formally and their ability to influence major community decisions is restricted to their ability to influence individual men.

For the Endo the control of language is not merely a rhetorical skill, but also part of a way of understanding their language which links public speaking to the communal nature of social knowledge. Knowledge, like language, is thought to be a male attribute, and although some older women are highly regarded and recognized as knowledgeable they still do not possess the peculiarly social knowledge which is the inheritance of men. Access to knowledge, like the control of language, is a prerequisite for full adult, male status. The process of becoming adult, of assuming social responsibility, is closely tied to the acquisition of certain types of esoteric knowledge. Such knowledge may only be gained by passing through various rites, of which initiation and marriage are probably the most significant. A man's knowledge, just like his control of language, increases with age and experience. The knowledge which old men acquire is not, however, a coherent set of beliefs, a kind of Endo theosophy. It may include fragments of ritual language, the interpretations given to particular symbols and the like, but it mostly consists of recollected experience and past strategies of procedure. Ritual knowledge consists first and foremost of an ability to recall incidents from the past and then to use that experience to locate the causes of misfortune in the present and to suggest a solution. The recollection of successful strategies is always an essential part of coping with contemporary misfortune.

For example, when there is a drought the men of the *kor* might meet and try to recall what they did last time there was a shortage of rain. The discussion is quite detailed, and the various characteristics of the drought (when did it start, are animals dying, what are the specific changes in vegetation, what is the rate of dessication, etc.) are discussed and compared to those of preceding dry periods. When a comparable case is suggested, the elders try

---

[3] By this I do not mean rigorously determined. I am talking of a generative capacity, not of rule following.

to remember what action was taken on the previous occasion. Usually it turns out that a particular man from a specific lineage was called upon to slaughter a goat, and the assembled men then blessed the animal and expressed a desire for rain. In such a case, the solution to the contemporary drought will be for the men to gather in the same place and ask the same man, or a member of his lineage, to slaughter an animal and to ask for rain. Everyone then believes there will be rain. Knowledge is thus a powerful mixture of tradition, experience, and repetition. Although individual men are respected for what they know, the Endo see this as an ability to articulate a traditional knowledge which is acquired through experience of living in the community. Ultimately, knowledge is not something which is possessed by specific individuals, but is a tradition of social experience which is held in common by a group of men who are related through residence and/or descent and whose past and future are bound together through such links. The communality of male knowledge is therefore a traditional knowledge which, exercised correctly and according to tradition, maintains the balance of the natural world and of "man's" place in that world.

The Endo use command over language to define social being; language and knowledge are intimately related and together they construct a discourse of power which regulates not only relations within the social group, but also relations between men (the social) and the natural world. But, since women are thought to have an incomplete command of language, and since they do not, by definition, possess social (i.e., male) knowledge, they are excluded from the exercise of power, whether it be political or ritual. It is men who command language, and as such they occupy a privileged position in the structure of society and in the structure of the symbolic order. The conceptual categories "male" and "female," and the social categories "men" and "women," are organized around the recognition of this privilege. Men and women occupy different positions vis-à-vis the symbolic order because meaning is constructed in such a way that to be male describes a particular relation to language and to power. The sexual division of labor, the social organization of marriage, the structure of the household and the differential jural status of men and women are not unrelated to the privileged position of the male, because it is impossible to separate a discussion of male and female as conceptual categories from the material practices in which actual men and women relate to each other. If the Endo use control of language to define social being, then men's and women's differing linguistic competence defines them as different sorts of social individuals. It is through language and other systems of signification that ideas about masculinity and femininity are constructed; and it is on the basis of these constructed categories that the proper behavior of men and women is formulated in Endo society. The categories "female" and "male" are part of a system of representation which assigns characteristics to each sex, and there is a strong and overdetermined connection between systems of representation and the relationship which exists between men and women in the social order.

THE DOMINANT REPRESENTATION

You will, I know, keep measuring me by some standard of what you deem becoming to my sex.
                                        −CHARLOTTE BRONTE, 1849

One of the problems with the study of gender is that cultural notions about men and women rarely reflect the true nature of gender relations, what men and women actually do, what men and women can be observed to contribute to society. For example, I showed in Chapter 7 that the popular depiction of gender roles and tasks among the Endo is a very inadequate description of the division of agricultural tasks between women and men. Statements about the proper behavior or dress of the sexes, their status and social responsibilities, their moral qualities and character dispositions, are all part of a common folklore whose very quotidian repetitiveness naturalizes it as the substance of life, makes it the rationale for observed behavior, and exercises the peculiar quality of its ever-present conventionality even as it is challenged and despised. "Just like a woman" is a phrase which tells us nothing, but says everything. When Marakwet men say, "Women are like children, they speak before they think," there is no intention to inform; nothing is to be understood about the locutionary and rhetorical skills of individual women. On the contrary, such a phrase tells us nothing precisely because it purports to say everything. The socially dominant representations of women and men are contained in a heavily condensed form in the most commonplace of phrases, the most conventional of attitudes and the most familiar of images. It is the habituated form of such representations that makes them so pervasive and so powerful, that provides them with an apparently universal relevance. The peculiar force of culturally dominant representations derives from their seemingly universal and very practical applicability. They are not mere phrases, mere images and attitudes, but actually serve to inscribe and construct practical responses to everyday situations. Forms of response, the competent analysis of social events, the delineation of strategies, and the like, are all structured with reference to culturally specific notions of what is considered appropriate.[4] This is not to say that individuals may not do, say, and think things which are inappropriate, or to deny that such behavior may have very varied consequences. But the meaning of what is inappropriate is only grasped through a practical understanding of what is thought to be appropriate: the recognition of the inappropriate may be a strategy for the manipulation of appropri-

---

[4] It is unfortunate that Ardener (1975a: 1976) has not discussed his ideas on female models more. For a critique of Ardener, see Lipshitz, 1978.

ate categories and is not necessarily a rejection of culturally given representations. It should not be understood from the foregoing argument that cultural
representations are, in their naked form, a kind of rule or structure of rules.
The crucial point is that they do not prescribe particular courses of action or
thought; what they provide is something which precedes any such thought
or action, a kind of orientation, a way of standing in relation to a cultural
context and to other individuals in that context. This does not mean that
cultural constructions or representations should be treated as some sort of communal psyche, or as something of undoubted cognitive value but little material
import. As I have said, in a society like the Endo, where notions of gender
and sexuality operate as organizing principles for other domains of social life,
the ideological categories "male" and "female" instill the differences which
create the social. I would argue that a discussion of "male" and "female" as
cultural constructs cannot be separated from the actual relations in which men
and women live their lives, because the symbolic value of representation is
indissolubly linked to its part in the renegotiation of asymmetrical power relations between the sexes.

If cultural notions about men and women rarely reflect the true nature
of gender relations, then the problem is to understand how and why this is
so. In Endo society, as we have seen above, the cultural representations of
men and women and of relations between the sexes (gender ideology) form
what is usually referred to as a "male" model. This model gives a partial and
refracted picture of the characteristics of both sexes and is constructed as much
through silence and absence as it is through assertion. On the one hand, the
sexes are "assigned" roles on the basis of affirmed connection; for example,
women are associated with the home, with mothering and with nurturing.
On the other hand, the absence of explicit connection, the not-said, is an equally important part of creating a highly eclectic representation. The Endo model
of gender relations "works" in favor of men – that is, it supports men's domination over women, it portrays men as superior, and it misrepresents the relations of production in such a way that women's contributions are trivialized.
Such a model has an obvious male bias, and, since it does not adequately reflect
"real" gender relations, then it could be assumed, as it has been by Ardener
and others, that there exists a female model of equal validity but much reduced
visibility. I think there are two points to be made here: The first concerns
the existence of an autonomous "female" model (which, I have already suggested, does not exist), and the second concerns the conceptualization of the
notion of model itself.[5] Both points may be developed by considering the
concept of the dominant representation and its ideological character.

[5] Strathern also argues that there is no separate women's model, but her emphasis is rather different from mine (Strathern, 1981b: 169).

Gender is a cultural construction which everywhere takes socially and historically specific forms. Not all cultures elaborate on notions of maleness and femaleness in the same way, but there is no culture which does not in some way create social categories from the observable differences between men and women (Ortner and Whitehead, 1981b: 6–7). One of the widespread features of gender ideologies is that the distinction between what is male and what is female is also used to structure other cultural contrasts (I showed how this works for the Endo in Chapter 7). Through such a process maleness may become associated with a series of things like "big," "up," "sky," "right"; while femaleness is associated with their opposite, "small," "down," "earth," "left." Such associations are, of course, culture-specific, but within their specific context they form a system of meanings which is acquired by individuals on both a conscious and an unconscious level. Men and women who share the same culture will share the same categories, but their position *vis-à-vis* those categories varies according to their sex. The individual is always a sexed individual and thus has a place in this system of categories, a pregiven "femaleness" or "maleness" to refer to. The individual is constructed and constructs herself/himself in relation to the cultural representations of what is male and what is female. To be so constructed is not merely to refer to some "free-floating" femininity or masculinity, but also to be inserted into a matrix of social meanings, and thereby into a mode of cultural discourse (see the argument about language above). Men and women are inserted into this matrix of meaning, this symbolic order, in different ways, because they take up different positions within it.

The socially dominant representations of women (and, of course, of men) play a crucial part in the location of the individual within the cultural system, not only on a symbolic, but also on a social, level. If this is so, then to posit the existence of an autonomous female model would be to imply that women have a way of representing themselves which exists outside the dominant (male) culture. In other words, to say that an autonomous female model exists is to imply that women have access to a different form of representation; whereas I would argue that it is not that women have access to a particular *form* of representation, but rather that they have a particular *relation* to cultural representation and discourse. When women articulate their own viewpoint, they are not providing an alternative model, reaffirming the position they occupy outside the male model. On the contrary, they are precisely attempting to locate themselves within culture, to recognize themselves in the contradictory representations which confront them. Women's models cannot be understood as independent of the dominant culture, for there is no neutral realm to which women could refer. Women cannot construct models of themselves outside that realm of socially constructed meanings and practices which is culture; nor can they articulate or represent their position without using the cultural categories and constructions within which such articulations and representations find meaning and structure. In contemporary anthropology, studies which focus on women and on the woman's point of view assume that such a focus is a method of correcting male bias. In other words, it is thought that what women have to say about themselves is more "real," of greater veracity, than what men say about them. It is only possible to hold this position if it is assumed that women are somehow outside or separate from the dominant model, running contrary to the dominant mode of cultural discourse. The point, however, is that women are just as enmeshed as men in the dominant structures of meaning and practice and I would argue that what women say about themselves is no more "real" than what men say about them. The female point of view is the way in which women represent for themselves their gender, their sexuality, and the social and symbolic relations in which they as gendered individuals are involved. Their representations are different from those of men, and they are normally less demeaning and less alienating than the pictures men present, but they are equally ideological and certainly no more "real." The way women represent themselves, and their lives, to themselves does not necessarily have anything "truer" to say about the real nature of sexual, social, and productive relations than what men have to say. Nevertheless, there is no denying that men and women do have different points of view and that in most societies, as among the Endo, the male view is predominant.

If the male view of the world constitutes the dominant model, then what has to be explained is how and why that dominance is maintained. This is, of course, what Ardener attempts to do by examining the theory of mutedness. He explains dominance in terms of a group's ability to generate modes of expression which silence alternative modes. Such domination does not necessarily involve (although it may in some circumstances) physical coercion of any kind, but is the product of a particular homology between the structures of language and the social structures of domination within a society. I have already discussed how the structures of language *are* the structures of power in Endo society and how that identity operates on both a symbolic and a material level to position women and men differentially within social discourse and social relations. The theory of "mutedness" is, in itself, useful and powerful, but I would want to take issue with what I take to be Ardener's rather static notion of the dominant model. To say that dominant groups retain their dominant position by suppressing (muting) alternative viewpoints is a beginning, but the real problem still remains: "How is this suppression achieved?" In the case of the Endo, I would argue that it is achieved by making the cultural constructions of gender, and the relations between the sexes appear inevitable and natural. This process of naturalization accounts for the ideological nature of gender relations and concepts, and is necessary precisely because male dominance is not a natural state, but an arbitrary imposition. The social and ideological dominance of men is not something which is given, but something which has to be constantly renegotiated and recreated. Ardener's notion of the dominant model would imply that male dominance exists and merely has to suppress challenge in order to be maintained; whereas I would argue that it is not enough to suggest that male dominance exists because the structures of society and the structures of language are male dominated. What has to be accounted for is how those structures are constantly created, and recreated, in the "male" idiom, how individuals' perceptions of the world, of self, and of social relations are shaped within particular sets of social and symbolic relations. It is too often assumed in anthropology that the male model exists as an ideological formation which, although it can be shown to misrepresent social and productive relations, is nevertheless rarely challenged directly. This encourages the idea that such models (and, by implication, male dominance itself) are essentially monolithic and homogeneous. There is no denying the strength of dominant models, or the almost unassailable ubiquity which historical tradition gives them; but the real power of a dominant model is in its ability constantly to produce and reproduce itself, continually to impose the principles of the construction of reality. The ideological work of a dominant model is to make the arbitrary basis of its domination appear natural, to construct a "common sense" world where the unthinking individualism of women and the social prerogatives of men are not just natural, but inevitable. The power to impose the principles of the construction of reality is, therefore, a major dimension of material power (Bourdieu, 1977: 165), but such power must be made to appear both legitimate and natural. In situations where subordinate groups are not directly censured or controlled, dominant groups must "win" consent for their view of the world: must make it seem "natural," beyond particular interests, in aid of the social good (Hall, 1978). The dominant model is not a static phenomenon, but a complex and continual process of renegotiation and recreation. The ability of the dominant model to reproduce itself is its ability to retain control over the principles of the construction of reality, to frame all competing constructions within its own definitions, to maintain and control the socially dominant representations.

In the following sections I shall discuss the position of Endo women and how what women say and do contravenes both the socially dominant representations of women and the ideology of complete male dominance and control. I shall also discuss how women represent themselves and how these representations are subsumed by the male order, which uses the cultural construction of gender and the socially dominant representations of men and women to renegotiate the asymmetrical power relations between the sexes.

THE FEMALE PERSPECTIVE

To come with a well-formed mind is to come with an inability of ad-
ministering to the vanity of others, which a sensible person should always
wish to avoid. A woman, especially, if she has the misfortune of knowing
anything should conceal it as well as she can.

—JANE AUSTEN, *Persuasion*

Endo women often take a particular delight in concealing things from men, and such "deceptions" are almost always an uneasy mixture of appeasement and challenge. The women view these responses as alternative types of strategy and speak openly of getting their own way by using a mixture of both. The woman who claimed, in the presence of her husband, that the family herd was a single unit and then carefully explained to me, in private, which animals were hers and why, was pursuing such a strategy. As far as she was concerned, she was not just acquiescing in male superiority, but was sensibly keeping quiet in a situation where it would not have been advantageous to push her claims. Much in male–female relations is actually about the way in which men's rights are constrained by women's claims. The images which men portray of women either ignore the whole issue of women's claims or depict them as illegitimate and/or disruptive. For example, the constant reiteration of the childlike qualities of women denies them the rights (claims) of adult status, and complaints about the irritating nature of domestic upheaval relegates women's protest (the furtherance of their claims) to the realm of selfish and unnecessary disruption.

I have already discussed in Chapter 4 how men's ownership/disposal rights over land and stock are circumscribed by the usufruct/consumption rights which women acquire in their husband's property when they marry. Women's use rights in their husband's resources are institutionalized, insofar as they are openly acknowledged, but the actual amount of land and stock a woman receives varies and is completely dependent on what her husband and her husband's family decide to make available. It is a feature of the difference between men and women's "rights" that men have rights, while women have to negotiate and make claims. This does not mean that men's rights are never in dispute; for example, fathers and sons are often in conflict over questions of inheritance, but the nature of male property-owning rights is unassailable and very different from the negotiable and potentially somewhat problematic claims which women are able to make. In spite of this, it must not be imagined that women's claims are insubstantial, for as I shall show this is not the case. The problem women face is that they have to pursue and defend their claims, and they acquire little without work and/or negotiation. This is in marked contrast to men, who often acquire much of what is theirs through patrimonial right. A woman's interests are most frequently pursued by making claims on her husband and on his property. Every woman apparently acts very much as an individual in negotiations with her husband: help from her natal lineage is unlikely to be forthcoming unless the marriage is in danger of complete collapse; and although an older woman can expect some help from her sons, this will depend upon their interests in the matter (see below). The image of the individual woman alone against the weight of male authority, is a "male" perception of the situation, inasmuch as it stresses the woman's lack of a wider, social network of support and obligation. It is also, however, very much the crux of the matter as far as women are concerned. It is clear that women are often frustrated – particularly when they are younger – by the lack of help they can expect from their natal kin in any dispute, and many women experience a sense of isolation in their dealings with their husband and their husband's lineage. Women combat this sense of isolation by combining to support each other. The form which such support takes is very varied, but a large part of it consists not of practical action *per se*, but of affirming and reinforcing female identity, sexuality, and solidarity.

The single most important and overt way in which women come together as a group, and actually reflect on their position as women, is in the women's initiation rite. Women's initiation is held almost every year in different villages (*kor*) and involves all the women of the community, and sometimes other female relatives from the surrounding area. The initiation rites are very extended and complex, and take place over two to three months. The main stages are the public circumcision ceremony (*chebyogone*; see Plate XXVI), the

PLATE XXVI. *Chebyogone*. This ceremony takes place at dawn and is part of the first stage of the initiation rites. It is a testing time for the girls, who must demonstrate their courage before the whole community.

period of seclusion, and the coming-out ceremony (*kibuno*; see Plate XXVII). Each stage has a number of special songs, dances, observances, and traditions associated with it, and many of the activities are carried out using a "secret" language which successive generations learn during their time in seclusion. The meanings of many words and gestures are obscure and are only known to the older women (those who have at least one circumcised granddaughter). The ritual knowledge of the seclusion house is, like the social knowledge of men, cumulative, and as a woman becomes older she gradually learns the complex meanings associated with the most secret parts of the rite. What follows is not intended to be a description or an analysis of female circumcision among the Endo. Instead, I want to focus on the ways in which the female point of view is expressed during the initiation rites, and on how this illustrates the socioeconomic status of women and the ambivalent nature of gender relations. It is during the initiation rites that women's representations of themselves and of their position in Endo society are most forcefully and completely expressed. It is thus possible to use women's initiation as a starting point for a discussion of the "female perspective."

Sexuality[6]

Woven into the fabric of the initiation rites and into the lengthy instruction which the initiates (*chemeri*) undergo is a series of themes which revolve around subordination and power, authority, and challenge. These themes are present in an overt fashion in the constant admonition and ridicule of initiates, the beatings they suffer in *kapkore,* the successive reiteration of the obedience which is owed to husbands and fathers, the revelation of past mistakes and arrogances, in the rigorous training, and, of course, in the nature of the clitoridectomy operation itself They also emerge in less obvious ways, because much of the teaching in *kapkore* is actually about the power of female sexuality, the difficulties of being a wife, the strength of women as a group, and the respect which is owed to older women and to female knowledge in general. The most important feature of a woman's initiation is that it legitimizes her right to have children. It is through initiation that a girl is granted full social and sexual status. Since mature social status is dependent upon marriage and motherhood, and because sexual maturity is understood as the social recognition of a woman's procreative powers, it is not hard to grasp the inseparable nature of a woman's sexual and social status. The perceived relationship between

---

[6] This discussion is based on four initiation ceremonies I attended in Endo and two I attended in Mokorro. I have also spent a considerable time inside *kapkore.* Elizabeth Meyerhoff's analysis of the Pokot ritual was an inspiration, and her material on the Pokot appears very similar to the data I collected on the Marakwet (see Meyerhoff, 1982).

PLATE XXVII. *Kibuno:* The release from seclusion. The dance of *kibuno* is the final stage of the initiation rites and is a time for celebration and rejoicing. The young men and women are decorated with ornaments belonging to their female kin.

the social and the sexual is what enables women to link the power of their sexuality with their ability to further their claims and those of their children. As a woman gets older much of her social status is related to her authority within the family, an authority which is directly dependent upon the resources (stock and land) she commands and on the influence she is able to exert over her sons (and, to a lesser degree, her daughters-in-law). A woman only acquires stock, land, and children through marriage, and it appears that many women feel that such things are bought or perhaps won with their sexuality. During the initiation rites women express a positive pride in their sexuality and thus in their womanhood, which is itself expressed as a pride in their membership of a women's group, defined in contradistinction to men and men's groups.

It is in the teaching which takes place during seclusion that the theme of sexuality is most often expressed. Initiates (*chemeri*) are not exactly taught how to use their sexuality strategically, but this comes across in what the older women do and say. The seclusion period is divided into a number of smaller periods by the performance of a series of rites (*kiborusco, tang'at, kimaget, en*) which mark the progress of the girls through their instruction and seclusion. As each rite is completed some of the restrictions of the seclusion house are lifted; for example, after *kiborusco* the girls can eat with their hands and can sit outside the house during the day. During *kiborusco* and *tang'at* the women who have gone to *kapkore* to train the initiates stand outside the seclusion house and shout abuse at men. The open expression of things which should never be said in public is an important part of the ritual.[7] This abuse takes varied forms and is sometimes couched in a language so "metaphorical" that few women know the meaning of the phrases. Whether the meaning of the phrases is clear or not, they are all obscene, and the women greatly enjoy shouting them out. There are quite a number of these phrases, but most either mention the size and other characteristics of the male organ or else ridicule men for their sexual desire and consequent dependence on women, and sometimes for their inability to give women sexual satisfaction. Such phrases are shouted out whether there are any men in sight or not, but if a man does pass close to *kapkore* then the women accompany their shouts with gestures; such gestures are always explicitly about the arousal of male desire and the actions of sexual intercourse. Men sometimes gesture back, and this only makes the women laugh harder!

Inside *kapkore* the initiates receive much of their instruction during the evening, and sometimes they dance and sing late into the night. The girls are not taught sexual techniques, but the relationship between sexuality, power and men is implicit in much of what is said and done inside the seclusion house. This part of the teaching prepares the girls for marriage and their role as wives, and consequently the teaching itself often reflects the very ambiguous and negotiable nature of gender relations. Both the socially dominant male perspective and the somewhat different female point of view are presented to the girls, and this is one of the reasons why the teaching frequently appears contradictory and confusing, not only to the anthropologist, but also to the initiates themselves. For example, the girls are constantly reminded to be faithful and obedient to their husbands while, at the same time, they are enjoined not to agree too quickly to have sexual intercourse on their marriage night. This reinforces the authority of the husband on the one hand and, on the other, makes an explicit link between sexuality and female power, since a girl knows that she will receive stock for consenting to sexual intercourse. On the whole, women view all the stock they are promised during the early stages of marriage as a kind of reward/payment for their sexual favors and procreative functions. However, it would be unusual to hear a young woman make an explicit statement of this kind; it seems such perspicacity comes with experience. A young wife would be much more likely to say: "If my husband loves me, then he will give me . . . [something]." However it is expressed, women are only too well aware that they can use their sex-

---

[7] Reversal of status and sex roles is often a feature of ritual contexts (see, e.g., Gluckman, 1954; 4–11; Turner, 1969: 183–5).

uality as a bargaining power. The fulcrum of power which this gives them, the point which it opens up for negotiation within the totality of male authority and control, is what is expressed in the obscene phrases which the women shout and in the instruction they give their "daughters" in the seclusion house. Women can, of course, use their sexuality in very direct ways. For example, a woman can refuse to sleep with her husband in an effort to influence him or as a way of expressing disapproval for some action taken or intended. Gossip is an equally effective strategy, and a woman may imply certain things about her husband in order to pressurize him. Women take an enormous pride in their sexuality because they see it as something which they have and men desire but cannot take away from them. Their sexuality literally gives them a bargaining point. The female control of sexuality must, however, be seen in the context of the husband's authorized control of his wife's person, including her sexual and procreative activities. In *kapkore,* the balance between male control and female power is expressed in an indirect, rather than a direct, form. Apart from particular dances, songs and ritualized sign systems, the teaching of *kapkore* is not particularly formalized. Women draw on their own experience and on their knowledge of the life histories of the individual initiates in order to make more general points. Thus, initiates learn of the ambivalent nature of the woman's position not through formal instruction, but through the way in which that position is dramatized in the exchanges which take place between other women. During the rituals in *kapkore* a considerable amount of beer is inevitably consumed. The social consumption of beer is an important statement about the social solidarity of women as a group and is, therefore, an integral part of the proceedings. However, the maize beer (*mayek*) is extremely strong and considerably enhances the excitement and emotion of these occasions. Women may break down and weep in remembering the difficulties of their own lives, and in moments of reflection and introspection the older women say things which would never normally be articulated. Since these narratives are about life experiences, they provide valuable instruction for initiates, who are also able to hear other women contradicting and reinterpreting the narrator's account. It would be misleading to suggest that these narrations are lengthy or complete. Rather, situations arise where one woman may be chastising an initiate in order to make a point, perhaps about the necessity of obeying her future husband, when a second woman will begin a story or make a remark about an occasion when the first woman disobeyed her husband, or took a lover, or refused to cook for her family. The women constantly test the initiates and give them advice by asking rhetorical questions which make a practical or moral point. At moments of heightened excitement women often contradict each other, give conflicting advice, and question the validity of behavioral norms. The result is a dramaturgical performance of bewildering complexity, where the possible courses of action, the socially approved behavior, and the alternative female perspective are all displayed, almost simultaneously, to the initiates. The effect of many such performances is to stress that although the female perspective is different from the socially approved male point of view, it is nonetheless of equal status and validity. At the same time, the juxtaposition of male and female perspectives, and the general confusion of competing claims, provides a realistic representation of the position of women in Endo society and of the negotiable, ambiguous nature of relations between the sexes.

The only other occasion, besides initiation, when female sexuality and solidarity are expressed overtly and publicly, is when women club together to chastise a man who has been mistreating his wife. Here is a description of such an event, provided by a male informant:

> If a man beat his wife badly, she may call together other women to abuse the man as a warning. Women tie the hands and legs of the man and beat him. Then the man cries out, "Leave me alone, I'll give you a goat – I'll give you two goats," until the women agree. Then the man goes and gives the women one or two he-goats, whatever the man agreed. Then the women slaughter the goats and divide between them.

Accounts from women informants suggest that the man is often quite severely beaten and that the women are verbally, as well as physically, abusive. Verbal taunts ridicule the man's sexual prowess and speak plainly of the mistreatment his wife has suffered. Women may also expose their genitals, which under normal circumstances is completely taboo and is considered to be an appropriately shocking reversal of normal standards of behavior. I have not witnessed an event of this kind, which Edgerton and Conant (1964) describe as a "shaming party." Their data from the Pokot suggest that such practices are not unusual, but both men and women among the Endo were reluctant talkers on the subject, and no woman actually admitted to having taken part in such an event. I cannot tell how common this practice is among the Endo, but it is certainly recognized, by men and women, as a legitimate way for a woman to express a particularly strong dissatisfaction with her husband. The binding and beating of a worthless or tyrannous husband is obviously a statement of female power and solidarity. The exposure of the female genitalia links that power to female sexuality. The fact that women claim stock as compensation is also significant. Animals represent a "male" wealth which is intimately associated with male prestige, and a man undoubtedly feels that he has "paid the price" in more than one way when he is forced to relinquish some of his herd. The only other occasions on which women may demand stock are related to marriage, the granting of sexual favors, and circumcision. Thus the demand for stock is linked to the more general exercise of "female power" through the manipulation of female sexuality.

Childbirth

The one point on which all women are in furious secret rebellion against
the existing law is the saddling of the right to a child with the obligation
to become the servant of a man.
                    −G. B. SHAW, *Getting Married,* 1908

The power of female sexuality is not unrelated to women's procreative abilities (see above). Since the Endo say that initiation legitimizes a woman's right
to have children, it is unsurprising that the initiation rites should contain a
number of implicit and explicit references to childbirth. It is acknowledged
that conception involves both men and women; but the physiological basis
of this involvement is more explicit in the case of men than it is in that of
women. The importance of the male's sperm is clearly recognized, since the
Endo practice *coitus interruptus* as a method of birth control. For women,
however, conception has a less obvious physiological basis and is associated
with a moment of heightened sexual pleasure, which is somehow linked to
the power of female sexuality. The relationship between conception and female power may be interpreted in a number of ways. In a straightforward
sense, conception merely demonstrates the natural fecundity of women, and
thus supports the male view that the social value of women is derived from
their "natural" role as mothers. However, it could also be said that conception is related to female power because men depend on women for the production of children and, what is more, if those children are sons they may work
with their mother to further her interests and theirs at the expense of their
father. The fact that men need women to produce children is made quite explicit at various stages in the initiation rite, particularly during *kiborusco* and
tang'at, when the women hurl abuse at the men. Women are fully aware of
their desirability as childbearers, and they use the training period in *kapkore*
to celebrate that power and the power of their sexuality. Inside the seclusion
house the initiates are repeatedly told that they must prepare themselves for
motherhood, and references are often made to their future lives as wives and
mothers. These references are sometimes contained in the texts of songs: "You
will not sing the songs of dawn (*chebyogone*) as you walk to the fields"; "When
you are feeding your child you will not sing the songs of *kapkore.*" Many
of the girls will marry as soon as they are released from seclusion, and these
repeated refrains have particular force and meaning (Plate XXVIII). There are
also many occasions on which the value of women as mothers is emphasized. For example, during *kibuno,* when female relatives anoint the heads of
the girls with oil, they praise the clan of the girl's mother and sing of the
importance of women as mothers.

Women say that initiation is a preparation for childbirth and it is quite
common to hear women comparing the pain of childbirth with that of

PLATE XXVIII. A young couple. Men and women may not marry before initiation, but after the release from seclusion many young people make preparations to set up a household together. Some couples are pledged to each other before initiation, while some meet at the *kibuno* ceremony itself.

clitoridectomy. Both childbirth and initiation are considered to be women's concerns from which men are rigorously excluded, and there are strong similarities between the two experiences. First, there is the shared experience of pain and the fact that both events involve the cutting of women: during childbirth most women have episiotomies, and these are performed by traditional, female midwives. After childbirth a woman is secluded for three to four weeks and is considered to be polluted in similar ways to the initiates in seclusion. Immediately after the birth she is not allowed to eat with her hands, or speak loudly, or move outside the "bed area" of the house during the day. Initiates suffer similar restrictions; they are not allowed to eat with their hands until after kiborusco, they must speak in whispers, and for about the first two weeks of seclusion they must sit quietly in the "bed area" of the house during daylight hours. Both men and women among the Marakwet draw parallels between initiation and childbirth. Women perceive the emotional and physical similarities between the experiences, and see each as a time when the importance of female sexuality and female knowledge is celebrated in seclusion from men. Men, on the other hand, would appear to have a different perspective. The similarities between childbirth and initiation are not restricted to the female rites. Men frequently draw direct parallels between the restrictions imposed on a woman after childbirth and the restrictions imposed on the boys in *kaptorus* (boys' seclusion house). Boys are considered polluted while in seclusion, and, although the men greatly enjoy going to *kaptorus* to train the initiates and to dance, there is a sense of vulnerability and perhaps portent while seclusion is still in force. The parallels between male initiation and childbirth focus on the unclean state of the boys who are not yet men, and thus on the polluting and possibly threatening qualities of childbirth. Women regard childbirth as something positive, while men regard it as something weak, as a quality which defines femaleness; and, although they rejoice in the successful birth of children, they are uneasy about childbirth in general and about the state of male initiates who temporarily partake of these female qualities. However, women are not, on the whole, considered polluting, and the Endo do not have strong taboos associated with menstruation, sex, or food.

A menstruating woman is not allowed to cook and must not move around the house unduly, but she is not prevented from working or from attending ceremonies. Endo men do not believe that menstrual blood is harmful or that women are unclean, but there are a number of restrictions which suggest that men are wary of aspects of female sexuality. A woman may not step over a man or climb onto the roof of a house; both these restrictions are said to be related to a fear of being below or underneath female genitalia, and this might imply a fear of menstrual blood. In Sibou, adult men and children may wash in the irrigation channels, but sexually mature girls and women may not.

Irrigation is an exclusively male concern and is strongly associated with clan affiliation and social responsibility. The men of Sibou curse the women on pain of death not to wash in the channels, for they say that should a woman do so the water will dry up. On the whole, men seem to view childbirth as an exclusively female domain which is governed by a "female" knowledge to which they have no access. (Men are not allowed to witness births, and it is said that in the past a man could not see his newborn child until it was a month old.) Childbirth, menstruation, and initiation all signify aspects of female sexuality, over which men have no control; this is underlined by the fact that men are dependent on women as the bearers of children. Women, on the other hand, see initiation and childbirth as experiences which celebrate female sexuality, a perception which is not unrelated to the way women are able to use their sexual and reproductive powers to further their interests.

Aspects of Female Solidarity and Control

Men acknowledge that women have a great deal of influence over their children, but the role of women as socializers is very much underplayed in Endo society (Plate XXIX). This is partly because "women are like children, they know nothing," and partly because of the favored emphasis on male traditions and the continuity of male knowledge and male kin. I have already suggested that, from the male point of view, women are less permanent and

PLATE XXIX. A mother with her sons. The celebration of links with maternal kin is an important part of male initiation rites, and mothers take great pride in their sons at this time.

less social beings than men. It is in the female initiation rites that women contradict this image and find strength in their communal identity. The emphasis on secrecy is very strong and is an everpresent theme. The initiates are repeatedly warned not to reveal any of the secrets of *kapkore;* the older women say that if a girl reveals such secrets she will grow thin and die. The women make much play of the fact that men are always supposed to be trying to find out what goes on in the seclusion house, and part of the abuse that the women shout contains such lines as, "He has gone to a high place to try and see what we are doing, but he cannot see." Such taunts have a particular relish and cause a considerable amount of hilarity. Initiation provides women with a body of ritual and practical knowledge which is distinct from male knowledge, and from which men are excluded. The women regard their knowledge as a traditional knowledge, and there are repeated references to the fact that the girls are experiencing something which their mothers and grandmothers experienced in the same way. The girls are also told that what they learn in *kapkore* is a "knowledge of the grandmothers." Tradition and continuity are clearly and repeatedly expressed throughout the whole seclusion period.

Access to knowledge is guarded by the old women, who are often respected for their knowledge and authority within the community as a whole, but who also play a particularly significant role in initiation. The most secret parts of the rite are only revealed to old women by other old women, and much of what the initiates are taught does not become clear to them until they themselves are old. The older women use their knowledge to exercise power and control over the initiates and over the younger women. This reinforces a hierarchy based on age which gives the older women status both with other women and within the community as a whole. The control of the young by the old is the basis for the solidarity and tradition which the women associate with themselves as a group. In a patrilineal, patrilocal society like the Marakwet, the networks of support and obligation are based on residence and descent and are thus male networks. Given the rules of exogamy, women are excluded from these networks and are in a position of potential isolation. But it is through the initiation rites that women incorporate new wives into the life of the community and establish themselves as a group with a communal knowledge and communal interests. Women challenge the accepted male view of their individualism and isolation by asserting their solidarity as a group. They also challenge the notion of female impermanence by establishing ritual links between successive generations of women and by asserting the value of traditional female knowledge. The bond which is established between women during initiation provides them with their own networks of support and obligation, which are separate from those of men. On a day-to-day basis women express their support for each other by sharing child care and by undertaking communal agricultural labor. Thus, the links which are established in the seclusion house have important socioeconomic consequences.

Endo society is a patriarchal society, where men own all the property and make all the decisions, and where the dominant social values are all defined by "masculine" characteristics. This dominant male view is structurally supported by laws (e.g., women owe obedience to their husbands; women cannot inherit land), traditions (e.g., the permanence of the patrilineage *vis-à-vis* the impermanence of women) and ritual requirements (e.g., men are responsible for the ritual and moral well-being of the whole community). I have shown that the social ideal of complete male dominance and control is only half the story. Women may owe obedience to their husbands, but men are very dependent upon their wives in certain crucial ways; and a woman can bring a number of sanctions to bear (refusing to cook, withholding of sexual favors, encouragement of gossip) if she disapproves of her husband's behavior or dislikes his decisions. Women may not be able to inherit land, but they have substantial and well-institutionalized use rights in a proportion of their husband's property. From the discussion of the women's initiation rites it should be clear that women possess a considerable body of ritual and practical knowledge which is not known to men, and which provides society with its future wives and mothers. The image which women portray of themselves is a positive one which takes pride in female sexuality and in the fact of being a woman. Women emphasize the positive aspects of motherhood and childbirth, and motherhood is seen as something which gives women both power and social responsibility. The initiation rites belie the male notion of the impermanence of women and their observances, and women see themselves as part of a social group which has both continuity and tradition. In other words, what women have to say about themselves, and the way they portray themselves, their lives and their responsibilities, is apparently in fairly direct conflict with the socially dominant representations of women.

THE RENEGOTIATION OF REPRESENTATION

If a coherent and powerful female perspective exists, why does it not have more impact on social values? Why does it not challenge the socially dominant representations of women? To put it another way: Why do the men always win out? The answers to these questions are complex and difficult to unravel, but their complexity is perhaps understandable when it is acknowledged that, whatever the answers are, they are to be sought not at the level of models, but at the level of practice. To ask why the female perspective has so little impact is to begin again with the notion of autonomous male and female models: to imagine that one could replace the other. The first point to be made in reply is that the female perspective does not constitute an alternative model, but is an attempt by women to identify and value themselves as women within the cultural structures which confront them. The second point is that the so-called male model is not a static and definitive structure, but an ideology which is inconsistent, incomplete, and nothing like as systematic as its self-presentations would suggest. These two points are not unrelated, because if the articulation of a female perspective is an attempt at location, rather than subversion, then the male order can continue to contain the female "alternative" through a process of renegotiation rather than overt domination. It should be said, however, that this renegotiation is an asymmetrical process through which the socially dominant becomes the socially acceptable.

Both men and women have to learn to locate themselves in culture, but for men this process is less ambiguous and less contradictory than it is for women. A male individual can identify himself with dominant social values and representations, and essentially there is no contradiction between what is socially valued and his own value as a social individual. For women the situation is more complex. Women cannot recognize their own value as individuals in the dominant representations of what it is that society values. Men have to learn to aspire toward what is socially valued and to recognize the desirability of those values. Women, on the other hand, have to learn the desirability and "naturalness" of social values, but they also have to learn that they do not have these desirable qualities and should not aspire to them. I would suggest that this is the root cause of women's contradictory position in Endo society – a contradiction which cannot be resolved merely by discovering and articulating an alternative "female" world which ignores the predominantly male values of the community.

The female point of view does not banish the contradictory nature of women's position, because it does not deconstruct the socially dominant representations of men and women. Culturally dominant representations acquire their status precisely because they are widely and consistently believed in, and because in spite of contradictions, they retain the ability to remain highly effective in providing people with explanations and definitions of themselves and others. Women are not "free" from the images society provides for them; they are socialized, just as forcibly as men, into accepting social norms and values. When women construct representations of themselves, they do so using the material which the socially dominant representations of women provide. It often appears that in constructing self-presentations women contradict the socially accepted view; for example, men see women as individualistic, while women present themselves as part of a social group with a tradition. It is this sort of opposition that is sometimes mistakenly assumed to indicate the existence of alternative models; whereas I would suggest that when women provide representations of themselves they are attempting both to value themselves within the dominant social frame as it exists and to participate in that dominant frame, and thereby to appropriate some of its dominant quality. This accounts for the fact that many actions and assertions can be interpreted as supporting an alternative female model on the one hand, and as reinforcing the dominant male structures on the other. A good example of this is the teaching in *kapkore,* which can either be interpreted as constructing and reinforcing female values, or be seen as a structural mechanism through which older women socialize younger women into accepting their rightful positions within the patriarchal order. These alternative interpretations arise precisely because women's representations are an attempt to locate and value themselves within the dominant social frame. In this sense, the female perspective is not at all autonomous from the accepted male view, and it is no accident that as a woman gets older she may acquire a certain degree of control and influence which signals her successful investment in the material and symbolic good of the dominant order. The fact that women may end up supporting the dominant male order in their efforts to value themselves within it does not imply that women's interests are ultimately identical with those of men, or that women want to become men. On the contrary, women recognize the conflict of interests between themselves and men, but are trying to identify themselves as valuable, social individuals. The continuing dominance of the male order, and the appropriation of apparently male values or interests by women, are the result of the powerful and reinforced homology between what is socially valuable and what is male. This brings the argument back to the problem of the male "model" itself.

The strength of the dominant male order resides in its ability to contain the contradictions which arise between the different male and female viewpoints. However, these contradictions are contained not through suppression, but through renegotiation. The socially dominant representations of men and women are often in conflict with the experiences of lived reality and, in particular, with the actuality of negotiations between husband and wife. Contradictions exist within the male "model" itself, and further contradictions are engendered by the "lack of fit" which consistently emerges between the social ideal and the social reality. The potential for conflict and contradiction is thus inherent in the male "model" itself, and is not just the product of a confrontation between male and female "models." The problem for any dominant ideology is one not of bringing the recalcitrant into line, but of constantly having to recreate and redefine the ideology itself. While the outlines of the dominant ideology are relatively stable and firm, there are also many absences and omissions. Thus, the solutions to specific problems are not pregiven: in a sense, not every eventuality is catered for. Solutions do not emerge automatically, but have to be negotiated and renegotiated. The socially dominant representations constitute the framework within which the negotiation proceeds, and it is the ability to negotiate that is the source of the ideology's effectiveness. However, such negotiation is not an exchange between equals, because, as I have said, it only proceeds within the framework of the socially dominant representations. Thus, it is the element of negotiability, the way in which the dominant ideology is only worked out in a "broad" perspective, rather than in minute detail, that allows it to contain contradictions and conflicts, and so to contain the vagaries of lived reality.

If ideology is in essence negotiable, then how does it prevent its own deconstruction? In other words, how do dominant groups make sure that they always win the negotiations? The answer to these questions lies in the nature of socially dominant representations. These often appear very stark and simplistic: A good example from Western culture might be the notion of the "wicked stepmother." However, this simplicity conceals a range of enormous flexibility and power. As I said earlier, dominant representations appear to say nothing and yet say everything. The enormous range of their applicability is, in fact, a direct consequence of their simplicity. It is the same simplicity that guarantees that they are never fully contradicted by lived experience. Dominant representations are constructed on the basis of socially and structurally dominant values, which are in turn produced and reproduced through the same set of dominant representations. There is, therefore, no "neutral" ground to which lived experience could refer, and from which it could deconstruct those representations which produce it and which it subsequently reproduces.

SPACE AND REPRESENTATION

At the beginning of this chapter, I posed a series of questions concerning women and the organization of space: For example, to what extent would it make sense to claim that women are invisible in the organization of space, and to what extent is space the product of a dominant male orientation in the world? In addition, I asked whether Endo women could be said to have an alternative model of the world and, if so, whether they wished to express it. These were the questions suggested by an initial investigation of the notion that women, as a subdominant group, have an alternative "model" of the world but are prevented from expressing it by the dominant male structures of society. Although the terms of the debate have now been altered slightly by the preceding discussion, aspects of these questions are still relevant. The traditional organization of space among the Endo works over a series of themes which are associated with the positive valuations given to masculine qualities and the correspondingly negative valuations given to female characteristics. The male–female distinction provides a way of thinking about the world and of assigning social value. The spatial organization of burial, refuse, and houses appeals to the structural hierarchy implicit in the male–female distinction, and is readily comprehensible in terms of the socially dominant representations of men and women. For example, the traditional segregation of ash and animal dung makes a fairly direct appeal to the distinction between what is social and what is individual, a distinction which recurs in the way relations between spouses and the relations between clan and household are represented. However, the elements which make up the spatial frame (ash, chaff, etc.) do not have fixed meanings, but can be used to represent a number of different concepts, in a variety of contexts. Ash, for example, has a large number of both positive and negative connotations and can be linked in one context to women and in another to men. Meaning does not adhere in the spatial frame, but must be invoked through action; thus, the meaning associated with ash is not inherent in the substance itself, but is given in the context of practice or use. This negotiability of meaning is what permits the expression of the female perspective within the spatial medium. In one context, ash may be associated with the positive power of female sexuality, and thus involved in the presentation of an alternative female perspective; while in another context it may be linked with the power and tradition of the patriclan, and thus support the representation of the dominant male structures. In short, space is a flexible medium of representation and communication, and elements may be used, in various contexts, to present both male and female points of view. In this sense, it could be argued that the question of whether women are visible or invisible in the organization of space is irrelevant. It would only be necessary to ask such a question if there were autonomous female models, and if the meaning of the spatial order were fixed and invariant. Under such circumstances it might be possible for a female model to exist and not be represented spatially.

Unfortunately, the problem of female invisibility cannot be dismissed so lightly, for it exists, though on quite another level. I have said that the meanings given to the organization of space are not fixed and immutable, but may be differentially invoked in varying contexts. However, this does not mean that the organization of space is open to an indefinite number of interpretations. Although the number of interpretations might in theory be indefinite, nevertheless in practice it is limited. Actual individuals provide interpretations of space by using physical elements of the spatial order in a particular way or in a particular sequence. These interpretations may be strategic–that is, consciously or subconsciously designed to achieve particular ends–and this is why the contextual meanings given to particular spatial elements can be used in the representation of both male and female perspectives. However, the strategic interpretations, and the contextual invocation of meaning on which they depend, are not random. All interpretations have a past and a future, and can only be constructed in relation to the already-existing spatial text. In other words, every interpretation is constrained, to some degree, by the existing order of space, which is no more than the sum of past and future interpretations of that space. As a result, interpretation is not value free, but is itself an ideological act which, because it takes place within a given set of historical relations, ensures that some interpretations are more favored than others. These favored interpretations are those imposed by the dominant group, and any alternative interpretations tend to be contained within them. The ability to impose particular interpretations is a political power and for this reason dominant interpretations tend to be very strongly linked to dominant representations.

The link between dominant interpretations and dominant representations is not necessarily easy to grasp. The dominant interpretations of space are those which are most consistently made; hence the term "favored." These interpretations acquire a particular power through their constant repetition, and, as a result, tend to provide the framework within which alternative interpretations are made. The reason for this, as I have said, is that the range of possible interpretations is constrained by the already existing spatial order, which is, in one sense, the cumulative result of a series of preferred interpretations. Thus alternative interpretations do not radically interrogate the values which inform the dominant interpretations, because, as interpretations, they are attempts to convey a point of view which cannot exist outside the dominant values of society. Dominant interpretations, like dominant representations, are of a very general, and apparently simple, kind. They are not "worked out" in detail, but have a very wide-ranging relevance which permits a considerable amount of reinterpretation which does not in any way affect their general structure.

Dominant interpretations, like the socially dominant representations of men and women, embody the cultural values of Endo society. These values are constructed in terms of a "male" idiom which makes appeal to a structural hierarchy between what is male and what is female, and within this hierarchy value is assigned to what is male. In this sense, the dominant interpretations of space enabody the male-oriented values of Marakwet society in a condensed form. Through the action taken in space, individuals interpret that space in such a way as to produce a spatial representation – that is, an image or a point of view which is expressed through the use of the spatial medium. Spatial representations express, in a very condensed way, the asymmetrical hierarchy between what is male and what is female, because they are the product of dominant interpretations. As a result, spatial representations are informed by the same set of cultural values as inform the socially dominant representations of the sexes. However, given the fact that gender distinctions are used to order cultural values, spatial representations actually turn out to be expressing, albeit in their own logic, the socially dominant representations of men and women. Ultimately, spatial representations help to produce and reproduce the distinctions on which the cultural constructions of gender are based. In other words, spatial representations help to support gender ideologies.

The problem with gender ideologies is that they do not reflect the true nature of gender relations, and it follows from this that the dominant spatial representations do not reflect the true nature of gender relations either. The values which both produce and are produced by the spatial text are the dominant male values of Endo society, and the spatial text is thus involved in the production and reproduction of the dominant male ideology. Consequently, the organization of space "works" in favor of men; it helps to construct a representation of gender relations which presents male authority as natural and pregiven. In such a situation, women are invisible, sunk, contained within the "naturalized" domain of the dominant ideology.

CHAPTER 10

Text, Ideology, and Power

Two things of opposite natures seem to depend
On one another, as a man depends
On a woman, day on night, the imagined
On the real. This is the origin of change.
    – WALLACE STEVENS,
        Notes Towards a Supreme Fiction

There are, of course, many ways to read a text, and space is only one cultural text among many. To read a text is always to read it in relation to other texts. In the case of the Endo, these other texts range from circumcision songs, through cuisine, to personal adornment. The choice of space as an object of study is partly the result of its materiality and everyday relevance, and partly because it is the context in which all other cultural representations are produced, and reproduced. The various cultural productions of a society are not necessarily homogeneous; they contain contradictions, and frequently conflict with each other. These conflicts take the form of disputation – a disputation which is continuous, and which allows for competing claims, ambiguities and reinterpretations. This openness to reinterpretation is the origin of change.

The ideal of cultural representation as text requires some comment both about reading the text and about its production. A theory of reading would necessarily be concerned with reception and interpretation. This immediately raises the point that interpretation, which is a form of consumption, is not independent of production. Contemporary literary theory has been much occupied with the interdependence of reader and text, and the extent to which it is possible to claim that the reader actually "creates" the text (Fish, 1980; Eco, 1979; Suleiman and Crosman, 1980). The enduring value of these discussions has been the realization that it is not enough to discuss "the meaning" of a text without some consideration of who reads it, and how. The interdependence of meaning and interpretation, and the mutuality of exegesis and praxis, is particularly important with regard to the analysis of space.

I argued in Chapters 5 and 7 that the organization of domestic space is not a reflection of cultural codes and meanings, but must be understood as a context developed through practice. I based this argument on the assertion that meaning is not inherent in any spatial order, but must be invoked. The invocation of meaning is achieved through the practical activity of individual actors who utilize the existing organization of space to give particular meanings both to their actions and to the spatial order. The idea that meaning is context dependent provides an opportunity to analyze individuals' actions as strategic. Individuals may be both conscious and unconscious of the effects of their strategies, but what is clear is that they are not unaware of the meanings and values associated with the organization of space. The question of how conscious particular individuals are of culturally given meanings is a vexed one. I do not wish to suggest that, if asked, a Endo person would be able to provide a catalogue of all the meanings related to the organization of space; on the contrary, it is clear from my fieldwork that individuals are almost never in a position to provide such an exegesis. However, as Bourdieu points out, it is important not to confuse the lack of an intellectual synthesis with the lack of practical awareness (Bourdieu, 1977: 122–3). I think that Bourdieu is correct to emphasize the practical nature of social knowledge. It is not necessary for an individual to be analytically or discursively aware of social values for her/him to invoke or use those values strategically. This is not to argue for a return to the slavish following of cultural norms or rules, neither is it a reiteration of the overarching and opaque nature of cultural codes and meanings. It is merely to emphasize that a knowledge of cultural values can be both discursive and practical, and that such knowledge is implied in the knowledge of how to proceed, of how to participate in social situations and of how to manipulate such situations. To emphasize the strategic invocation of meaning, and the practical mastery of social schemes and values, provides a way of understanding how individuals are involved in the production and reproduction of social and symbolic practices, without excluding the possibility of social change and transformation. The possibility of social change is inherent in the strategic invocation and use of cultural values, or if one prefers in their interpretability.

To emphasize the creative and constitutive power of the reader, or in this case the actor, raises the problem that texts have a material existence independent of their readers. The meaning of the spatial text may be invoked through the practical and knowledgable activities of social actors but the fact remains that the organization of space has a physical form which endures in a recognizable fashion over certain periods of time. This form is, however, the product, at least in part, of past readings or interpretations. The spatial text is "read" through the activities which take place therein, and, as a result, its final form is the dual product of both its past and its present meanings: "of its past genesis and present functioning." Reading is always recreating the text but under conditions and consciousness inherited from the past–a past which is not just the historical past, but is also the immediate biographical and experiential past. The materiality of the spatial text suggests a solidity and rigidity which it does not in fact possess.

The acknowledged historicity of the spatial text emphasizes the importance of locating the text within a particular historical ensemble of social conditions and practices. In Chapter 7 I demonstrated that in order to understand why particular concerns become the subject of the spatial text it is necessary to investigate the social and economic conditions which give rise to them. Thus, I was able to link the opposition between ash and animal dung to a series of conflicts and tensions which arise between men and women concerning control of productive resources. In order to analyze the organization of space as a cultural representation which produces meanings, it is necessary to link those meanings to the natural conditions which give them authority and force. As a result, space may be understood as neither the reflection of cultural codes and meanings, nor the reflection of practical activities and functional requirements; it must instead be understood as the product of both. In Chapters 5 and 8 I argued that this dual determination of the organization of space means that there can be no fixed way to characterize the relationship between the spatial text and the ideology which informs it; nor is there necessarily any direct way to link the organization of space with the objective conditions of its existence.

In relation to Sibou sample Ia I argued that changes in the organization of space could not be directly related to changing social, economic, and gender relations. Often in studies concerned with social change, factors like wage-labor and the desire to emulate or follow fashionable trends are thought to be causally and self-evidently related to the changes observed. However, I suggest that the introduction of square houses is not a matter which can be unproblematically "read" off from the fact that emulation and information-exchange are recognized instigators of social change. It is undoubtedly true that the organization of domestic space is changing in response to wage labor and other "external" pressures, but the way it is actually changing has to do with how particular social and economic conditions make certain ideological or symbolic forms both possible and authoritative. Social change cannot be understood merely in terms of causal relationships which act independently of the particular forms of discourse and the particular cultural representations which must necessarily sustain such relationships (Asad, 1979). In Sibou, the introduction of square houses and "modern" household items is only viable in the context of a prestige system which values the "modern" over the "traditional," and which encourages a particular view of gender relations. The view that changes in the ordering of space are the product both of changing ideas and of changing social and economic conditions is what provides the clue to the relationship between cultural ideologies and the organization of space in general.

In Chapter 5 I argued that the relationship between a spatial text and the ideology which informs it is one of produced representation. What the text speaks about or works over is not "real"/objective historical relations, but the same historical relations construed in terms of an ideological production. Thus, it can be said that history "enters" the text as ideology. Such a statement immediately invokes the problem of ideology as "false consciousness." But to say that the text takes as its object (i.e., as its subject for representation) certain ideological forms is not to say that the "real"/objective conditions are hidden in the text or present there in a disguised form. It is important to stress that the "truth" of a spatial text cannot be conceived as something which is obscured by the processes of ideological representation, and which remains hidden there until revealed through analytical excavation. It is necessary, instead, to consider the notion of ideology as representation, rather than as "false consciousness." Ideology takes as its ultimate source and referent the material conditions of existence themselves, and can be understood as "providing" material for the spatial text in the form of certain representations of those conditions. This does not mean, however, that the relationship between the text and its objective conditions is one of fantasy or illusion. Ideological forms are not mere illusions, for they constitute the actuality of lived relations; they are not so much distortions of reality as the "lived" conditions of social reality itself. Thus, ideology is not just a passive and "imaginary" representation of social and economic conditions, nor is it some sort of independent illusion; rather, it is a mode of discourse, a way of understanding, which constitutes the way people actually live out the objective conditions of their existence. Social, economic, and gender relations are not empirical relationships which exist outside or behind ideology, for such relationships cannot exist outside the ideology which gives them form. In consequence, there is no set of objective conditions which could exist outside the lived reality of human beings – and such realities are always ideological.

However, the actual character of ideological formations, and the details of their representation and authority, cannot be predicted from a given set of historical determinants alone. This is because there is no fixed way to characterize the relationship between the spatial text and the ideology which informs it. The relationship between ideology and text is one of production, and as a result ideology may be present in the text in a number of different ways. For example, in Chapter 7 I argued that the opposition between ash and animal dung could be related to conflicts between male and female interests. In the case of this "traditional" Endo material, the organization of space could be understood as working over the theme of male and female opposition within the context of the actual interdependence of men and women. However, in Chapter 8 I argued that tensions between men and women are not necessarily represented spatially, because the spatial text works over a theme of unitary family interests and prosperity. In both cases tensions between the sexes exist, but in one case they are overemphasized and in the other they are virtually denied. If this problem is approached from the point of view that, in both instances, the ideological representations which form the object of the spatial text are just distortions of reality, then there is no hope of understanding either the relationship between text and ideology or the nature of ideological distortions themselves. It is for this reason that, if one wishes to understand the relationship between text and ideology, it is necessary to analyze the work which ideological representations (space) must do within a given set of material conditions to be produced and maintained as authoritative systems of discourse (Asad, 1979: 620). To analyze the work ideological representations do within a given set of historical conditions is part of the task of finding out how space is active in the production and reproduction of social and symbolic practices. To illustrate this point further it is necessary to turn to a consideration of gender relations and the position of women.

SEXUALITY AND POWER

We should admit rather that power produces knowledge (and not simply by encouraging it because it serves power or by applying it because it is useful); that power and knowledge directly imply one another; that there is no power relation without the correlative constitution of a field of knowledge, nor any knowledge that does not presuppose and constitute at the same time power relations.
—MICHEL FOUCAULT, 1977: 27

Sexuality must not be thought of as a kind of natural given which power tries to hold in check, or as an obscure domain which knowledge tries gradually to uncover. It is the name that can be given to a historical construct: not a furtive reality that is difficult to grasp, but a great surface network in which the stimulation of bodies, the intensification of pleasures, the incitement to discourse, the formation of special knowledges, the strengthening of controls and resistances, are linked to one another, in accordance with a few major strategies of knowledge and power.
—MICHEL FOUCAULT, 1979: 105–6

One of the most interesting aspects of Foucault's work concerns the relationship between discourse and power. Foucault argues that all discourse is a discourse of power; its aim is the control and manipulation of knowledge, and ultimately of society. Texts are, of course, included in discourse, and Foucault views texts as hiding something, as having a form which intentionally obscures power (Foucault, 1972; 1979). As far as the analysis of space is concerned, this relationship between power and text is of particular interest with regard to relations between men and women. As I showed in Chapter 9, the Endo themselves make an explicit link between gender, knowledge, and power – a link which is given daily credence in the meetings of the all male *kok,* and reinforced and celebrated in other ways in both men's and women's rituals. In a very important sense Chapter 9 is the crucial chapter in this book, because it is in discussing the problems of women that it is possible to link the idea of space as a cultural representation with the theory of interpretation, and then to combine both these perspectives to show how ideological discourse is produced forcefully and authoritatively within a given set of material conditions. The relevance of Foucault's work to this point is that he establishes the relevance of power to the maintenance of ideological discourse. However, he also emphasizes that power is not the "privilege" of a dominant group who exercise it upon the dominated. Relations of power are not exterior to other types of relationships (economic, social, and sexual), but are immanent in those relationships (Foucault, 1979: 94). As a result, power relations are the product of the "divisions, inequalities, and disequilibriums" which occur in human relationships. This argument is, I think, a familiar one in anthropology because anthropologists are acquainted with the diffuse and immanent nature of power relations in small-scale societies which lack formalized offices, stations, and bureaucracies. The value of Foucault's argument is that he stresses that "power comes from below," that the dominated are implicated in the production, and reproduction, of power relations (Foucault, 1977; 1979: 94).[1] One of his main points is that power is not unitary; it is not the possession of a single group; power is an effect or product of the operation of social relationships. In the end, there are as many forms of power as there are types of relationship. "Every group and every individual exercises power and is subject to it" (Sheridan, 1980: 218). Certain categories of people – women and the young – have a limited ability to exercise power, but they do seek to use it if they can. A good example is the way postmenopausal women can actively seek and exercise power in Endo society. Power does not operate in a uniform and monolithic way: it is made up of a multiplicity of intersecting elements which offer themselves as instruments and effects of power, and also as points of resistance to that power. Cultural representations produce and reproduce power relations; they also undermine and expose them. Ultimately, the dominated are as involved in the use and maintenance of power as the dominant, because there are no available forms of discourse which do not appeal to the given categories, divisions and values which simultaneously produce and expose the relations of power.

The impossibility of standing outside social relations, which are also power

---

[1] Said criticizes Foucault's concept of power for its "unworldliness." He points out that Foucault does not make it clear why and how people actually seize and use power in the real world. Foucault's discussion is more about how power works (Said, 1984: 220).

relations, is relevant to a final point. As we have seen, among the Endo the traditional organization of space works over a series of themes which are associated with the positive valuations given to what is male and the negative valuations assigned to female characteristics. I therefore argued that the male–female distinction can be understood as a way of thinking about the world and of assigning worth or value. The spatial organization of compounds – in particular the relationships between houses, burials, and refuse – makes a direct appeal to the hierarchy implicit in the male–female distinction and is thus readily comprehensible in terms of the socially dominant representations of men and women. However, the remaining problem is that, if the meanings given to the organization of space are not fixed but may be differentially invoked in varying contexts, how is it possible to maintain the "authority" of certain cultural values? The answer to this problem is that acts of interpretation work on two levels. First, there is a practical level where the meaning of space is extremely negotiable and almost entirely context dependent. This level corresponds to the situations I have described concerning the renegotiation of meanings associated with the substance ash. It also corresponds to the level at which women's rituals and power songs can be seen to challenge the social order. Secondly, there is a level at which dominant representations are much more authoritative and determining. This is because, although the organization of space is in theory open to an indefinite number of interpretations, in practice these interpretations are limited. The reason for this is that the strategic use of space and the contextual invocation of meaning are not random. Interpretations have a past and a future and are always constrained by the existing order of space, which is no more than the sum of past and future interpretations of that space. Thus, the fact that interpretations must take place within a given set of historical relations ensures that some interpretations are more favored than others. These favored interpretations are those imposed by the dominant group, and they make a direct appeal to the dominant representations and cultural values which are also imposed by the same group. As a result, dominant interpretations are always closely linked to dominant representations and cultural values. Any alternative interpretations, including the quotidian, practical interpretations of space, tend to be contained within the set of dominant interpretations. Thus, certain ideological forms are maintained through the articulation of representation and interpretation. However, in the midst of this particular line of argument, it must not be forgotten that the ability to make strategic interpretations of the organization of space, and the possibility of changing social and economic conditions, are the factors which allow for the possibility of social change. How dominant interpretations and representations could be undermined, and ultimately overthrown, through a cumulative shift in interpretations – which might become possible in the context of favorable socioeconomic change – is perhaps best left to the people themselves.

APPENDIX 1

Kinship Terminology

The system of kinship terminology known as the "Omaha type" is almost always associated with patriliny and serves to make a distinction between agnatic and affinal relationships. Clan or lineage membership is very strongly expressed and crosscuts some principles of generation organization, so that the matrilateral cousins are raised a generation (MoBrSo = MoBr, MoBrDa = Mo) and the patrilateral cousins are lowered, FaSiSo = child, FaSiDa = child. Marakwet terms are presented here in the vocative with their nearest English equivalents. The sex of the speaker is only indicated where relevant and the reciprocal usage of some terms is made clear in the lists of applicable kin. This terminology and its usage are based on my fieldwork in Endo, but there is some evidence to suggest regional variation in the terms, although not – as far as I could establish – in their usage.

English	Marakwet	Applicable kin
Father	Abor	Fa, FaBr, Father's age mates, MoSiHu, MoBrDaHu, WiFa
Mother	Mama	Mo, FaWi, FaBrWi MoSi, MoBrWi, WiMo, MoBrDa, women of mother's clan, wives of father's age mates, MoBrSoDa
Sibling	Kitupche[1]	Si, Br, FaSo, MoSo MoSiDa, MoSiSo, FrBrDa, FaBrSo
Brother/son	Weri	Br, FaSo, FaBrSo, clan brother, MoSiSo: So, BrSo, FaSiSo, BrDaSo, BrSoSo, MoBrDaSo, HuSo, son of age mate

[1] I am still unsure as to whether this term covers all children of father's age mates.

Sister/daughter	Cheby	Si, FaBrDa, MoSiDa, Da, BrDa, MoBrDaDa, daughter of age mate
Child	Lakwe	Da, SiDa, BrDa, FaBrSiDa, daughter of age mate, SoWi BrSoWi, SiSoWi: ♂ So, SiSo, BrSo, son of age mate, MoSiSoDa MoSiSoSo, FaBrSoSo
Uncle (maternal)	Mamaa	MoBr, MoBrSo, all males of mother's clan except MoFa, MoBrSoSo: ♂ SiSo
Aunt (paternal)	Sanga	FaSi, FaMoSiDa, clan sisters of father, FaFaSi: ♀ BrSo BrDa
Grandfather/grandchild	Kuko	FaFa, MoFa, FaFaBr, FaMoBr, MoFaBr: ♂ SoSo, SoDa, DaSo, DaDa, BrDaDa, FaSiSoDa, FaSiSoSo
Grandmother/grandchild	Koko	MoMo, MoMo clan women, MoBrWi, FaFaSi, FaFaBrWi: SoSo, SoDa DaSo, DaDa, HuSiSo, HuSiDa, HuBrSo, HuBrDa, HuBrSoSo, FaSiSoDa, FaSiSoSo
Husband	Ponde	Hu, possibly HuBr, husband's age mates
Wife	Chebyosos	Wi, wives of age mates, Mo
Wife	Korgei	Wi
Cowife	Korgeinyon	HuWi
Sister-in-law	Barsinda	BrWi
Sister-in-law	Bugot[2]	WiSi, BrWi, HuBr, WiBrDa, HuSi, husband's clan brothers
Brother-in-law	Abor	WiBr, WiBrSo, wife's clan brothers
Brother-in-law	Beito or Barsinmwa[3]	WiSiHu, SiHu, SiHuBr
Father-in-law	Abor	WiFa, WiFaBr, WiFaBrSo, HuFa
Mother-in-law	Borgerr	WiMo, WiFaBrWi, WiFaBrDa, WiBrWi

[2] I was unable to discover the difference between *barsinda* and *bugot*. From the information I do have, it seems probable that it is a dialectical variation.

[3] Some informants claimed that *bugot* was the term of address for any wife of a barsinmwa. This seemed to be the case, but I could not establish if *barsinmwa* was always the term for the husband of BrWi, HuSi, and WiFaBrDa.

APPENDIX 2

Burial

The Endo bury their dead in shallow rock graves, without clothing or grave goods of any kind. The grave is usually unmarked, although a large stone or a collection of cactus branches may be placed on the grave if people believe there is any danger of accidental disturbance. The people of the highland Kapsowar region bury their dead in shallow earth graves, and with the increasing influence of Christianity many people are now buried in coffins, especially if they are interred in the hospital graveyard. The highland Marakwet say that they used to cover the body with sheep- or goatskins, although nowadays a white sheet may be used. The Marakwet as a whole claim that the color white is not associated with death, although many informants spontaneously mentioned the fact that if a sheet were used for covering the body then it ought to be white. It would seem that "whiteness" is actually associated with inauspiciousness rather than with death *per se,* and this was borne out in a number of contexts where informants indicated a dislike of white substances, including ash.

In Chapter 6 I discussed the relevant criteria by which the Endo determine the positioning of graves, and I pointed out that such criteria are never fixed, but are actually relative principles which operate according to the needs of the particular context. Unfortunately, I was not able to document or observe any situation where such cross-cutting criteria had been operationalized. The Endo were, quite naturally, extremely sensitive to being questioned on the subject of death, and the general lack of grave markers meant that the position of each grave and the details concerning its occupant had to be ascertained from a knowledgeable informant.[4] While such informants were always courteous and quite willing to provide a certain amount of information, they were nevertheless distressed by repeated requests for help of this kind. However, I did manage to obtain information on the burials associated with all the houses I sam-

[4] In point of fact the Endo are only reluctant to talk about the death and burial of known individuals. They talk openly and freely about burial in general, and there is often talk of the positioning of graves, etc., because it is a matter of concern to the elderly that they should be buried properly.

pled in Sibou. I believe the information I received to be correct, and I was careful to
crosscheck all the relevant details.

Burials in Sibou

Sex	Age	Positions of grave[5]	Reasons for death
M	50–60	Right of his house under goat dung	Natural causes
M	65–70	Right of his house under goat dung	Natural causes
M	1.5 years	Left of father's house	Dysentery
M	60–65	Right of his house under goat dung	Natural causes
F	2 yrs	Left of mother's house	Pneumonia
M	60	Right of son's house under goat dung	Natural causes
F	3 yrs	Left of mother's house	Unknown disease
F	3 yrs	Right of mother's house	Unknown disease
M	65	Right of son's house; no goats in compound	Natural causes

A total of nine graves is an extremely small sample, from which it is not possible
to draw inferences of any kind. However, although the information may be patchy,
it is quite clear that, as far as it goes, it supports the idealized statements concerning
the disposal of the dead which I recorded in Chapter 6.

---

[5] As I said in Chapter 6, all burials are positioned on the lower side of the compound, and it
is therefore only necessary to give the relative positioning of the graves *vis-à-vis* houses and refuse placements.

Afterword

$\mathcal{C}$

There are, perhaps, many ways of synthesizing Endo experiences of space/time, but the perspective which the Endo themselves take most often is based on the pivotal relationship between men and women.

(CHAPTER 4, P. 52)

The male–female distinction provides a way of thinking about the world and of assigning social value.

(CHAPTER 9, P. 186)

This book is about theories of agency and the production and interpretation of spatial texts, but more crucially it is concerned with the difference that gender makes. Marakwet metaphysics is premised on sets of binary oppositions, where dominant terms define the ground of contrasting terms, placing them in a subordinate position. The relations between the male and the female in Marakwet thought appear all too familiar to postmodernist and feminist thinkers. As symbols, they may be combined and recombined with other pairs of contrasts in a variety of contexts, but the relationship between what is male and what is female is always hierarchically organized. The structural nature of the male–female distinction is so marked that it can be used to think about a range of contexts, where the only reason for "gendering" the contrasting terms is to imply a hierarchical relation between them. However, the male and the female are not independent of each other; to invoke one term is to imply the other: "As symbols, they always contain their own opposites . . . they are simultaneously what they represent and what they oppose" (Chapter 7, p. 123).

BINARY LOGIC AND DECONSTRUCTION

A number of feminists, following the work of French scholars, notably Derrida, have argued that presence is always dependent on absence, that the posi-

tive binary terms – man, culture, identity – are always inextricably bound up
with the negative ones – women, nature, difference.[1] Derrida shows, through
a series of deconstructive readings of texts, that the privileged term only derives its position from the suppression and curtailment of its opposite or other.
For Derrida, this is the différance which makes the difference. Deconstruction is thus partly the dismantling of hierarchical systems of thought and partly
the searching out of moments of inconsistency and self-contradiction within
the text.[2] The analysis contained within this book is in a sense a deconstructive reading of Marakwet spatial texts and of sedimented actions considered
as a text. The larger question remains, however, as to whether or not Marakwet women intend this deconstructive reading themselves, and/or whether
resistance to cultural discourses and texts can be usefully likened to deconstruction in a general sense.[3]

The answer to these questions depends in large part on whether or not
it is possible or desirable, either aesthetically or politically, to think outside
the binary economy of symbolic thought. This is a question that must be
posed in very specific terms because it is evident from an anthropological perspective that the nature and content of binary economies is not the same in
all cases. Binary logics are culturally variable, and in each context they necessarily take on a specific inflection and force. Logically, this must be so since
symbol systems and philosophies only become persuasive and powerful within specific social and economic conditions.[4] The question then of the similarities between Marakwet and Western metaphysics must be examined because
to assert that both share a hierarchical and overdetermined relationship between what is male and what is female is not to say very much. Or, to put
it another way, it is the texts themselves and the power relations that constitute them that are of interest rather than just the abstract generative principles of their making.

Feminist scholars have asked how they might think outside the dichoto-
mous structures of woman and man, and find alternative ways of characterizing difference.[5] Their critics have asserted that the task is an impossible

---

[1] See Derrida, 1976; 1978. The feminist literature on the exclusion of woman as constitutive
of Western philosophy and theorization is very large (see, e.g., Lloyd, 1984).
[2] Deconstruction for Derrida is a series of devices disigned to reveal the presuppositions on which
logocentric texts are based rather than a method. It involves the strategic reversal of binary terms,
the displacement of the subordinate term into a position where it becomes the precondition
of the dominant term, and the discovery of an intermediate undecidable term within the binary
logic which "includes" both binary terms.
[3] Deconstruction has been criticized as an elite practice requiring a master intellect with the ability to overview the text.
[4] Bourdieu (1990a: 4) makes the same point and argues that one way of exposing the hidden
oppositions in academic discourses is to examine anthropological examples which appear similar, but actually operate in a different way.
[5] The work of Irigaray (1985a; 1985b) and Kristeva (1974; 1980; Moi, 1986) has been very influential in this regard, but the literature is very large (see, e.g., Jardine and Eisenstein, 1980).

one because at the very moment one engages with the deconstruction of dualist principles they reinsert themselves into the text as its structuring principles.

However, I have argued in this text that Marakwet women are not seeking to deconstruct the binary logic of Marakwet metaphysics; rather they are trying to locate themselves within discourses, practices, and social structures thus constructed. Their task is not one of deconstruction, but of self-valuation through a process of self-identification. This poses a challenge to what I term the "dominant male ideology," but instead of deconstructing it, it reworks it from a female or feminine perspective. The purpose is to create a positive female space or place within dominant discourses and practices. For this reason, I argue that we cannot properly speak of a separate female model of the world. This argument has not been popular with many of my feminist colleagues who point out that women do have particular perspectives or standpoints which inform their social strategies and are engaged in their struggles over power with men. I do not dispute this; the question however is whether they are independent or autonomous from so-called male models. I would argue that they are not and cannot be because they cannot be located outside the binary economy. It is not that Marakwet women have access to a particular *form* of representation, but rather that they have a particular *relation* to cultural representation (Chapter 9, p. 179). Women and men are inserted into matrixes of cultural meanings, but within this symbolic order they are positioned differently.

THE RELATIONSHIP BETWEEN LANGUAGE AND PRAXIS

This is particularly evident for the Marakwet given the different relationship that women and men have to language. However, it is also apparent at the level of practice. Bourdieu argues that the habitus, as a set of cultural dispositions, defines the individual's relation not only to the social, but to their psyche and to their body (Bourdieu, 1977: 92). Women's and men's different relationships to the cultural order are made concrete through a set of discursive practices that organize the spatiotemporal rhythms of their lives, both quotidian and biographical. As Bourdieu argues for the Kabyle, this includes everything from the nature of their work during the different seasons of the year, to their roles in childbirth, their involvement in rituals, and the dress and management of their bodies. It is not necessary for an actor to be consciously aware of cultural meanings in order to act in accordance with them. Bourdieu's emphasis on the intersection of social location with sets of structuring principles is the basis for his contention that praxis is itself a moment of interpretation and thus of potential change. Forms of practical enactment can be moments for the strategic interpretation of meanings and outcomes. These moments can be brought to discourse, but few of them will be conscious in the sense

of thought-out strategies that can be expressed in language.[6] Women's and
men's different positions within social relations and dominant cultural discourses are given substance by their specific space/time locations within socially and symbolically structured contexts. Bourdieu grounds the differences
in women's and men's perspectives in the physical orientation and positioning of their bodies.

> One or other of the two systems of oppositions which define the house . . . is
> brought to the foreground, depending on whether the house is considered from
> the male point of view or the female point of view: whereas for the man, the
> house is not so much a place he enters as a place he comes out of, movement
> inward properly befits the woman. (Bourdieu, 1977: 91)

Praxis for Bourdieu is not about learning cultural rules by rote, but about
coming to an understanding of social distinctions through your body and recognizing that your orientation in the world will be based on that incorporated
knowledge. Thus, it should not be surprising that many of the strategies wom-
en employ to challenge or counter the dominant male ideology and the socially given nature of power relations between the sexes involve practical
actions rather than overt verbal statements. These actions may often employ
a mixture of verbal statement and practical acts, and their force can be the
result either of conjunction or of conflict between the two.

It could certainly be argued – and it would be true for the Marakwet – that
women may favor covert action rather than overt statement because of their
powerlessness. However, this is rather to miss the point. Both women and
men can employ practical action as a strategic method for the interpretation
and reinterpretation of sedimented cultural meanings. Men find it easier to
do this, both because they are less vulnerable than women and because their
interests are often perceived as congruent with general social interests (Chapter 9, p. 182). As Bourdieu argues, the power to impose the principles of the
representation of reality is a political power, and it is not one which is shared
equally in Marakwet life.

RESISTANCE AND CONSCIOUSNESS

The unequal nature of power relations in Marakwet life raises the question
of forms of resistance and most particularly those which are incorporated in
praxis rather than verbal statement. Forms of resistance based on foot drag-
ging, petty pilfering, and noncooperation are well documented from around
the world, but the issue of whether they are always conscious and intention-

---

[6] See Moore, 1994c, for a fuller discussion of Bourdieu's work on bodies and positionality.

al acts is unresolved (Scott, 1985). Resistance, as the term is used in the social science literature, normally implies a conscious and coherent strategy: you cannot resist unless you know you are resisting. The issue here is whether it is possible to challenge power relations and forms of social domination without being consciously aware of doing so. Certain actions are unthought and unthought out; that is, they do not come into language and are not consciously formulated strategies. Many actions are merely half apprehended and they become effective only in the light of others' reactions to them, or perhaps after their consequences are known (Moore, 1994c: 82). If these actions come into discourse at all, it will often be *after* not before the event. Yet, such actions are strategic and effective. They are calculated and calculating in that they require no more then the knowledge of how to proceed. The analytical dilemma is further compounded by the fact that certain actions, and particularly those involving resistance, can be of an indeterminate nature. It can be very difficult to tell whether someone has just made a mistake or is deliberately doing something differently. The problem is perhaps one of identifying the borderline, but it is worth recalling that language and behavior are frequently at odds with each other, and behavior can reveal what language would seek to hide.

Dominant discourses are not impervious to change, and shifts in meaning and interpretation can occur as a result of the reordering of practical activities: simply doing something differently, placing something where it should not be, drawing attention to something. It is no accident that utopian communities wishing to bring about changes in gender relations have frequently approached this task through a reordering of spatial, and particularly domestic, relations (Moore, 1994c: 83–4).

The reorganization of space, or of items within constructed space, is a powerful means of social change. Relations of social dominance can themselves be challenged by the positioning and repositioning of persons and things in space–time relations. However, analysts differ as to the degree of radical social change that is possible in such circumstances. Bourdieu argues, for example, that women's resistance to male domination inevitably takes place within the symbolic categories of the male world view, and thus can never be the origin of radical social change (Bourdieu, 1990a: 13, 15, 30).[7] Leaving aside, for the moment, the question of how to determine degrees of social change, and of whether the kind of change Bourdieu seems to envisage is more radical than most societies experience in most historical periods, it is worth pursuing the relationship of dominant ideologies to forms of change.

---

[7] Bourdieu (1979) certainly believes resistance is possible, but he sees it as the product of collective rather than individual action, and he is critical of what he terms "spontaneous populism" because he believes that the dominated rarely escape the power relations of the dominated/dominant divide (1991: 90–102).

In this book, I argue that it is in the nature of dominant gender ideologies that their basic premises are rarely challenged. They are seldom threatened by change because they do not function through coercion, but through renegotiation and omission. Dominant ideologies operate in "broad brush-strokes," they are not worked out in detail but contain contradictions and absences; it is their very inconsistency and incompleteness which gives them their power. The simplicity and pervasiveness of dominant ideologies guarantees their applicability to disparate contexts and ensures that they are never fully contradicted by the vagaries of lived experience (Chapter 9, pp. 194–6). Bourdieu makes a similar point when he suggests that it is the very indeterminacy of certain elements of the ritual–mythological system of the Kabyle which creates the opportunity and/or the space for women to take a form of revenge on the symbolic system and to revalue themselves in a positive light (1990a: 15). Dominant ideologies retain their power through a form of radical indeterminacy, and this is why their effects can never be specified completely either by social actors or by social scientists.

Issues of indeterminacy are also at the root of an individual's identifications with collective representations, and this is particularly important with regard to dominant gender ideologies. I argue in this book that a recognition of power differentials, and an engagement with strategies designed to limit male control and promote alternative interests, do not mean that Marakwet women reject dominant gender ideologies. Much of the issue here rests on what we might mean by the term "gender ideology." Anthropology has moved in recent years from a view that stressed intercultural variation in gender discourses to one that emphasizes the existence of multiple discourses of gender within single social settings. A "gender ideology," properly speaking, is thus made up of several discourses on gender which may conflict with and contradict each other. These different discourses on gender are frequently hierarchically organized, with the result that some overdetermine others. In many contexts, the dominant discourse is one that emphasizes the mutually exclusive and hierarchically ordered nature of the categories male and female, as in the Marakwet case (Moore, 1994d). This does not mean, as I point out in the book, that other discourses do not exist, that women are always viewed negatively, for example. But, it does tend to mean that other discourses on gender difference are overdetermined by the dominant discourse. It is for this reason that the dominant discourse is rarely threatened by the existence of alternative discourses on gender, and thus may be termed a "dominant gender ideology."

However, dominant gender ideologies do not work through coercion, as I have argued, but through the fact that they overdetermine the ways in which gender differences may be expressed and in doing so they make use of indeterminacy. Dominant gender discourses may appear rigid and fixed, but in practice their very broad applicability, the fact that they are never specified in detail, is what allows for interpretation and reinterpretation. Women are often the victims of such latitude, as when men use power differentials to impose a particular interpretation or social regime. However, it is also this latitude that allows for individual identification; it makes it possible for there to be several ways of being a woman – or indeed a man – within the dominant gender ideology.

BODIES AND THE (MIS)RECOGNITION OF DIFFERENCE

The process of identification is complex and is achieved more often through practice than through critical reflection. Thus Bourdieu argues that a correspondence exists, as a result of the functioning of the habitus, between mental structures and social structures. In other words, ways of life give rise to ways of thought and categories of perception. However, he also maintains that practical belief is not a "state of mind," but rather a "state of the body." "The pre-verbal taking-for-granted of the world that flows from practical sense" ensures that the body acts as a living memory pad for cultural symbols and social values (Bourdieu, 1990b: 68). The relationship between collective representations and individual identifications is not therefore an intellectualist one, but one forged through practical engagement in a social world. Gender is an embodied process and not just because sex is a matter of physically embodied difference. Since self-identity and social relations are formed through the same sets of practical activities, unconscious desires are part of an embodied relation to the world, and one that is always already gendered. Individual women thus have an investment in their own identities which is simultaneously an investment in social categorizations.

This does not imply, of course, that these categories are immutable, but it does suggest that resistance and identification will not always be completely separable, that there might always be a form of ambiguity that escapes the knowing actor. Social scientists, like social actors, are bound up with their own problems of resistance and identification, and this is never more obvious than in the field of gender analysis. The ambiguities and indeterminacies we identify as analysts are always thus a mixture of our own and of the people we analyze.

If self-recognition and self-identification invariably involve an embodied process of practical engagement, then we must recognize the importance of praxis for understanding the unconscious and desire. However, recognition is always an intersubjective, social process. Csordas (1993) has used the notion of "somatic modes of attention" to describe the way in which we attend to the world and to the bodies of others through our own bodies. We understand social distinctions, and particularly gender differences, through our bodies and through attending to the bodies of others. If our world is an intersubjective world, where we only come to an understanding of our own subjectivity through engagement with the subjectivities of others, then we must acknowledge that much of this engagement is embodied and practical.

Intersubjectivity involves much more than people simply speaking to one another. It includes the recognition of bodily dispositions and the eliciting of responses in others through the medium of the body: comportment, gestures, and the like. It involves the monitoring of others' responses to one's own body and the concrete realization of similarity and difference through the engagement of embodied subjectivities. Social experiences are always embodied experiences and bind both body and consciousness together. Human beings are able to recognize themselves simultaneously as subject and object in social engagements, and thus the perception of the other and the comprehension of the other's intentions are always partly based on perceptions and understandings of self. This is what intersubjectivity entails. These human abilities build on deep-rooted patterns of muscular movement and postural stances that give rise to inhabited memories of the body and states of mind. However, this is not simply a matter of learning habitual behavior; it is a question of developing relations with oneself and with others, and, in so doing, investing in those relations. These processes begin very early in human life, but they are never completely finished. The mimesis that is such an important part of socialization is not a mere copying, but an enactment and reenactment of embodied processes of recognition and identification.[8]

However, processes of recognition and identification always involve a form of misrecognition. Bourdieu argues that it is a feature of human social and symbolic systems that power works to make its arbitary impositions appear natural and pregiven. Dominant gender ideologies present themselves as legitimate and natural features of the social world, and as they do so they work a form of symbolic violence (Bourdieu, 1990a: 5–8). This symbolic violence is made possible by the concordance that exists, as a result of the functioning of the habitus, between social structures and cognitive structures. Women and men thus identify with the taxonomic principles that construct gender difference. These principles themselves, as I have argued, are rarely brought into question. Consequently, recognition and identification are implicated in power relations. There can be no way of specifying analytically how power will be challenged – in advance of those challenges being brought to bear – because the relationship between individual identifications and collective representations is always one bound up with desire and is thus based on forms of indeterminacy which cannot be captured completely by social analysis.

---

[8] For further discussion of various phenomenological approaches to the body, based primarily on the work of Merleau-Ponty (1962), and their potential for social theory, see Grosz, 1994; Giddens, 1991; Csordas, 1993; and Jackson, 1983; 1989.

References

꒝

A. KENYA NATIONAL ARCHIVES: COLONIAL RECORDS

Records of the Provincial Commissioner, Rift Valley Province (PC/RVP); District Commissioner, Baringo District(DC/BAR), Elgeyo–Marakwet (DC/ELM); miscellaneous reports and correspondence; Annual Reports of the Native Affairs Department; District Political Record Books (PRBs); Handing Over Reports (HORS) concerning Baringo and Elgeyo–Marakwet Districts, were consulted in the Seeley Historical Library, Cambridge.

B. REFERENCES

Abrahams, R. G., 1978. "Aspects of labour, age and generation grouping and related systems" in *Age, Generation and Time: Some Features of East African Age Organizations,* ed. P. T. W. Baxter and U. Almagor. London: C. Hurst & Co.; 37–67.

Agar, M., 1980. "Hermeneutics in anthropology: a review essay." *Ethos 8* (3): 253–72.

Agnew, J., and Duncan, J. (eds.), 1989. *The Power of Place: Bringing Together Geographical and Sociological Imaginations.* London: Unwin Hyman.

Allen, J. van., 1972. "Sitting on a man: colonialism and the lost political institutions of Igbo women." *Canadian Journal of African Studies 6*: 165–81.

1974. "Women in Africa: modernization means more dependency." *The Centre Magazine* May/June: 60–7.

Althusser, L., 1969. *For Marx.* London: Allen Lane.

and Balibar, E., 1970. *Reading Capital.* London: New Left Books.

Anzaldua, G., 1987. *Borderland/La Frontera.* San Francisco: Spinsters/Aunt Lute.

(ed.), 1990. *Making Face, Making Soul: Haciendo Caras.* San Francisco: Spinsters/Aunt Lute.

Ardener, E., 1975a. "Belief and the problem of women" in *Perceiving Women,* ed. S. Ardener. London: J. M. Dent; 1–17.

1975b. "The problem revisited" in *Perceiving Women,* ed. S. Ardener. London: J. M. Dent; 19–27.

1978. "Problems in the analysis of events" in *Yearbook of Symbolic Anthropology*, ed. E. Schwimmer. London: C. Hurst & Co.; 103–23.

Ardener, S., 1981. "Ground rules and social maps for women: an introduction" in *Women and Space: Ground Rules and Social Maps*, ed. S. Ardener. London: Croom Helm; 11–34.

Asad, T., 1979. "Anthropology and the analysis of ideology." *Man* (NS) 14: 607–27.

1983. "Anthropological conceptions of religion: reflections on Geertz." *Man* (NS) 18: 237–59.

Auge, M., 1982. *The Anthropological Circle*. Cambridge: Cambridge University Press.

Austin, J. L., 1960. *How To Do Things with Words*. Oxford: Clarendon Press.

Barrett, M., *et al.* (eds.), 1979. *Ideology and Cultural Production*. London: Croom Helm.

Barth, F., 1975. *Ritual and Knowledge among the Baktaman of New Guinea*. New Haven, CT: Yale University Press.

Barthes, R., 1973. *Mythologies*. London: Paladin.

Baxter, P. T. W., and Almagor, U., 1978. "Introduction" in *Age, Generation and Time: Some Features of East African Age Organizations*, ed. P. T. W. Baxter and U. Almagor. London: C. Hurst & Co.; 1–35.

Beattie, J. H. M., 1968. "Aspects of Nyoro symbolism." *Africa* 38: 413–42.

Beech, M. W. H., 1911. *The Suk*. Oxford: Clarendon Press.

1913. "Endo vocabulary." *Man* 13: 70–2.

Beneria, L., 1981. "Conceptualising the labour force: the underestimation of women's economic activities" in *African Women in the Development Process*, ed. N. Nelson. London: Frank Cass; 10–28.

Berger, P., and Luckmann, T., 1967. *The Social Construction of Reality*. Harmondsworth: Penguin.

Bhabha, H., 1990. "Interrogating identity: the postcolonial prerogative" in *Anatomy of Racism*, ed. D. Goldberg. Minneapolis: University of Minnesota Press.

Black, M., 1962. *Models and Metaphors*. Ithaca, NY: Cornell University Press.

Bloch, M., 1971. *Placing The Dead*. London: Seminar Press.

1977. "The past and the present in the present." *Man* (NS) 12: 278–92.

Boserup, E., 1970. *Women's Role in Economic Development*. London: Allen & Unwin.

Bourdieu, P., 1973. "The Berber House" in *Rules and Meanings*, ed. M. Douglas. Harmondsworth: Penguin; 98–110.

1977. *Outline of a Theory of Practice*. Cambridge: Cambridge University Press.

1981. *Le Sens Pratique*. Paris: Editions Minuit.

1977. *Outline of a Theory of Practice*. Cambridge: Cambridge University Press.

1979. *Algeria 1960*. Cambridge: Cambridge University Press.

1990a. "La domination masculine." *Actes de la Recherche en Sciences Sociales* 84: 2–31.

1990b. *The Logic of Practice*. Cambridge: Polity Press.

1991. *Language and Symbolic Power*. Cambridge: Polity Press.

Bulmer, R., 1973. "Why the cassowary is not a bird" in *Rules and Meanings*, ed. M. Douglas. Harmondsworth: Penguin; 167–93.

Burke, K., 1966. *Language as Symbolic Action*. Berkeley: University of California Press.

Butler, C., 1984. *Interpretation, Deconstruction and Ideology*. Oxford: Clarendon Press.

Callaway, H., 1981. "Spatial domains and women's mobility in Yorubaland, Nigeria" in *Women and Space*, ed. S. Ardener. London: Croom Helm; 168–86.

Caplan, P., and Bujra, J. (eds.), 1978. *Women United, Women Divided*. London: Tavistock.

Carney, J., and Watts, M., 1990. "Manufacturing dissent: work, gender and the politics of meaning in a peasant society." *Africa* 60: 207–241.

Clayton, A., and Savage, D. C., 1974. *Government and Labour in Kenya, 1895–1963.* London: Frank Cass.

Conant, F. P., 1965. "Korok: a variable unit of physical and social space amongst the Pokot of East Africa." *American Anthropologist* 67(2): 429–34.

Cornelisen, A., 1977. *Women of the Shadows.* New York: Vintage Books.

Coward, R., and Ellis, J., 1977. *Language and Materialism.* London: Routledge & Kegan Paul.

Critchley, W., 1983. "Agricultural developments in Marakwet: some controversial issues" in *Kerio Valley: Past, Present and Future,* ed. B. E. Kipkorir, R. C. Soper, and J. W. Ssennyonga. Nairobi: Institute of African Studies; 19–26.

Csordas, T., 1993. "Somatic modes of attention." *Cultural Anthropology* 8(2): 135–56.

Culler, J., 1980. "Prolegomena to a theory of reading" in *The Reader in the Text,* ed. S. Suleiman and I. Crosman. Princeton, NJ: Princeton University Press; 46–66.

1981. *The Pursuit of Signs: Semiotics, Literature, Deconstruction.* London: Routledge & Kegan Paul.

Deere, C. D, Humphries, J., and Leon de Leal, M., 1982. "Class and historical analysis for the study of women and economic change" in *Women's Roles and Population Trends in the Third World,* ed. R. Anker *et al.* London: Croom Helm; 87–114.

Derrida, J., 1974. "White mythology." *New Literary History* 6(1): 5–74.

1976. *Of Grammatology.* Baltimore: John Hopkins University.

1978. *Writing and Difference.* London: Routledge.

Deutsche, R., 1991. "Boys town." *Society and Space* 9: 5–30.

Dey, J., 1981. "Gambian women: unequal partners in rice development projects?" in *African Women in the Development Process,* ed. N. Nelson. London: Frank Cass; 109–22.

Diamond, S., 1974. "The myth of structuralism" in *The Unconscious in Culture: The Structuralism of Claude Lévi-Strauss in Perspective.* New York: E. P. Dutton & Co.; 292–335.

Distefano, J. A., 1976. "Lagokap Miot: an enquiry into Kalenjin pre-colonial history." Unpublished staff seminar paper, no. 7, Dept. of History, University of Nairobi.

Douglas, M., 1966. *Purity and Danger: An Analysis of Concepts of Pollution and Taboo.* London: Routledge & Kegan Paul.

1973. *Natural Symbols.* Harmondsworth: Penguin.

1975. *Implicit Meanings: Essays in Anthropology.* London: Routledge & Kegan Paul.

1978. *Cultural Bias,* Occasional paper, Royal Anthropological Institute, 34. London: RAI.

Duncan, J., and Ley, D. (eds.), 1993. *Place/Culture/Representation.* London: Routledge.

Dundas, K. R., 1910. "Notes on the tribes inhabiting the Baringo District, East African Protectorate." *Journal of the Royal Anthropological Institute* 40: 49–72.

Durkheim, E., 1976. *Elementary Forms of Religious Life,* trans. J. W. Swain, 1915. New intro. by Robert Nisbet. 1976. London: Allen & Unwin.

and Mauss, M., 1963. *Primitive Classification,* trans. R. Needham, 1963. London: Cohen & West.

Dyck, I., 1990. "Space, time and renegotiating motherhood: an exploration of the domestic workplace." *Society and Space* 8(4): 459–84.

Eagleton, T., 1976. *Criticism and Ideology*. London: Verso.

1983. *Literary Theory: An Introduction*. Oxford: Basil Blackwell.

Eco, U., 1979. *The Role of the Reader: Explorations in the Semiotics of Texts*. Bloomington: Indiana University Press.

Edgerton, R. B., and Conant, F. P., 1964. "Kilapat: the 'shaming party' among the Pokot of East Africa." *Southwestern Journal of Anthropology* 20: 404–18.

Ehret, C., 1968. "Linguistics as a tool for historians." *Hadith* 1: 119–33.

1971. *Southern Nilotic History*. Evanston, IL: Northwestern University Press.

Ennew, J., 1980. "The material of reproduction: anthropological views on historical materialism and kinship." *Economy and Society* 8(1): 99–124.

Epstein, T. S., 1982. "A social anthropological approach to women's roles and status in developing countries: the domestic cycle" in *Women's Roles and Population Trends in the Third World*, ed. R. Anker *et al.* London: Croom Helm; 151–70.

Evans-Pritchard, E. E., 1940. "The political structure of the Nandi-speaking peoples of Kenya." *Africa* 13: 250–67.

Fernandez, J. H., 1971. "Persuasions and performances: of the beast in every body . . . and the metaphors of everyman" in *Myth, Symbol and Culture*, ed. C. Geertz. New York: Norton & Co.; 39–60.

1974. "The mission of metaphor in expressive culture." *Current Anthropology* 15(2): 119–45.

1977. "The performance of ritual metaphors" in *The Social Use of Metaphor*, ed. J. D. Sapir and J. C. Crocker. Philadelphia: University of Pennsylvania Press; 100–32.

et al., 1981. "Toward a convergence of cognitive and symbolic anthropology." *American Ethnologist* 8: 422–50.

Fish, S., 1980. *Is There a Text In This Class?* Cambridge, MA: Harvard University Press.

Fortes, M., 1971. "Introduction" in *The Developmental Cycle in Domestic Groups*, ed. J. Goody. Cambridge: Cambridge University Press; 1–14.

Foucault, M., 1972. *The Archaeology of Knowledge*, trans. A. Sheridan. London: Tavistock.

1977. *Discipline and Punish*, trans. A. Sheridan. London: Allen Lane.

1979. *The History of Sexuality*. London: Allen Lane.

Fox, J., 1972. "Sister's child as plant: metaphors in an idiom of consanguinity" in *Rethinking Kinship and Marriage*, ed. R. Needham. London: Tavistock; 219–52.

Friedmann, J., 1974. "Marxism, structuralism and vulgar-materialism." *Man* (NS)9: 444–69.

Geertz, C., 1971. *Myth, Symbol and Culture*, ed. C. Geertz. New York: Norton & Co.; 1–37.

1973. "Person, time and conduct in Bali" in *The Interpretation of Culture*, ed. C. Geertz. New York: Basic Books; 360–411.

1984. *Local Knowledge: Further Essays in Interpretative Anthropology*. New York: Basic Books.

Gennep, A. van, 1960. *The Rites of Passage*, trans. M. Vizedom and G. Caffee. London: Routledge & Kegan Paul.

Giddens, A., 1976. *New Rules of Sociological Method*. London: Hutchinson.

1979. *Central Problems in Social Theory: Action, Structure and Contradiction in Social Analysis*. London: Macmillan.

1984. *The Constitution of Society: Outline of the Theory of Structuration*. Cambridge: Polity Press.

1985. "Time, space and distanciation" in *Social Relations and Spatial Structures*, ed. D. Gregory and J. Urry. London: Macmillan; 265–95.

1991. *Modernity and Self-Identity*. Cambridge: Polity Press.

Gluckman, M., 1954. *Rituals of Rebellion in South-East Africa*. Manchester: Manchester University Press.

1965. *Politics, Law and Ritual in Tribal Society*. Chicago, IL: Aldine.

Godelier, M., 1977. *Perspectives in Marxist Anthropology*. Cambridge: Cambridge University Press.

Goffman, E., 1971. *The Presentation of the Self in Everyday Life*. Harmondsworth: Penguin.

Goldschmidt, W., 1967. *Sebei Law*. Berkeley: University of California Press.

1976. *The Culture and Behaviour of the Sebei*. Berkeley: University of California Press.

Goody, J., 1971. *The Developmental Cycle in Domestic Groups*. Cambridge: Cambridge University Press.

1977. *The Domestication of the Savage Mind*. Cambridge: Cambridge University Press.

Greenberg, J. H., 1963. "The languages of Africa." *International Journal of American Linguistics* 29(2): 1–171.

Gregory, D., 1989. "Presences and absences: time–space relations and social theory" in *Social Theory of Modern Societies: Anthony Giddens and His Critics*, ed. D. Held and J. Thompson. Cambridge, Cambridge University Press; 31–53.

1994. *Geographical Imaginations*. Oxford: Blackwell.

Gregory, J. W., 1896. *The Great Rift Valley*. London: Frank Cass (1968).

Griaule, M., 1965. *Conversations with Ogotomeli*, trans. R. Butler. London: Oxford University Press.

Grosz, E., 1994. *Volatile Bodies*. London: Routledge.

Hall, S., 1978. "The hinterland of science: ideology and the 'Sociology of knowledge' " in *On Ideology*, Centre for Contemporary Cultural Studies. London: Hutchinson; 9–32.

Hardin, K., 1983. *The Aesthetics of Action: Change and Continuity in a West African Town*. Washington: Smithsonian Institution Press.

Harris, O., 1981. "Households as natural units" in *Of Marriage and the Market*, ed. K. Young, C. Wolkowitz, and R. McCullagh. London: CSE Books; 40–68.

and Young, K., 1981. "Engendered structures: some problems in the analysis of reproduction" in *The Anthropology of Pre-Capitalist Societies*, ed. J. S. Kahnand & J. R. Llobera. London: Macmillan; 109–47.

Hebdige, D., 1979. *Subculture: The Meaning of Style*. London: Methuen.

Hennings, R. O., 1941. "The furrow makers of Kenya." *Geographical Magazine* 12: 169–79.

1951. *African Morning*. London: Chatto & Windus.

Hertz, R., 1960. *Death and The Right Hand*, trans. R. Needham. London: Cohen West.

Hindess, B., and Hirst, P., 1975. *Pre-Capitalist Modes of Production*. London: Routledge & Kegan Paul.

1977. "A reply to John Taylor," *Critique of Anthropology* 8: 49–58.

Hirschon, R., 1978. "Open body/closed space; the transformation of female sexuality" in *Defining Females*, ed. S. Ardener. London: Croom Helm; 66–88.

Hobart, M., 1978. "The path of the soul: the legitimacy of nature in Balinese conceptions of space" in *Natural Symbols in South-East Asia*, ed. G. B. Milner. London: SOAS; 5–28.

Hodder, I., 1979. "Social and economic stress and material culture patterning." *American Antiquity*, 44: 446–54.

Hohnel, L. von, 1894. *Discovery by Count Teleki of Lakes Rudolf and Stephanie*, 2 vols. London: Longman & Co.

Hollis, A. C., 1969. *The Nandi: Their Language and Folklore*. Oxford: Clarendon Press. First published 1909.

Holy, L., 1976. *Knowledge and Behaviour*. Belfast: Queen's University Papers.

1983. "Symbolic and non-symbolic aspects of Berti space." *Man* (NS) 18(2): 269–88.

Hugh-Jones, C., 1978. "Food for thought: patterns of production and consumption in Pira–Parana society" in *Sex and Age as Principles of Social Differentiation*, ed. J. S. La Fontaine. London: Academic Press; 41–66.

1979. *From the Milk River*. Cambridge: Cambridge University Press.

Hugh-Jones, S., 1979. *The Palm and the Pleiades*. Cambridge: Cambridge University Press.

Huntingford, G. W. B., 1950. *Nandi Work and Culture*, Colonial Research Studies, 4. London: HMSO.

1953. *The Nandi of Kenya*. London: Routledge & Kegan Paul.

1963. "The peopling of the interior of East Africa by its modern inhabitants" in *History of East Africa*, vol. 1, ed. R. Oliver and G. Mathew. Oxford: Clarendon Press; 58–73.

Huxley, E., 1959. "African water engineers." *Geographical Magazine* 32: 170–5.

Irigaray, L., 1985a. *This Sex Which is Not One*. Ithaca: Cornell University Press.

1985b. *Speculum of the Other Woman*. Ithaca: Cornell University Press.

Jackson, M., 1983. "Knowledge of the boy." *Man* 18(2): 327–45.

1989. *Paths Toward a Clearing: Radical Empiricism and Ethnographic Enquiry*. Bloomington: Indiana University Press.

Jardine, A., and Eisenstein, H. (eds.), 1980. *The Future of Difference*. Boston: G. K. Hall.

Katz, C., and Monk, J. (eds.), 1993. *Full Circles: Geographies of Women over the Life-Course*. London: Routledge.

Keith, M., and Pile, S. (eds.), 1993. *Place and the Politics of Identity*. London: Routledge.

Kenya Land Commission Report, 1933. Kenya: HMSO.

Kettel, D. W. W., 1975. *Passing Like Flowers: The Marriage Regulations of the Tugen of Kenya and their Implications for a Theory of Crow-Omaha*. Unpublished doctoral thesis, Illinois University.

Kipkorir, B. E., 1983. "Historical perspectives of development in the Kerio valley" in *Kerio Valley: Past, Present and Future*, ed. B. E. Kipkorir, R. C. Soper, and J. W. Ssennyonga. Nairobi: Institute of African Studies; 1–11.

and Welbourn, F. B., 1973. *The Marakwet of Kenya: a preliminaty study*. Nairobi: East African Literature Bureau.

Kirby, V., 1989. "Capitalizing difference: feminism and anthropology." *Australian Feminist Studies* 9: 1–24.

1991. "Comment on Mascia-Lees, Sharpe and Cohen's 'The postmodernist turn in anthropology: cautions from a feminist perspective.'" *Signs* 16(2): 394–400.

1993. "Feminism and postmodernisms: anthropology and the management of difference." *Anthropological Quarterly* 66(3): 127–33.

Kohler, O., 1954/5. "Die ausbreitung der Sudniloten." *Tribus* 9(4–5): 78–86.

Komma, T., 1979. "The dwelling and its symbolism among the Kipsigis" in *Themes in Socio-Cultural Ideas and Behaviour among the Six Ethnic Groups of Kenya,* ed. N. Nagashima. Japan: Hitotsubashi University; 91–123.

Krieger, S., 1991. *Social Science and the Self: Personal Essays on an Art Form.* New Brunswick, NJ: Rutgers University Press.

Kristeva, J., 1974. "La femme, ce n'est jamais ça." *Tel Quel* 59: 19–25.

1980. *Desire in Language.* New York: Columbia University Press.

Kuhn, A., 1981. *Women's Pictures: Feminism and Cinema.* London: Routledge & Kegan Paul.

Kuper, A., 1980. "Symbolic dimensions of the Southern Bantu homestead." *Africa* 50(1): 8–23.

Lacan, J., 1980. *Ecrits: A Selection.* London: Tavistock.

Lakoff, G., and Johnson, M., 1980. *Metaphors We Live By.* Chicago, IL: University of Chicago Press.

Langley, M., 1979. *The Nandi of Kenya.* London: C. Hurst & Co.

Leach, E., 1964. "Anthropological aspects of language: animal categories and verbal abuse" in *New Directions in the Study of Language,* ed. E. H. Lenneberg. Cambridge, MA: MIT Press.

1970. *Claude Lévi-Strauss.* New York: Viking Press.

1976. *Culture and Communication: The Logic by Which Symbols Are Connected.* Cambridge: Cambridge University Press.

Leacock, E. B., 1975. "Class, commodity and the status of women" in *Women Cross-Culturally: Change and Challenge,* ed. R. Rohrlich-Leavitt. The Hague: Mouton; 601–16.

Lévi-Strauss, C., 1962. *La Pensee sauvage.* Paris: Plon.

1963. *Structural Anthropology.* New York: Basic Books.

1969. *The Elementary Structures of Kinship.* Boston, MA: Beacon Press.

1971. *L'Homme nu.* Paris: Plon.

1978. *Myth and Meaning.* London: Routledge & Kegan Paul.

Lipshitz, S., 1978. *Tearing the Veil.* London: Routledge & Kegan Paul.

Llewelyn-Davies, M., 1981. "Women, warriors and patriarchs" in *Sexual Meanings: The Cultural Construction of Gender,* ed. S. Ortner and H. Whitehead. Cambridge: Cambridge University Press; 330–58.

Lloyd, G., 1984. *The Man of Reason: "Male" and "Female" in Western Phiolsophy.* Minneapolis: University of Minnesota Press.

MacCormack, C., and Strathern, M. (eds.), 1980. *Nature, Culture and Gender.* Cambridge: Cambridge University Press.

Macherey, P., 1978. *A Theory of Literary Production,* trans. G. Wall. London: Routledge & Kegan Paul.

Mackenzie, S., 1989. "Restructuring the relations of work and life: women as environmental actors, feminism as geographical analysis" in *Remaking Human Geography,* ed. A. Kobayashi and S. Mackenzie. London: Unwin Hyman.

Mascia-Lees, F., Sharpe, P., and Cohen, C. B., 1989. "The postmodernist turn in anthropology: cautions from a feminist perspective." *Signs* 15(1): 7–33.

1991. "Reply to Kirby." *Signs* 16(2): 401–8.

Massam, J. A., 1927. *The Cliff-Dwellers of Kenya.* London: Sampson & Co.

Merlau-Ponty, M., 1962. *Phenomenology of Perception.* London: Routledge.

Meyerhoff, E., 1982. *The Socio-Economic and Ritual Roles of Pokot Women.* Unpublished doctoral thesis, Cambridge University.

Miller, N., 1991. *Getting Personal: Feminist Occasions and Other Autobiographical Acts.* London: Routledge.

Milton, K., 1979. "Male bias in anthropology?" *Man* (NS) 14: 40–54.

Moi, T. (ed.), 1986. *The Kristeva Reader.* Oxford: Basil Blackwell.

Moore, A., 1981. "Basilicas and king posts: a proxemic and symbolic event analysis of competing public architecture among the San Blas Cuna." *American Ethnologist* 8(2): 259–77.

Moore, H. L., 1983. "Anthropology and development: some illustrations from the Marakwet of Kenya" in *Kerio Valley: Past, Present and Future,* ed. B. E. Kipkorir, R. C. Soper, and J. W. Ssennyonga. Nairobi: Institute of African Studies; 132–8.

1985. "Problems in the analysis of social change: an example from the Marakwet of Kenya" in *The Archaeology of Historical Meanings,* ed. I. Hodder. Cambridge: Cambridge University Press.

1988. *Feminism and Anthropology.* Cambridge: Polity Press.

1994a. "The feminist anthropologist and the passion(s) of New Eve" in *A Passion for Difference.* Cambridge: Polity Press; 129–50.

1994b. "Master narratives: anthropology and writing" in *A Passion for Difference.* Cambridge: Polity Press; 107–28.

1994c. "Bodies on the move: gender, power and material culture" in *A Passion for Difference.* Cambridge: Polity Press; 71–85.

1994d. "Fantasies of power and fantasies of identity: gender, race and violence" in *A Passion for Difference.* Cambridge: Polity Press; 49–70.

1996. "The changing nature of anthropological knowledge: an introduction" in *The Future of Anthropological Knowledge.* London: Routledge; 1–15.

Moore, M. P., 1974. *"Some Economic Aspects of Women's Work and Status in the Rural Areas of Africa and Asia."* Discussion Paper no. 43. Brighton: Brighton Institute of Development Studies.

Moore, R. O., 1977. "Unraveling the Kalenjin riddle." Unpublished staff seminar paper no. 6., Dept. of History, University of Nairobi.

Moraga, C., and Anzaldua, G. (eds.), 1981. *This Bridge Called My Back: Writings by Radical Women of Color.* Watertown, MA: Persephone Press.

Murgatroyd, L., 1989. "Only half the story: some blinkering effects of 'malestream' sociology" in *Social Theory of Modern Societies: Anthony Giddens and His Critics,* ed. D. Held and J. Thompson. Cambridge: Cambridge University Press; 73–101.

Ogot, B. A., 1967. *A History of the Southern Luo.* Nairobi: East African Institute Press.

and Kiernan, J. A. (eds.), 1968. *Zamani: A Survey of East African History.* Nairobi: East African Publishing House.

Ong, A., 1987. *Spirits of Resistance and Capitalist Discipline: Factory Women in Malaysia.* Albany: State University of New York Press.

Ortner, S., 1974. "Is female to male as nature is to culture?" in *Woman, Culture and Society,* ed. M. Rosaldo and L. Lamphere. Stanford, CA: Stanford University Press; 67–87.

1984. "Theory in anthropology since the sixties." *Comparative Studies in Society and History* 26(1): 126–66.

and Whitehead, H. (eds.), 1981a. *Sexual Meanings: The Cultural Construction of Gender and Sexuality*. Cambridge: Cambridge University Press.

1981b. "Introduction: accounting for sexual meanings" in *Sexual Meanings: The Cultural Construction of Gender and Sexuality,* ed. S. Ortner and H. Whitehead. Cambridge: Cambridge University Press; 1–27.

Peacock, J., 1981. "The third stream: Weber, Parsons and Geertz." *Journal of the Anthropological Society of Oxford* 7: 122–9.

Peristiany, J., 1939. *The Social Institutions of the Kipsigis*. London: Routledge & Kegan Paul.

1954. "Pokot sanctions and structure." *Africa* 24: 17–25.

Peters, C., 1891. *New Light on Darkest Africa*. London: Ward Lock.

Pred, A., 1990a. *Making Histories and Constructing Human Geographies*. Boulder, CO: Westview Press.

1990b. "In other wor(l)ds: fragmented and integrated observations on gendered language: gendered spaces and local transformation." *Antipode* 22: 33–52.

and Watts, M., 1992. *Reworking Modernity: Capitalisms and Symbolic Discontent*. New Brunswick, NJ: Rutgers University Press.

Probyn, E., 1990. "Travels in the postmodern: making sense of the local" in *Feminism/Postmodernism,* ed. L. Nicholson. London: Routledge, 175–89.

Quinn, N., 1977. "Anthropological studies of women's status." *Annual Review of Anthropology* 6: 181–225.

Rabinow, P., and Sullivan, W. (eds.), 1979. *Interpretative Social Science: A Reader*. Berkeley: University of California Press.

Rapoport, A., 1977. *Human Aspects of Urban Form*. Oxford: Pergamon Press.

Rapp, R., 1979. "Review essay: anthropology." *Signs* 4(3): 497–513.

Reiter, R. Rapp, 1977. "The search for origins: unraveling the threads of gender hierarchy." *Critique of Anthropology*, 3(9–10): 5–24.

Remy, D., 1975. "Underdevelopment and the experience of women: a Nigerian case study" in *Towards an Anthropology of Women,* ed. R. Reiter. New York: Monthly Review Press; 358–71.

Richards, A., 1939. *Land, Labour and Diet in Northern Rhodesia. An Economic Study of the Bemba Tribe*. London: Oxford University Press.

Ricoeur, P., 1976. *Interpretation Theory: Discourse and the Surplus of Meaning*. Fort Worth, TX: Texas Christian University Press.

1978. *The Rule of Metaphor,* trans. R. Czerny *et al.* London: Routledge & Kegan Paul.

1981. *Hermeneutics and the Human Sciences,* trans. and ed. J. B. Thompson. Cambridge: Cambridge University Press.

Rogers, B., 1980. *The Domestication of Women: Discrimination in Developing Societies*. London: Tavistock.

Rosaldo, M., 1975. "Man the hunter and woman: metaphors for the sexes in Ilongot magical spells" in *The Interpretation of Symbolism,* ed. R. Willis. London: Malaby Press; 177–203.

Rose, G., 1993. *Feminism and Geography: The Limits of Geographical Knowledge*. Cambridge

Rosen, L., 1978. "The negotiation of reality: male-female relations in Sefrou, Morocco" in *Women in the Muslim World,* ed. L. Beck and N. Keddie. Cambridge, MA: Harvard University Press; 561–84.

Rottland, F., 1981. "Marakwet dialects: synchronic and diachronic aspects" in *Kerio*

Valley: Past, Present and Future, ed. B. E. Kipkorir, R. C. Soper and J. W. Ssennyonga. Nairobi: Institute of African Studies; 139–46.

Sacks, K., 1974. "Engels revisited: women, the organization of production and private property" in *Woman, Culture and Society,* ed. M. Z. Rosaldo and L. Lamphere. Stanford, CA: Stanford University Press; 207–22.

Said, E., 1984. *The World, the Text and the Critic.* London: Faber & Faber.

Sapir, J. D., 1981. "Leper, hyena, and blacksmith in Kujamaat Diola thought." *American Ethnologist* 8(3): 526–43.

Scott, J., 1985. *Weapons of the Weak: Everyday Forms of Peasant Resistance.* New Haven, CT: Yale University Press.

Searle, J., 1969. *Speech Acts: An Essay in the Philosophy of Language.* Cambridge: Cambridge University Press.

Shankman, P., 1984. "The thick and the thin: on the interpretive theoretical program of Clifford Geertz." *Current Anthropology* 25(3): 261–79.

Soja, E., 1983. "Redoubling the helix: space–time and the critical social theory of Anthony Giddens." *Environment and Planning A* 15: 167–72.

1989: *Postmodern Geographies: The Reassertion of Space in Critical Social Theory.* London: Verso.

Sommer, D., 1988. "Not just a personal story: women's testimonies and the plural self" in *Life/Lines: Theorizing Women's Autobiography,* ed. B. Brodzki and C. Schenk. Ithaca: Cornell University Press; 107–30.

Soper, R., 1983. "A survey of the irrigation systems of the Marakwet" in *Kerio Valley: Past, Present and Future,* ed. B. E. Kipkorir, R. C. Soper, and J. W. Ssennyonga. Nairobi: Institute of African Studies; 75–95.

Southall, A. W., 1961. "Introductory summary" in *Social Change in Modern Africa,* ed. A. W. Southall. London: Oxford University Press; 1–66.

Spencer, P., 1965. *The Samburu: A Study of Gerontocracy in a Nomadic Tribe.* London: Routledge & Kegan Paul.

Sperber, D., 1975. *Rethinking Symbolism.* Cambridge: Cambridge University Press.

Stacey, M., and Price, M., 1980. "Women and power." *Feminist Review* 5: 33–52.

Strathern, M., 1981a. "Self-interest and the social good: some implications of Hagen gender imagery" in *Sexual Meanings: The Cultural Construction of Gender and Sexuality,* ed. S. Orthner and H. Whitehead. Cambridge: Cambridge University Press; 166–91.

1981b. "Culture in a netbag: the manufacture of a subdiscipline in anthropology." *Man* (NS) 16(4): 663–88.

1987. "An awkward relationship: the case of feminism and anthropology." *Signs* 12(2): 276–92.

Suleiman, S., and Crosman, I. (eds.), 1980. *The Reader in the Text: Essays on Audience and Interpretation.* Princeton, NJ: Princeton University Press.

Sutton, J. E. G., 1968. "The settlement of East Africa" in *Zamani: A Survey of East African History,* ed. B. A. Ogot and J. A. Kiernan. Nairobi: East African Publishing House; 70–97.

1973. *The Archaeology of the Western Highlands of Kenya.* Nairobi: British Institute in Eastern Africa.

1976. "The Kalenjin" in *Kenya Before 1900,* ed. B. A. Ogot. Nairobi: East African Publishing House; 21–52.

Tambiah, S. J., 1969. "The magical power of words." *Man* (NS) 3: 175–206.

1973. "Classification of animals in Thailand" in *Rules and Meanings,* ed. M. Douglas. Harmondsworth: Penguin; 127–66.

1981. *A Performative Approach to Ritual.* London: Oxford University Press.

Thompson, J. B., 1981. "Introduction" in *Hermeneutics and the Human Sciences,* ed. J. B. Thompson. Cambridge: Cambridge University Press; 1–26.

Thomson, S., 1885. *Through Masai Land.* London: Sampson Law & Co.

Thrift, N., 1983. "On the determination of social action in space and time." *Society and Space* 1: 23–57.

1985. "Bear and Mouse or Bear and Tree? Anthony Gidden's reconstitution of social theory." *Sociology* 19: 609–23.

Tinker, L., 1976. "The adverse impact of development on women" in *Women and World Development,* ed. I. Tinker, M. Bo Bramsen, and M. Buvinic. New York: Praeger; 22–34.

Tucker, A. N., and Bryan, M. A., 1962. "Noun classification in Kalenjin: Pakot." *African Language Studies* 3: 137–181.

Turner, V., 1967. *The Forest of Symbols.* Ithaca, NY: Cornell University Press.

1968. *The Drums of Affliction.* London: Routledge & Kegan Paul.

1969. *The Ritual Process: Structure and Anti-Structure.* Chicago, IL: Aldine Press.

1974. *Dramas, Fields and Metaphors: Symbolic Action in Human Society.* Ithaca, NY: Cornell University Press.

1975. "Symbolic studies." *Annual Review of Anthropology,* 4: 145–61.

Turton, A., 1978. "Architectural and political space in Thailand" in *Natural Symbols in South-East Asia,* ed. G. B. Milner. London: SOAS; 113–32.

Valentine, G., 1989. "The geography of women's fear." *Area* 21(4): 385–90.

Walkerdine, V., 1986. "Video replay: families, films and fantasies" in *Formations of Fantasy,* eds. V. Burgin, J. Donald, and C. Kaplan. London: Methuen; 26–42.

Were, G., 1968. *A History of the Abaluyia.* Nairobi: East African Publishing House.

Whiting, B., 1972. "Work and the family: cross-cultural perspectives." Paper presented at an International Conference on Women, Radcliffe Institute, Massachusetts.

Wolff, J., 1981. *The Social Production of Art.* London: Macmillan.

Worsley, P., 1984. *The Three Worlds: Culture and World Development.* London: Weidenfeld & Nicolson.

Index

Abaluyia, 18
Adult. *See also* Initiation, Marriage
  control over children and young, 60
  life stages, 63–4
  transition to adulthood, 60–4
Age sets. *See also* Ancestors, Elders, Initiation, Time
  function of, 60
  method of dating, 60
  opening and closing of, 61
  order of, 59–60
  origins of, 60–1
  principle of social organization, 65
  warriors, 61
Ancestors. *See also* Child, Clan, Elders
  and age sets, 60
  and fireplace, 125, 134
  naming children, 62
  and time, 58
Animal dung. *See also* Refuse
  and burial, 110
  and men, 110, 112
  position of, 110, 151–2
  as symbol, 120–3, 197
Arawa. See Moon
Ardener, E., 173, 177, 180–1
Ardener, S., 81
Aret. See Clan
Argumentation, 92, 200
Asad, T., 6–7
Ash. *See also* Refuse
  and burial, 110
  and circumcision, 125
  position of, 110, 112, 151–2
  as symbol, 120–3, 125–6, 197
  and women, 112, 120, 206
Asis. See Sun
Aunt (*sanga*), 67. *See also* Kinship

Baringo, 32
Barthes, R., 5, 127

Beech, M. W. H., 13–4. *See also* Pokot
Beer, 117–18, 166
  drunk in *kapkore,* 187
  for ceremonies, 73
Birth control, 189
Bourdieu, P., 5, 8, 83–5, 91, 95, 98, 201
Brother. *See* Siblings
Bridewealth
  composition and amount of, 66–7, 69
  origins of, 66
Burial, 110–13, 153, 209–10
Burke, K., 81
Butler, C., 82–3

Chaff. *See also* Refuse
  position of, 110, 112
  as symbol, 120–3, 197
  and women, 110, 112, 117, 122–3
Change
  social, 6–7, 26, 93–4, 96–7, 138, 140, 202
  associated with prestige, 152
Cherangani hills, 9, 26
Chiefs, 25
Child. *See also* Ancestors, Parents
  activities of, 165–9
  and ancestors, 62
  death of, 110
  disputes over inheritance, 74, 103–4
  education, 64–5
  labor of, 64–5, 105, 116
  life stages, 63–4
  naming of, 62, 118, 153
  sleeping arrangements, 100, 102, 105, 108–9
  socialization of, 64–5
Childbirth, 189–91. *See also* Initiation
  exclusion of men, 191
  parallels with initiation, 189–90
Circumcision, 57, 59, 190. *See also* Initiation
  and change of status, 63, 174–5
  receipt of stock and other presents, 69–70

Clan (*aret*). *See also* Marakwet, Marriage,
    Sibou
  conflict between household and, 74,
    118–19, 121–3
  continuity of, 62–3, 74
  men's and women's different relations to,
    62–3, 72–3
  rights to land and water, 30–2
  totems, 22
  women's natal clans, 189
Colonialism
  affect on Endo, 27
  affect on indigenous groups, 13–5, 20
  period of, 9
  and Westernization, 129–30, 138, 157
Compounds, 11, 34, 39, 48. *See also*
    Houses, Sibou, Space
  activities in, 165–70
  factors affecting residence, 105–6
  life cycle of, 52, 98–110
  position of graves in, 111
  position of houses in, 111
Conant, F. P., 22, 188. *See also* Pokot
Cooking, 121–3, 167–9
  restrictions during childbirth and menstru-
    ation, 189–91
Council (*kok*), 20–2, 24–5, 74, 165–6, 174–5
Critchley, W., 18, 130
Crops. *See also* Foodstuffs, Stores
  acreage, 18
  cash, 116–17
  food, 18–19, 116–17
  storage of, 52–3, 117
  types of, 18–19
  and women, 116–21, 154–5
Culler, J., 88
Culture
  as a set of texts, 86–7
  conventions of, 92
  definitions of, 7, 80–1
  plurality of, 80
  relations between society and, 81

Death, 120, 209–10. *See also* Burial
Discourse, 88–90, 94
Distanciation, 88–90
Douglas, M., 6–7
Dundas, K. R., 13
Durkheim, E., 4

Eagleton, T., 5, 93–4
Edgerton, R. B., 188
Education, 138, 146–7. *See also* Child
  of girls, 65
  school fees, 146–7
  valued over traditional instruction, 138, 152
Egypt (*Misre*), 18, 30
Ehret, C., 16–17

Elders, 25, 58, 166. *See also* Ancestors, Clan
  control over young, 152
  distinguished from young, 61
Endo, 9–12, 19–21, 25–32, 39, 48–59,
    61–3, 68–74, 85, 100, 102, 105,
    109–15, 118–20, 129–30, 138, 152–3,
    176, 199, 205. *See also* Kalenjin,
    Marakwet
Evans-Pritchard, E. E., 13–14

Fernandez, J. H., 83
Fertility, 121–3
Foodstuff. *See also* Crops
  associated with modernity, 155
  recently introduced, 155
Fortes, M., 100
Foucault, M., 204–6

Geertz, C., 86
Gender. *See also* Men, Women
  cultural construction of, 176–82
  expressed in organization of space, 10–11,
    97, 115–16, 159–61, 197–9
  models of, 178, 199
  relations of, 11, 116–19
  as symbol, 115, 118, 123–4, 178–9
Giddens, A., 8
Goats. *See also* Stock
  absence of, 151–2
  bridewealth, 69
  and burial, 112
  houses (*kano*) for, 53–4, 103, 165
  and men, 116
  position of *kano* in compound, 54, 113–14
  slaughtered at ceremonies, 73, 117
Goldschmidt, W., 20, 22, 67, 141. *See also*
    Sebei
Grandparents, 33–4. *See also* Kinship
Greenberg, J. H., 16

Handmills, 154, 156
Hennings, R. O., 26
Hobart, M., 80
Hollis, A. C., 110
Houses, 9–11. *See also* Compounds, Space
  changes in as indices of modernity,
    130–4, 136–8, 142–5, 152
  construction of, 99–109
  contents of, 142–50
  gender association of, 99–106, 111–13,
    120–1
  internal arrangements of, 49–51, 131–138
  position in compound, 51–2
  position in village, 99
  square houses, 11, 140–2, 152
  types of, 48–9, 130–2
Huntingford, G. W. B., 17, 19–22, 24, 31.
    See also Nandi

Ideology. *See also* Representation
  conflicts within, 96
  male control, 74, 196
  relationship between text and, 93–5,
    160–1, 202–4
Initiation. *See also* Circumcision
  celebration of women's power, 186–8, 191–4
  and marriage, 61–2
  and maturity, 110–11
  of men, 62
  of women, 62, 183–4
Interpretation, 10. *See also* Representation,
    Text
  akin to reading, 86–93
  competing and alternative, 95–6, 198–9
  dominant, 80, 96, 198–9
  metaphor, 89–90
  multiplicity of, 92–3
  representation, 92–3, 128
  temporality of, 91
Irrigation
  furrows, 13, 190–1
  history of in Sibou, 30–1, 119. *See also*
    Clan, Sibou

Johnson, M., 82

Kabor. See Lineage
Kabyle, 83, 98
Kalenjin, 60–1. *See also* Endo, Marakwet
  composition of, 13–15
  history of, 15–18
  language of, 14–17
  migrations of, 17
Kapchogo. See Stores
Kapkore, 125–6, 184–9, 192–3, 195. *See also*
    Initiation, Women
  rites of, 184–6
Kaptorus, 126, 190. *See also* Initiation, Men
Kenya, 9, 16, 30, 129, 138, 147
Kerio valley, 13, 18–19, 26–8
  as axis of orientation, 57–8
Kerio Valley Development Authority, 138
Keyo, 16. *See also* Kalenjin
Kinship
  classification and usage of, 65–8, 207–8
  obligations of, 31–2, 100, 102, 106–7, 158
Kipkorir, B. E., 19, 22–3, 67
Kipsigis, 16, 19–22, 60–1. *See also* Kalenjin
Kitupche. See Siblings
Knowledge, 11, 55
  defined as male, 175–6
  and language, 175–6
  and status, 152–3
  text as an instrument of, 95
  tradition, 175–6
  of women, 184, 191–3
Kok. See Council

Labor. *See also* Child
  agricultural, 68, 71–2, 166
  changes in organization of, 154–9
  description of, 79
  domestic, 71–3, 121, 156, 166–9
  sexual division of, 116–19, 156
  waged, 138, 146–7, 151, 155–6, 158–9
Lagam (escarpment), 21
  associated with tradition, 49, 130–1, 145,
    152–3
Lake Turkana, 57
Lakoff, G., 82
Land. *See also* Sibou
  control and division of, 117
  leasing of, 32
  men's and women's different access to,
    68–72
  named divisions of, 56–7
  ownership of, 32
  rights through marriage, 68–71
Language
  in *kapkore,* 184
  and knowledge, 175–6
  and social being, 175–6
  women's control of, 174–6
Lévi-Strauss, C., 7–8
Lineage (*kabor*), 99–100, 102–4. *See also*
    Marakwet, Sibou
  men's and women's different relation to,
    73–5
  perpetuation of, 74
  relations to clan, 21–2, 29–32
  relations between women, 154–160
  residence of, 23–4
  rights to land, 32
Llewelyn-Davies, M., 63
Luo, 18

Maasai, 63
MacCormack, C., 124
Mamaa. See Uncle
Manufactured goods, 138
  as indices of modernity, 142–52, 158–60
  valued over stock, 150–3
Marakwet, 9–26. *See also* Endo, Kalenjin
  age sets, 59–62
  clans, 22–5
  councils (*kok*), 21–2, 24–5
  divisions within section, 21–4
  kinship, 65–8
  life stages, 63–5
  lineages, 23–4
  links between residential units and land, 21–2
  sections of, 13, 19–21
  villages, 21–4
Marriage. *See also* Kinship, Men, Women
  changes in, 153–60
  description of, 69–71

gaining control of resources, 65, 73
instructions given in *kapkore,* 186–8
men's and women's roles in, 68–73, 119–21
polygamy, 71, 103
property and rights associated with, 68–72, 182
rules governing, 33–4
and social maturity, 61–2, 64, 101–2, 184–5
and social reproduction, 65
Mauss, M., 4
Meaning. *See also* Interpretation, Representation, Space
classification, 3
defined by context, 4, 89–91, 125–8, 197–9, 206
and interpretation, 128, 200
invoked through practice, 84–5, 91, 124–6, 201
of organization of space, 83–4
polysemy, 90
simultaneity of, 126
Men, 67–9, 116–19. *See also* Gender, Initiation, Marriage, Women
activities of, 165–7, 169
age sets, 59–62
behavior of, 176–9
changes in gender relations, 153–61
conflicts between sexes, 11, 72, 115, 117–19, 128–9, 159
dependence on women, 67–74, 117–19
dominance of, 68, 72, 75, 156
models of, 11, 170–1, 178–80, 194–9
and permanence, 57, 62–3, 118
rights and duties in marriage, 68–73
as social beings, 73, 118–19, 121
social responsibilities of, 73–4, 117
social status of, 61–2
Menstruation, 190–1
Metaphor, 124, 126–8. *See also* Interpretation, Meaning, Space
analysis of in anthropology, 81–2
as interpretation, 82–3, 85–6, 95–6
nature of, 81–4, 120
as strategy, 83, 128
Meyerhoff, E., 184
Misre. See Egypt
Missions, 138, 140–2
Moon (*arawa*), 57
Muted groups, 80, 173, 180–2

Nandi, 16, 19–20, 22, 24, 31, 60, 110. *See also* Kalenjin
Nilotes. *See* Kalenjin

Parents, 65–6. *See also* Adult, Child, Kinship, Marriage
care of by children, 104
children and reproduction, 72–4

sleeping arrangements, 102, 105, 108–9
teknonymy, 73
Peristiany, J., 20, 22, 24. *See also* Kipsigis
Pokot, 13–14, 16, 21–2, 61, 184. *See also* Kalenjin
Power, 11, 95–6, 123, 125–6
asymmetries between the sexes, 176–9
and sexuality, 204–6
Psychoanalysis, 173

Rainfall, 18–19
Refuse, 11. *See also* Animal dung, Burial, Chaff
and burial, 109–13
and gender, 123–4
and houses, 110
prohibition on mixing of 110, 112, 120, 122–3, 151–3
spatial ordering of, 109–13, 151–3
types of, 109–10
Representation, 159–61. *See also* Ideology, Interpretation, Meaning, Space
of gender relations, 176–81
as interpretation, 92–3, 128
as reflection of historical conditions, 93–4, 203–4
socially dominant forms of, 9, 178–81, 194–7, 204–6
Ricoeur, P., 86–90
Rosen, L., 170

Said, E.
Samburu, 61
Sanga. See Aunt
Saussure, F. de, 3
Sebei, 16, 20, 22, 61, 67, 141. *See also* Kalenjin
Seclusion. *See* Initiation
Semiotics, 3–5, 82, 93, 128
critiques of, 3–8
Siblings (*kitupche*)
brother–sister relations, 66
Sibou. *See also* Marakwet, Tot
clans of, 33
clan histories of, 29–32
compounds, 34, 39, 48
geographical location of, 28–9
houses, 48–52
land ownership, 32–4
location of study, 9, 25, 125
observable changes, 129–31, 148–9, 152–3
organization of, 29–34
other structures, 52–4
sample choice, 33–4, 37
Sister. *See* Siblings
Social action. *See also* Social actors
principles informing, 84
theory of practice, 84

Social actors
  interpretations of, 85–6, 91, 128
  as knowledgeable, 84, 201–2
  models of, 7–8
  practical activity of, 87–8, 128
  strategic intentions of, 85–6, 96–7
Space. See also Goats, Houses, Ideology, In-
    terpretation, Meaning, Metaphor,
    Representation
  analogous to language, 3–4
  analysis of, 80–81
  axes of orientation, 56–7
  different experiences of men and women,
    79–80
  gender associations of, 10, 124
  and invisibility of women, 170–4, 197–9
  life-cycle of, 98–9
  mutuality of space–time, 55–9
  meaning of, 81–86
  and modernity, 129, 144, 150–3, 202–3
  organization of, 9–11
  readings of, 87–90, 200–6
  as a reflection of ideology, 93–95,
    159–61, 202–4
  as a reflection of social categories, 4–6
  as representation, 95–6, 128, 161, 197–9,
    204–6
  and status, 158–61
  as a text, 86–93, 160–1
Spencer, P., 61
Stock. See also Circumcision, Goats, Marriage
  bridewealth, 68–70
  and circumcision, 69
  and female sexuality, 188
  and marriage, 69–71, 74, 102
  and men, 116
  misfortune concerning, 106
  ownership and inheritance of, 68, 103
  and prestige, 117
  replaced by other prestige structures, 150–3
  rights to, 68–9
Stores (kapchogo). See also Crops
  construction of, 52, 103
  control of, 72, 103, 117
  position of, 53, 114
  use of, 52–3
Strathern, M., 124, 178
Structuralism, 3–4, 82, 93
  critiques of, 3–9
Structures. See also Meaning, Metaphor,
    Space
  informing the organization of space, 83
  relationship between activity and, 87–8
Sun (asis). See also Ancestors
  and men, 57, 62
  tropics of Capricorn and Cancer, 57–8
  and space–time orientation, 58
Sutton, J. E. G., 16–18

Teknonymy, 73
Terik, 16. See also Kalenjin
Text, 10. See also Ideology, Interpretation,
    Meaning, Metaphor, Representation,
    Space
  activity as, 86–8
  authorship of, 87–8, 200
  as cultural representation, 3, 93, 200
  and history, 88, 92–4, 203
  and ideology, 93–5, 160–1, 202–4
  irreducibility of, 87
  literary texts, 81, 88
  and power, 204–6
  readings of, 86, 88, 90–3
  referring ability of, 86–90
  space as, 86–7, 128, 201–4
Thompson, J. B., 88
Thomson, J., 13
Time, 10. See also Age sets
  genderization of, 55, 62
  and generations, 58
  mutuality of space–time, 55–9
  repetition of, 59, 62
Tot
  and change, 129–32, 138, 140–4, 146,
    148–150, 153
  history and location of, 26–30
Tugen, 16, 21. See also Kalenjin
Turner, V., 80–1, 127
Turton, A., 80

Uncle (mamaa), 67. See also Bridewealth,
    Kinship

Widow, 109
Widower, 109
Witchcraft, 67
Women, 67–9, 116–19. See also Gender, In-
    itiation, Kapkore
  activities of, 165–170
  age sets, 59–62
  behavior of, 176–9
  change in gender relations, 153–61
  conflict between sexes, 11, 72, 115–19,
    128–9, 159
  cooperative links between, 154–60, 183
  and household, 117–23
  as impermanent, 57, 62, 118
  as individualistic, 73–4, 118–19, 121
  as invisible, 170–4, 197–9
  location in culture, 174–82, 194–6
  models of, 11, 170–1, 173, 178–81, 194–5
  negative valuation of female qualities,
    123–4, 171, 197
  power of female sexuality, 123–6, 184–9
  rights and duties in marriage, 68–73, 182–3
  social status of, 61–2, 171, 173, 184–5
  transformation from wife to daughter, 79–80
Worsley, P., 80